FAITH
&
CULTURE

*I believe in Christianity as I believe that the sun has risen:
not only because I see it, but because by it I see everything else.*

C. S. LEWIS

FAITH
&
CULTURE

THE GUIDE TO A CULTURE
SHAPED BY FAITH

Previously published as
A Faith and Cultural Devotional

KELLY MONROE KULLBERG
& LAEL ARRINGTON

ZONDERVAN

ZONDERVAN.com/
AUTHORTRACKER
follow your favorite authors

ZONDERVAN

Faith and Culture
Copyright © 2008 by Kelly Monroe Kullberg and Lael Arrington
Previously published as *A Faith and Culture Devotional*

This title is also available as a Zondervan ebook. Visit www.zondervan.com/ebooks.

Requests for information should be addressed to:

Zondervan, *Grand Rapids, Michigan 49530*

This edition: ISBN 978-0-310-33138-4 (softcover)

The Library of Congress has cataloged the original edition as follows:

Kullberg, Kelly Monroe, 1960–
    A faith and culture devotional : daily readings on art, science, and life / Kelly
Monroe Kullberg and Lael Arrington.
       p.   cm.
    Includes index.
    ISBN 978-0-310-28356-0 (printed caseside)
    1. Christianity and culture—Meditations. 2. Christianity and art—Meditations.
3. Religion and science—Meditations. 4. Christian life—Meditations. I. Arrington,
Lael F., 1951– II. Title.
BR115.C8K825   2009
261—dc22   2008036169

Cover design: Extra Credit Projects
Cover photography: © Robert Daly / gettyimages
Interior photography: iStockphoto.com®
Interior design: Beth Shagene

Printed in the United States of America

11 12 13 14 15 16 /DCI/ 23 22 21 20 19 18 17 16 15 14 13 12 11 10 9 8 7 6 5 4 3 2 1

CONTENTS BY TOPIC

History

Philosophy

Science

Literature

Arts

Contemporary Culture

For millennia, faith has inspired believers to take the raw material of God's creation and *create culture* — to build in the ruins, to farm, to study, to dance, to paint, to sing, to write books, to love and nurture new life, to drill wells for fresh water, to visit prisoners with hope, to find cures for disease. Faith sees "the glory of God in the face of Jesus Christ" and, in response, worships and creates.

Why a "faith and culture" devotional? To marvel at the wonders of God and his world. To learn of ancient empires. Dark matter. String theory. Rembrandt. *Uncle Tom's Cabin.* U2. Quantum physics. To worship. In fifteen weeks of two- or three-page daily readings that fit your busy life, you can explore the significance of great ideas, events, and people. We invite you to enjoy the connections between faith and culture that outstanding Christian thought leaders offer in seven key subjects — one for each day of the week: bible and theology, history, philosophy, science, literature, arts, and contemporary culture.

And like Forrest Gump's box of chocolates, "You never know what you're going to get!" The assortment is rich and varied, yet patterns emerge: one week you'll find several pieces that speak to a theme like the goodness of God in the face of evil. Another week you'll explore a theme connecting Picasso as entertainer and life as entertainment.

We've written sections for reflection and discussion at the end of each reading to help you process the meaning and see how each relates to your relationships, work, leisure, worship — all of your life with God. Book groups can process the questions together. Special-interest groups may choose to study certain topics, such as the arts and literature. Also note that this devotional is not meant to substitute for daily Bible reading but to enrich it. Please visit *www.culturedevo.com* for more inspiration from great ideas, events, and people.

Our hope is that this devotional catalyzes a kind of kingdom education from master kingdom teachers, expanding our knowledge, strengthening our beliefs, and inspiring our love for God and others. We long to pass on a sense of wonder at the genius, the power, and the beauty of Jesus Christ, and the futility of life apart from him. Put rather urgently, try to imagine cultures without Christ. As the eminent Charles Malik wrote not long before his death, "I really do not know what will remain of civilization and history if the accumulated influence of Christ is eradicated from literature, art, practical dealings, moral standards, and creativeness in the different activities of mind and spirit."[1]

Cultures fall but can rise again. How great is our opportunity to, right now, be the church in the world God loves. The more we've explored these great ideas, people, and events, the more we've discovered how great is our God and how large is the story in which we live. We hope you might drink deeply and live out of that which you've first received. Enjoy!

In these pages songwriter Michael Card reflects on art and beauty. The former director of the U.S. Human Genome Project, Francis Collins, tells us about DNA and his journey of faith. Painter Bruce Herman explores the connections between intimacy and worship. Sociologist Os Guinness teaches us about the Beatles in one entry and the genius of Blaise Pascal in another. Philosophy professor Dallas Willard offers insight on hearing God. John Eldredge probes the major and minor themes of the Bible and life.

Pastor Erwin McManus helps us understand the gospel from the perspective of a Muslim audience. Philip Yancey discusses the life and work of Leo Tolstoy. Chuck Colson explores the legacy of 9/11. A former president of the United Nations General Assembly, Charles Malik, speaks on the wonder of Christ. And Randy Alcorn reminds us of the reality of heaven.

Faith and Culture invites you, the reader, into a spirited conversation with these and many others who think and live creatively in the largest "story." They offer a Christ-centered education — in a devotional. We believe that, of all people, Christians are to be curious and free to explore, to try new things and make mistakes — to learn and grow.

Theologian Thomas Dubay wrote in *The Evidential Power of Beauty*, "People with lively minds and sparks in their hearts are blessedly prone to wonder, to be astonished, and to marvel. They are the normal ones — and happy too. They are alive."[2]

Discover so many — and so much — that came before us: Julian of Norwich, Copernicus, Rembrandt, Wilberforce, C. S. Lewis, Vincent van Gogh, Francis Schaeffer. Read about Handel's *Messiah*, Melville's *Moby-Dick*.

Meet believers now among us who glorify God through their lives and words. We thank each friend, scholar, professional, and publisher for their contribution to this devotional.

Kelly Monroe Kullberg and Lael Arrington	Michael J. Behe
	James Scott Bell
Randy Alcorn	Darrell Bock
Kerby Anderson	Ray Bohlin
Jack Arrington	Keith Bower

Walter L. Bradley
Michael Card
G. K. Chesterton
Betsy Childs
Francis S. Collins
Charles Colson
William Lane Craig
Robert Durfey
William Edgar
John Eldredge
Keith Getty
Chris Gilbert
Sandra Glahn
Terry Glaspey
Guillermo Gonzalez
Os Guinness
Gary R. Habermas
Fred Harburg
Archibald D. Hart
Bruce Herman
Phillip Johnson
Joy Jordan-Lake
Mark Joseph
Walter C. Kaiser
Patrick Kavanaugh
Dick Keyes
Greg Koukl
David Kullberg
Catherine Claire Larson
Frederick Larson
Martha D. Linder
Jerry MacGregor
Charles Malik
Frederica Mathewes-Green

Scot McKnight
Erwin McManus
Eric Metaxas
J. P. Moreland
Richard W. Ohman
Marvin Olasky
Nancy Pearcey
Mary Poplin
Stephanie Powers
John C. Rankin
John Mark Reynolds
Hans Rookmaaker
Hugh Ross
Jody Hassett Sanchez
Francis Schaeffer
Vera Shaw
R. C. Sproul
Sue Stewart
Sam Storms
John Stott
Michael G. Strauss
Lee Strobel
Sarah Sumner
Charles Thaxton
Drew Trotter
Gene Edward Veith
Catherine Hart Weber
James Emery White
Benjamin Wiker
Dallas Willard
Jennifer Wiseman
Jonathan Witt
Philip Yancey

For a decade I lived in the Harvard community of Cambridge, Massachusetts. Whether on a Vermont ski lift, or building a medical clinic in Haiti, or over jazz and coffee in Harvard Yard, friends would discuss the nature of reality and *how* we know what we think we "know." The implications of the big bang, DNA, and quantum chemistry. The moral law as an invisible wall that we keep bumping into. Our desire for the joy a friend said he'd been searching for and finally encountered as he read Augustine's *Confessions* written sixteen hundred years ago. We marveled at the veracity and relevance of the gospel for today's questions. How did its ancient writers know that electromagnetic energy preceded visible light (Genesis), or that "darkness" resided somewhere (Job) as physicists are now pondering, or that only forgiveness breaks a cycle of vengeance in a fractured world.

After one spring dance, friends ended up on the roof of the Harvard observatory, taking turns at the telescope. We discussed the mass and density of Jupiter in relation to the infamous cranberry sourdough bread I was known to bake. Telescopes and microscopes and our new eyes for God's world were windows into an enchanted creation. More than arguing timelines or mechanisms, we were captivated by the wonder and meaning of it all. Such conversations would continue with endless variations, laughter, sometimes prayer, and often someone breaking into a song of praise drawing in curious students who had rarely heard such singing.

As founder and director of project development of the Veritas Forum (*www.veritas.org*) I visit campuses around the world, where I continue to find kindred spirits in labs, art studios, and concert halls. Together we host conversations and service projects, diving into life's hardest questions and the relevance of Jesus Christ to all of life. May this devotional be such a treasure hunt for you. Welcome.

One day, early in my teaching career, I sat spellbound in a dark Southern Methodist University auditorium, like Alice staring through the keyhole, as Francis Schaeffer introduced his film series *How Should We Then Live? The Rise and Decline of Western Thought and Culture.* All my study of the Bible — creation, fall, redemption — and all my course work in biology, government, literature, and the rest came together in this entirely new panorama of the larger "story." I showed the films to my students and invited them into this great conversation as we took our discussions on the road to art museums and private pipe organ concerts. Their questions sent me digging deeper into the history of ideas and aesthetics at the University of Texas at Dallas.

With friends at Schaeffer's Swiss study center, L'Abri, we peered down the railroad tracks of God's will and man's will, trying to make out how they merged in the distance. In evenings by the fire with fellow pastors' wives and our husbands, our conversations have flowed from astonishing reports of God drawing people to his Son in hostile territories to the encouragement we've needed to keep going in difficult stretches. And while I've struggled at times, trying to distill an ounce of pure meaning out of the sludge of twenty-eight years with rheumatoid arthritis, the written counsel of gifted thought leaders has reminded me of my own theology and God's presence.

On our weekly radio program (*www.thethingsthatmattermost.org*), my co-host, Rick, and I discuss the big questions about origins, morality, meaning, and destiny with thought leaders and culture makers. Bart Ehrman and Darrell Bock probe the evidence for "new" gospels of Jesus. John Eldredge invites a *GQ* journalist into a transcendence more enduring than what he has found on a surfboard. *Time* magazine humorist Joel Stein and Randy Alcorn get serious about heaven. Dick Keyes exposes the hidden "omniscience" behind cynicism.

My life has been enriched by master kingdom teachers, radio guests, and friends, and it is a joy to share the feast with you in these pages.

To my mother, Kay Anderson Monroe Van Meter,
and my husband, David Bard Kullberg,
for your partnership in this book and your friendship in this life.
Thank you for loving beauty. And me. And for the joy.
K. M. K.

To Don and Rose Fitzgerald
who gave me books, showed me the world.
And to Jack, my kindred spirit,
partner in learning and life.
Your steadfast love is my great comfort and delight.
L. A.

DAILY READINGS ON
ART, SCIENCE, AND LIFE

A Christian Theory of Everything

By **Sam Storms**, PhD, former professor of theology, Wheaton College. Adapted from his book *One Thing: Developing a Passion for the Beauty of God*. Storms left Wheaton to found Enjoying God Ministries in Kansas City, Missouri; *www.enjoyinggodmin istries.com.*

Physicists and cosmologists are ever in search of what they call "a theory of everything," an all-encompassing theory that can account for everything from the subatomic world of particle physics to the galactic expanse of super-novas and black holes.

Brian Greene, professor of physics and mathematics at Columbia University, argues that for the first time in the history of physics we have a framework with that capacity. Scientists call it *string theory*. The idea is that everything in the universe at its most microscopic level consists of combinations of vibrating strings. According to Greene, "string theory provides a single explanatory framework capable of encompassing all forces and all matter."

The problem isn't that Greene and others have gone too far in making this claim. The problem is they haven't gone nearly far enough! Greene is clearly drawn to this theory because strings make sense of every fundamental feature of physical reality. But what makes sense of strings? Why do *they* exist? If they explain "all forces and all matter," *what explains them*? What accounts for the shape they take and the functions they serve?

The answer is that everything exists for the glory of God. Everything — from quarks to quasars, from butterflies to brain cells — was created and is sustained so that you and I might delight in the display of divine glory. Only humans are fashioned in the image of God. We are the only species that establishes schools and conducts research and preserves archives of information. We alone have been granted remarkable capacities to reason and reflect, deduce and conclude. We alone can glorify God by *rejoicing* in the beauty of his creative handiwork and *relishing* the splendor of his self-revelation in the person and redemptive work of Jesus Christ.

We're touching here on the most profound question anyone could ever ask: Why is there something rather than nothing? The simple answer is that God chose to create. This was certainly not from the anguish born of need, as if creation might supply God what he lacked. God didn't take inventory and suddenly realize there was a shortage that only you and I could fill. So what prompted God to act?

The source of God's creative energy was the joy of infinite and eternal abundance! *God chose to create from the endless and self-replenishing overflow of delight in himself.*

We must begin with the recognition that God delights infinitely in his own eternal beauty. When God the Father gazes at the Son and sees a perfect reflection of his own holiness, he is immeasurably happy. The Father rejoices in the beauty of the Son and Spirit, and the Son revels in the beauty of the Spirit and Father, and the Spirit delights in that of the Father and Son. God is his own fan club! God created us out of this eternal community, this overflow of mutual love, delight, and admiration, so that we might joyfully share in it, to God's eternal glory.

God doesn't simply think about himself or talk to himself. He *enjoys* himself! He celebrates with infinite and eternal intensity the beauty of who he is as Father, Son, and Holy Spirit. And we've been created to join the party!

To relish and rejoice in the beauty of God alone accounts for why we exist. Enjoying God is the soul's sole satisfaction, with which no rival pleasure can hope to compete. Glorifying God by enjoying him forever. It's the Christian Theory of Everything.

For reflection or discussion

- Does this view challenge your assumptions about life and the universe? If so, how?
- What are the greatest barriers to your enjoyment of God?
- Perhaps you're not enjoying God as much as you would like. What step could you take to begin to change that (Psalms 84:2; 16:11)?
- How might today be different if you lived as though you were created to enjoy God as your greatest treasure?

Abraham, Father of Three Faiths

Note: *You'll discover a fairly serendipitous arrangement of topics in each subject area with the exception of history. God is telling a larger story and, as meaning-seeking creatures, we are always looking to discover what he is up to. So history unfolds chronologically, tracing his drama of redemption through the ages.*

By Kelly Monroe Kullberg and David Kullberg

Though their antecedents are rarely explored in the evening news, present tensions in the Middle East are rooted in a family story that is more than four thousand years old. This drama begins with Abraham, a model of faith and a father to Muslims, Jews, and Christians. Muslims learn about Abraham through the Qur'an (Koran) of Islam. Jews and Christians learn about Abraham through what the Jews call the Torah and Christians call the Old Testament, beginning in Genesis.[1]

The first chapters of Genesis shed light on some basic questions — our origins and purpose, why we fight, why we die, and how we live meaningfully. We find glory, beauty, love, deception, shame, blame, punishment, sibling rivalry, murder, expulsion — all in the first *four* chapters of Genesis. Before long, God grieved the sin among his people and re-created the world through a flood, a baptism, if you will. As author Madeleine L'Engle suggested, "The flood was God's tears."[2] But God found one righteous family, Noah's, through which he rebirthed a freshly storied world.

From Genesis 10 on, the focus of Scripture is on covenant relationships. In the context of cultural confusion in ancient Babel, where men were building a great city for personal glory, the Lord not only separated people through unique languages, he also planted the seed of a remarkable people who were asked to reject idolatry and live in love. Like us, these were fallible and three-dimensional people, making Genesis a vivid, candid, R-rated page-turner.

Through it all God was faithful, and over many generations the seed grew into a life-giving tree. Any person could be grafted into that tree, not by fortune of lineage or wealth but simply by faith in God and in his promised Messiah. God begins with a remarkable father and mother, a patriarch and matriarch. Abram and Sarai (whom God renamed Abraham and Sarah) were citizens of Ur, a great center of ancient Mesopotamia. And the Lord said to Abraham, "Go from your country, your people and your father's household to the land I will show you. I will make you into a great nation" (Genesis 12:1 – 2).

Muslims honor Abraham as the first monotheist, worshiper of the one true God they call Allah. Muslims trace their heritage through Abraham and Hagar, the servant who was Sarah's childbearing surrogate, and their son, Ishmael (Abraham's firstborn child). Muslims prize the promise God made to Hagar when she was abandoned in the wilderness: "Lift the boy [Ishmael] up and take him by the hand, for I will make him into a great nation" (Genesis 21:18). Indeed, Ishmael was blessed with life and progeny, for he had twelve sons, and his numbers quickly grew.

Jews and Christians trace their lineage through the son God promised Sarah and Abraham — Isaac, the miraculously conceived son of the free woman, through whom God would foreshadow and fulfill his covenant promises. Isaac's son Jacob then bore twelve sons, whose descendants became the twelve tribes of Israel.

The account of Abraham and Sarah continues the theme of God's covenant (beginning with Noah) to one particular family. The Lord said to Abraham,

> I will bless those who bless you, and whoever curses you I will curse; and all peoples on earth will be blessed through you.
>
> GENESIS 12:3

> I am God Almighty; walk before me faithfully and be blameless.... I will make you very fruitful; I will make nations of you, and kings will come from you.
>
> GENESIS 17:1, 6

The branches of this family tree would be known by their fruit. They would, as a way of life, turn curses into blessings. Joseph, son of Jacob, grandson of Isaac, converted the curse of exile into blessing: not only did Joseph save his own brothers who'd sold him into slavery but he saved non-Jews as well, including all of Egypt, from famine. The children of God would, and will, become a blessing to the nations. "Thus there were fourteen generations in all from Abraham to David, fourteen from David to the exile to Babylon, and fourteen from the exile to the Messiah" (Matthew 1:17).

This shared respect for Abraham, with differing ideas of the past, present, and future, makes the conflicts among Jews/Christians and Muslims — from the medieval crusades to today's Middle Eastern clashes — surprising on one hand and understandable on the other. But embedded within the tension there is also hope — that any cousin who so chooses will be present at the family reunion.

For reflection and discussion

- How do you see this ancient story unfolding in our time?
- At the age of one hundred years, "Abraham gave the name Isaac to the son Sarah bore him" (Genesis 21:3). Why do you think Abraham chose a name that means, in Hebrew, "he laughs"? Sarah also laughed. Why?

The theme of Abrahamic covenant is so essential that the apostle Paul revisited it two millennia later. In his letter to the Galatians, Paul tells Christ-followers that they are not children of slavery but of freedom. In Galatians 3:26 – 28 and Galatians 5:1, he writes:

> You are all children of God through faith, for all of you who were baptized into Christ have clothed yourselves with Christ. There is neither Jew nor Gentile, neither slave nor free, neither male nor female, for you are all one in Christ Jesus. If you belong to Christ, then you are Abraham's seed, and heirs according to the promise. . . . It is for freedom that Christ has set us free. Stand firm, then, and do not let yourselves be burdened again by a yoke of slavery.

- What is it to be a child of slavery? What is it to be a child of freedom and the Spirit? How might people in freedom *bless* those in slavery?
- What resources have you been given to share as a blessing to another?

Belief, Knowledge, and Truth

By Lael Arrington

Truman Burbank was born and raised on a TV set, the star of his own show. He is completely unaware of reality. He believes he lives on a coastal island. He believes that his wife and friends, all paid actors, really love him. Christoff, the producer in the film, says, "While the world he inhabits is ... counterfeit, there's nothing fake about Truman himself." Truman is real. That's what makes him "so good to watch."[3]

The 1998 film *The Truman Show* illustrates the often confusing distinctions between belief and knowledge, truth and untruth. What constitutes knowledge? Most philosophers would agree that knowledge is justified true belief. It is belief, something we take to be true by at least 51 percent, that agrees with the evidence. At the beginning of the movie, Truman *believes* that his life on Seahaven is real, not a scripted TV show. But his belief does not qualify as *knowledge* because it is not justified by the evidence of which the viewing audience is clearly aware.

What is truth? Truth is telling it like it really is. Truth is not a thing, but rather a *relationship* between our words or ideas and *reality*. Whether Truman can see it or not, whether he believes it or not, whether his words agree with it or not, his life is entertainment for the masses. Truman's beliefs do not correspond to reality. They are false.

We may think of belief as an all-or-nothing proposition. But belief is more of a continuum. In the course of the movie, we see Truman's confidence in what he believes to be true steadily diminish. Lighting canisters fall out of the "sky." The man he knew as "Dad" shows up one day, trying to warn him before he is hustled onto a bus. He catches on to his wife doing product placement commercials. You can almost see the needle on the continuum between belief and unbelief falling, falling past the 50/50 point. He suspects he is being deceived and controlled. When he escapes on a sailboat, the producer creates a ferocious storm. Truman shouts to the sky, "Is that the best you can do? You're going to have to kill me!" He survives and sails on until the ship reaches the edge of the watery set and, quite literally, pokes a hole in the bubble of deceit that has been his life.

In the same way, we can live in deceit and illusion until one day we hit the wall of reality. When our false beliefs collide with reality, we then have a choice: Will we live according to knowledge — true belief justified by good evidence? Or will we settle for illusion? The producer promises Truman an illusion of safety. Truman chooses the truth that sets him free. The cheers from the audience gradually subside as they stare at their blank screens, then grope around for their TV guides and some other virtual adventure to soothe and distract. But that is another story.

To seek knowledge, we weigh all our beliefs against the best evidence — God's revelation, both general and special. In order to live and speak with truth, we do so "in the sight of God" (2 Corinthians 4:2). That is, we live and speak words that correspond to reality as God created it and as The One Who Sees Everything sees it. Frederica Mathewes-Green has said, "Reality is God's home address."[4] To be a person of truth is to live before God in the reality he created rather than to settle for illusions, even those of our own making.

For reflection and discussion

As I look back over seasons of pain and escape into distraction and daydreams, I think of how I described my journey in my book *Godsight*:

"I think how the emptiness I often felt came from being in a place, either in my head or on a screen, where I was not present to God. My life did not correspond to his reality.

"I sensed the lack of integrity deep in my bones. The reality of my own life, full of potential moments of love and service to God and others was ticking by. My escapes were killing me softly — one evening of entertainment, one daydream at a time.

"What is most real is eternal life. Jesus said, 'Now this is eternal life: that they may know you, the only true God, and Jesus Christ, whom you have sent' (John 17:3). If we truly want to love and seek God, we find him when our words and lives correspond to reality, even painful reality. Not in untruth, fantasy or distraction."[5]

- Have you experienced hitting the wall of reality? Did you discover that any of your beliefs were untrue?
- What counts for true knowledge in today's world? What limitations might you find with today's approach to knowledge?

- When Truman discovered his life was an illusion, the director begged him to stay in the safety of Seahaven. He didn't stay. Why do you think it is so hard to live in an illusion? Why not enjoy the safety?
- Are there places in your life or heart that do not correspond to reality as God sees it? What reality have you constructed?
- What greater reality might God be inviting you into?
- What might you want to say to God about being a person of truth?

Francis Collins, God, and the Human Genome

By Francis S. Collins, MD, PhD, former director of the US Human Genome Project and author of *The Language of God: A Scientist Presents Evidence for Belief.* In Veritas forums, Collins has presented these ideas to thousands of students at Massachusetts Institute of Technology, University of California at Berkeley, and Ohio State University. A more complete discussion is on *www.veritas.org/media/talks/537.*

DNA is the instruction book of all living things. This marvelous code that each of us inherited from our parents is written in a language that is shared with all plants, animals, and other organisms. Its scaffold is a remarkable double helix, carrying information in a digital code made up of a series of chemical bases we abbreviate as A, C, G, and T.

How many of these base pairs (letters) does it take to provide the information for a human being? If we were to read it out loud, without stopping, it would take thirty-one years. We have all that information inside each cell of our body.

We only learned about the double helix in 1953. Just exactly fifty years later, more than 2,000 scientists announced that they had worked together to complete the sequence of all 3.1 billion letters of the human instruction book. I had the privilege of leading that effort.

We learned, among many things, just how few genes are encoded in our instruction book. We only have about 20,000 genes, which is amazing, given how much they have to do. Also, we learned that we humans are all 99.9 percent the same at the genetic level, but none of us are perfect DNA specimens. In fact, we all have dozens of glitches in our DNA that can help us understand genetic propensities for illnesses. We're involved now in producing a map of how we differ, and what contributes to the risk of disease, in order to better diagnose, treat, and prevent disease.

Though many scientists may have been raised in a faith tradition, that is not my story. I didn't know much about faith as a child, and in college at the University of Virginia I realized that I didn't believe in God, nor did I want to consider the evidence.

I went to graduate school in physical chemistry and my doctoral project was in quantum mechanics. I decided that second-order differential equations were "truth." What else did I need to "understand" the universe? I became an atheist with little tolerance for belief in God. That kind of faith seemed superstitious and irrational.

But I soon discovered life science and decided on medical school, due to my growing interest in DNA and RNA. One afternoon, an elderly patient with advanced heart disease shared with me her deep faith in God. She said, "I've told you about my faith, but you didn't say anything. What do *you* believe?" It was such a simple question, but suddenly I felt the ice cracking under my feet.

I found her honest question about faith, and my reaction, very troubling. What was that about? I realized I had work to do. After all, I was a scientist — right? I wasn't supposed to come to conclusions without considering the evidence. But I had never done that for the question of God.

Expecting an investigation of the rational basis of faith to shore up my atheism, I began to study world religions. A pastor down the street gave me *Mere Christianity* by C. S. Lewis. I thought, okay, at least it's short. But within the first three pages, a major source of my skepticism was laid to ruins by the straightforward logical argument of an Oxford scholar who had traveled my same path. Readers, beware!

What arguments got to me? A major one was the idea that something deep within all of us knows right from wrong, and that down through history, all peoples in all cultures seem called to do the right thing (even though we often fail). Why do we embrace such altruism and self-giving? Evolution would call that a scandal, instructing us only to take care of ourselves and to be sure our DNA gets propagated.

This so-called Moral Law was an intriguing signpost: potential evidence of a Mind interested in interaction with human beings. It seemed to be a signpost calling me to be more than I probably want to be, to be holier, thus giving me a sense of the potential character of God.

Another signpost for me was the unreasonable effectiveness of mathematics. Why should the laws of the universe be expressed in simple, beautiful equations? And what about the characteristics of our universe, with fifteen constants that determine the behavior of electromagnetism, the strong and weak nuclear forces, and the gravitational force perfectly calibrated to make complexity possible in the universe? Any minuscule change would yield catastrophe or utter sterility.

Coincidence was no longer a reasonable explanation. My atheism emerged as the least rational of all perspectives.

But the more I contemplated the significance of all this, the more I realized how far away from God's plan I was. He gave me the Moral Law, but all too often I broke it. My deepening gloom in feeling so far away from God was resolved by the discovery of the person of Jesus. He made astounding statements about forgiving sins, turning the other cheek, and helping widows, orphans, and our neighbors. And he not only claimed to know about God, he claimed to *be* God. Suddenly his death on the cross, which had always been a complete mystery, made sense — he did that for me, to set me right with God, despite my many imperfections.

One day while hiking in the beautiful Pacific Northwest, I found I was ready to make a decision. And so, in my twenty-seventh year, I became a believer and follower of Jesus. For thirty years now I've found no conflicts in what I know as a scientist and what I believe as a follower of Jesus.

Science is the only way to understand the natural world. But science is powerless to answer many of our deepest questions, such as "Why are we here?" "What is the meaning of life?" "What happens when we die?" Those questions can only be answered by faith. I can find God in a cathedral or in the science lab. I can read his words in the Bible or in the genome. There's no conflict, only joy, in discovering the harmony of science and faith.

For reflection and discussion

"Bio" means *life*. "Logos" means *word*, or *study of*. In light of this entry, *biolog-y* can be thought of as the "study of life" and "how the Word becomes life." In John chapter 1 we learn, "In the beginning was the Word ... and ... The Word became flesh." How intriguing it is that God speaks life into being — the universe, our lives, and his perfect "Word made flesh" in the person of Jesus.

• How do you hear God speaking life into you, and your story?

Collins humbly explained, "The experience of sequencing the human genome was both a stunning scientific achievement and an occasion of worship." As with Francis Collins' journey, the more we look, the more we see. Thank God for his brilliance that we are only beginning to discover.

• What unresolved questions are asking you to find out more about God? What "signposts" have found you along the way?

Paradise Lost —
Milton's Epic of Cosmic Betrayal

Note: *While science explores the laws and processes of God's creative work, we long for glimpses of reality that transcend molecules and machines. Literature and the arts invite us into stories and music, forms and images that reveal the truth in ways words cannot express.*

By Gene Edward Veith, PhD, provost and professor of literature, Patrick Henry College. Adapted from *Reading Between the Lines: A Christian Guide to Literature*. Veith is culture editor of *World* magazine; *www.geneveith.com*.

John Milton, a staunch Puritan (1608 – 1674), worked tirelessly as an official in Britain's Commonwealth government. He went blind in the midst of his career and struggled bravely to overcome his handicap. When the monarchy was restored, he was ousted in defeat and faced persecution and the collapse of everything he had worked for. At his life's lowest point, this blind exile from power wrote his greatest poetry by dictating it to his daughters.

Paradise Lost describes the pivotal event of human history — the fall of Adam and Eve. What the Bible succinctly states in the first three chapters of Genesis, Milton explores in thousands of lines of poetry.

In exalted style, Milton plays with the English language like Bach playing the organ. Consider these lines on Satan being cast out of heaven:

> *… Him the Almighty Power*
> *Hurled headlong flaming from the ethereal sky*
> *With hideous ruin and combustion down*
> *To bottomless perdition, there to dwell*
> *In adamantine chains and penal fire,*
> *Who durst defy th' Omnipotent to arms.*

Milton's long narrative poem is perhaps best approached as a novel. We see Satan's perspective. When he says, "Better to reign in Hell, than serve in Heaven," we, sinners that we are, can understand and relate to his furious pride and rebelliousness. Milton imagines Satan is holding a council in hell with all of the defeated demons. Their one way to hurt an omnipotent God, they decide, is to seduce away from him those whom he loves — the newly created human race. We next see the counsels of heaven as the Father works all of Satan's malice into his saving plan through the work of his Son.

We then get to know Adam and Eve. The unfallen couple are innocent, yet not naive or simpleminded. They are both strong, intelligent, and in love with each other. They love too the lush world God has given them, and they love God. An angel visits them and provides flashback accounts of the war in heaven and the creation, rendered with Milton's sublime descriptions. Later, Satan, enraged by their happiness, assumes the form of a serpent. As Satan is deceiving Eve, the arguments seem so plausible that, putting ourselves into this scene, we can admit that we too might have succumbed. We can see our own complicity in her fall. Adam falls without being deceived, knowing exactly what he is doing but choosing to reject God's word. According to Milton, Adam does not want to be separated from the woman he loves. To share Eve's fate, he eats the fruit.

The result of this romantic but idolatrous gesture is hateful recrimination between the two of them, the breaking of all natural harmony, and the tragic flaw that underlies human history. Milton has Eve come to her now-hateful husband and, in a memorable scene, repent of the wrong she has done to him. Adam comes to his senses and turns to God for mercy. God's judgment is tempered with the promise of salvation through the coming of his Son. An angel gives Adam a vision of subsequent human history, and the two must leave paradise in order to begin the human story.

For reflection and discussion

Milton shows how the ones we love most can become our idols — the things we love more than God — and how this can destroy the very relationships we treasure.

- Is there any person you love and give yourself to more than God? How might your joy be at risk in that kind of relationship?

In *The Sacred Romance*, John Eldredge observed, "Satan mounted his rebellion through the power of one idea: God doesn't have a good heart. He deceived a multitude of the heavenly host by sowing the seed of doubt in their minds that God was somehow holding out on them. After the insurrection is squelched, that question lingers in the universe like smoke from a forest fire. Power isn't the same thing as goodness."[6]

- Looking beyond Satan's rebellion and the fall, what does the crucifixion of Jesus Christ show us about his use of power? About his goodness?

Art — A Response to God's Beauty

By **Lael Arrington**, adapted from *Scribbling in the Sand* by Michael Card, recording artist and author, *www.michaelcard.com*; and from *Art and the Bible* by Francis Schaeffer, founder of the L'Abri Fellowship and a philosopher, theologian, and author.

When we contemplate one of those long theological lists of God's attributes, we can hardly help but conclude that he is above all beautiful, writes Michael Card. Yet "we rarely ponder his beauty, much less seek 'to gaze upon [it]' (Psalm 27:4). Rarely does our theology include God's beauty in its outlines. But the beauty of God is a biblical reality. Throughout the Word of God, he is recognized by and praised for being beautiful.... God is beautiful. His beauty demands a response that is shaped by that beauty. And that is art."

Card reminds us that God loves beauty. Not for the sake of some useful purpose, but because he *is* beautiful. Just as he loves mercy because he is merciful. God loves beauty for beauty's sake. In 2 Chronicles 3:16 – 17 we see God's beautiful design for the temple in Jerusalem: "He made interwoven chains and put them on top of the pillars. He also made a hundred pomegranates and attached them to the chains. He erected the pillars in the front of the temple, one to the south and one to the north."

Francis Schaeffer comments, "Here are two freestanding columns. *They supported no architectural weight and had no utilitarian engineering significance.* They were there only because God said they should be there as a thing of beauty. Upon the capitals of those columns were pomegranates fastened upon chains. Artwork upon artwork. If we understand what we are reading here, it simply takes our breath away. This is something overwhelmingly beautiful."

God loves and even commands beauty. Schaeffer continues, "God himself showed Moses the pattern of the tabernacle.... God was the architect, not man.... God told Moses what to do in detail. These were commands, commands from the same God who gave the Ten Commandments."

How does a Christian create art that reflects God's beauty? Is the artist limited to representing only what we observe in God's creation? Schaeffer finds God's design for the Jewish priest's garments to be instructive: "Make pomegranates of blue, purple and scarlet yarn around the hem of the robe, with gold bells between them" (Exodus 28:33). "In nature," he wrote, "pomegranates are red, but these pomegranates were to be *blue, purple* and *scarlet*. Purple and scarlet could be natural changes in the growth of a pomegranate. But blue isn't. The implication is that there is freedom to make something which gets its impetus from nature that can be different from it, and it too can be brought into the presence of God. In other words, art does not need to be 'photographic' in the poor sense of photographic!"

Schaeffer concludes, "What a Christian portrays in his art is the totality of life. Art is not to be solely a vehicle for some sort of self-conscious evangelism.... Christians ought not to be threatened by fantasy and imagination.... The Christian is the really free man — he is free to have imagination. This is our heritage. The Christian is the one whose imagination should fly beyond the stars."

For reflection and discussion

- Think of a time when beauty has taken your breath away or brought you to tears (or nearly so). What does this tell you about the beauty of God?
- How can this understanding of beauty deepen our appreciation of bringing beauty into our homes? Our churches and communities? Of artists who labor to create beauty?
- The enjoyment of beauty is always fleeting. The flower fades. The sun sets. The ballet ends. The moment of sexual transport passes. As Robert Frost put it, "Nothing gold can stay." How might the ephemeral nature of the beauty of our world invite us into God's presence?

A Conversation with Muslims

By **Erwin McManus**, lead pastor and cultural architect of Mosaic, a diverse community of followers of Christ in Los Angeles. Adapted from his book *Soul Cravings*. McManus is also distinguished lecturer at Bethel University; *www.erwinmcmanus.com*.

On a visit to the Middle East, I was invited to speak to a group of Muslims about Christianity. I had been describing my own disappointments with the religion of Christianity, and they all quickly agreed that there were deep problems and inconsistencies between beliefs and practices.

But eventually they wanted to know what exactly was the meaning behind the coming of Jesus. Somewhat apprehensively, I began my best effort to translate back into a Middle Eastern context the story of Jesus (after all, this was Jesus' home turf) and, more specifically, why it would be necessary for God to become human. This, from my vantage point, was the story of God. It's a love story, by the way.

"I once met a girl named Kim."

My translator stopped translating and just looked at me. I encouraged him to simply translate.

"I once met a girl named Kim, and I fell in love."

I continued, "I pursued her with my love and pursued her with my love until I felt my love had captured her heart. So I asked her to be my wife, and she did not say yes." I could feel their empathy.

"I was unrelenting and asked her again, pursuing her with my love, and I pursued her with my love until she said yes."

There was huge relief throughout the entire room.

I went on, "I did not send my brother, nor did I send a friend. For in issues of love, you must go yourself.

"This is the story of Jesus, that God has walked among us and he pursues us with his love. He is very familiar with rejection but is undeterred. And he is here even now, still pursuing you with his love."

The images we often receive of Muslims are angry, hostile, and violent. In this moment I knew there was something transcendent that connected all of our hearts and souls together. The belief that was supposed to divide us strangely united us. Every human being longs for love. The possibility that God is love is an almost overwhelming prospect.

In that moment the story of Jesus was not about who is right and who is wrong, what God's name is and who his prophet is, but what exactly is God's motivation toward humanity. If the message that God wants to get across to us is just about getting our beliefs right, then he didn't need to come himself. If God's entire intent was to simply overwhelm us with the miraculous so that we would finally believe, no personal visitation was necessary.

There is only one reason for God to come himself, because in issues of love, you just can't have someone else stand in for you.

When it comes to love, it has to be face-to-face. Love cannot exist where there is only distance. Love can survive distance, but only by the strength of what comes through intimacy.

Like Solomon's lover, God is going up and down the streets of the city, traveling the most obscure paths and untamed wilderness, searching for the one he loves — and that one is you and it's me.

Religion exists not because God loves too little but because we need love so much. We've been told that God is a reluctant lover and that his standards must be met before there can be any talk of love. This is lunacy. Love exists because God is love. Our souls will never find satisfaction until our hearts have found this love that we so desperately yearn for.

God is not passive, for love is never passive, but always passionate; and passion always leads to action.

For reflection and discussion

- How does this view of God enlarge your understanding of God's relationships with humans?
- What does it mean to you to be pursued by a God who longs to give you his presence?
- How have you experienced God's initiatives of love toward you?

The Grand Affair:
The Imago Dei and Intimacy

By **John Eldredge**, bestselling author and founder of Ransomed Heart Ministries. Adapted from *Desire: The Journey We Must Take to Find the Life God Offers*; www .ransomedheart.com.

It is a mystery almost too great to mention, but God is the expression of the very thing we seek in each other. For do we not bear God's image? Although the glory of God is not fully restored in us yet, we find his image in our creativity, consciences, memory, and imagination. We even find his image in a surprising place — in our gender. "So God created human beings in his own image,... male and female he created them" (Genesis 1:27). "I thought that there was only one kind of soul," said a shocked friend. "And God sort of poured those souls into male or female bodies." Many people believe something like that. But I believe Scripture indicates that we bear his image as men and women, and since God does not have a body, his image must be at the level of the soul — the eternal part of us that reflects God.

God wanted to show the world something of his strength. Is he not a great warrior? Has he not performed the daring rescue of his beloved? And this is why he gave us the sculpture, animated from within, who is man. Men bear the image of God in their dangerous, yet inviting, strength. Women too bear the image of God, but often in a different way. Is not God a being of great mystery and beauty? Is there not something tender and alluring about the essence of the Divine? And this is why he gave us the sculpture, animated from within, who is woman.

God is the source of all masculine power; God is also the fountain of all feminine allure. Come to think of it, he is the wellspring of everything that has ever romanced your heart. The thundering waterfall, the delicacy of a flower, the stirring capacity of music, the richness of wine. The masculine and the feminine that fill all creation come from the same heart. What we have sought, what we have tasted in part with our earthly lovers, we will come face-to-face with in our True Love. The incompleteness we seek to relieve in the deep embrace of our earthly love is never fully healed. The union does not last, whatever the poets and pop artists may say. Morning comes and we've got to get out of bed and off to our day, incomplete once more. But oh, to have it healed forever — to drink deeply from that fount of which we've had only a sip, to dive into that sea in which we have only waded.

And so a man like Charles Wesley can pen these words, "Jesus, Lover of my soul, let me to thy bosom fly," while Catherine of Siena can pray, "O fire surpassing every fire because you alone are the fire that burns without consuming." The French mystic Madame Guyon can write, "I slept not all night, because Thy love, O my God, flowed in me like delicious oil, and burned as a fire." The Bible is rich with romantic imagery.

Is there sex in heaven? It would be better to ask, Is there worship in heaven?

God creates a kingdom so rich in love that he should not be our all, but others should be precious to us as well. Even in Eden, before the fall, God said, "It is not good for the man to be alone" (Genesis 2:18). He gives us the joy of community to share in the "Sacred Romance."

For reflection and discussion

- How do you experience the strength of God? The tenderness and allure of God?
- How does the idea of feminine and masculine souls strike you? What questions does it raise?
- Does John Eldredge's focus on intimacy, and the beauty and romance of God, help or hinder your own relationship to God? How so?
- What does the "grand affair" imply for relationships with our family and friends? With church?
- As the love of God flows in and through us, the joy is multiplied in the giving. How might you be led to advance community and a culture of life — a kingdom of love?

Sodom: What Archaeology Tells Us

By Walter C. Kaiser, PhD, Old Testament, Gordon-Conwell Theological Seminary. Kaiser is president emeritus of Gordon-Conwell as well as executive editor of *The Archaeological Study Bible*, with more than five hundred articles on topics like "Sodom."

The destruction of the cities of the plain in Genesis 19:24 – 25 happened, says the text, when "the LORD rained down burning sulfur on Sodom and Gomorrah … [and] overthrew those cities and the entire plain." From that time on, Sodom, in particular, became a byword for any future threatened divine judgments on Israel.

Archaeologists have not firmly established the exact location of Sodom, but if you were to visit the southeastern shore of the Dead Sea, you would find several Early Bronze Age (3200 – 2200 BC) sites that present fascinating possibilities.

The Scriptures link five cities of the plain: Sodom, Gomorrah, Zoar, Admah, and Zeboiim. In Madeba, Jordan, on the southeastern shore of the Dead Sea, a sixth-century AD mosaic drawing of a map on the floor of the church marks Zoar, the city where Lot fled when the other four cities were threatened with destruction.

Some eight miles north lie the ruins of Numeira, a site occupied at the same time as Zoar. Some observe that the consonants of the Arabic name Numeira fit nicely the Hebrew for "Gomorrah," thus preserving the ancient name.

Another ten miles north, still on the southeastern side of the Dead Sea, you would come to one of the largest ruins in the area, Bab edh-Dra — the prime possibility for the site of ancient Sodom. Archaeologists have explored several Early Bronze occupation levels along with a nearby cemetery. There the dead were put into mausoleum-like houses called "charnel houses." Excavations show that five of these above-the-ground charnel houses were burned, but the surprising feature was that the fire began on the roofs of these houses. The site also yielded a surprising layer of ashes connected with the Early Bronze level. Whether this destruction was connected with an invader or with a shower of fire from heaven cannot be determined at this time, but archaeologists are determined to excavate the ruins more extensively. The ash layer is a bit too early for the days of Abraham, who is more comfortably placed from approximately 2150 to 2075 BC.

The name "Sodom" was early on identified in the Ebla Tablets, also said to be from the Early Bronze period. So the story continues. It is impossible to say that Sodom and Gomorrah have been discovered, but the new data from archaeology is tantalizing and encourages us to continue our search.

In his scholarly book *Sodom and Gomorrah: History and Motif in Biblical Narrative*, W. Fields concluded recently that "Biblical narrative cannot be primarily defined as historiography; it is didactic socioreligious commentary on the experience of Israel and of humankind in general as discerned by the writers and garbed in 'history.'" Even though Fields used the word "primarily," he seemed more interested in separating the events of history from the claims of faith. However, biblical faith, contrary to other world religions, insists on the close association of faith and history.

Staking everything on the historical reality of the resurrection, Paul asserted in 1 Corinthians 15 that if Christ was not actually raised from the dead, then our faith would be "in vain!" To divorce faith from history was to render our faith as worth nothing. If the biblical depiction of the Christian faith cannot be trusted in the details, how can we be expected to trust it on the big ideas — assuming we can sort out which is which in every instance. So, to echo Paul, if Sodom was not razed, could it be that our faith is also in vain? History is still his-story, for God in his sovereignty is Lord of all that happened, still happens, and will happen in the future.

For reflection and discussion

Most religious texts are compilations of wisdom literature (like the book of Proverbs) or stories that intersect geography very sparingly. For example, the events of the Qur'an take place between Mecca and Medina in the Arabian peninsula. The Bible is unique for the vast span of history and geography it covers: 1,600 years (in composition) and three continents.

- Perhaps you've been to the Middle East or seen pictures. What insight does it give you to investigate or even touch the physical reality of the biblical settings?
- How does the physical evidence for the Bible (or lack of it) challenge or encourage your faith?

- God told Abraham that if he could find even ten righteous people in Sodom, he would spare the whole place "for the sake of the ten" (Genesis 18:32). If you could stand among these burned charnel houses, what picture might it paint of God's judgment? And, if he could have found just ten people seeking him, his mercy?
- As you consider both our accountability to God and his mercy, how do you want to respond to him in prayer? In your actions?

The Mind, the Spirit, and Power

By John Stott, PhD, British minister, author of *The Living Church*. In 2005, *Time* magazine called eighty-six-year-old Stott "one of the 100 most influential people on the planet." And the Rev. Billy Graham humbly called Stott "the most respected clergyman in the world today." His legacy includes the Langham Partnership, which provides educational support to the developing world (*www.langhampartnership .org*). In this excerpt, from a 2001 message to The London Institute of Contemporary Christianity, Stott encourages the integrity and power of a unified person — heart, soul, mind, and strength.

I believe that anti-intellectualism and fullness of the Holy Spirit are mutually incompatible. And I dare to say it because the Holy Spirit is the Spirit of Truth. Jesus our Lord himself referred to the Holy Spirit as the Spirit of Truth, and therefore, it is only logical to say that wherever the Holy Spirit has given his freedom, truth is bound to matter. So I have argued, and argue still, that a proper, conscientious use of our minds is an inevitable part and parcel of our Christian life.

First, a proper use of our minds glorifies our Creator. We believe that he is a rational God who has made us in his own image and likeness, as rational men and women. And he has given us a rational revelation of himself.

Second, a proper use of our mind enriches our Christian discipleship. There is no aspect of our discipleship which can be developed without the use of our mind. Whatever part of discipleship you are reflecting on — worship, faith, guidance — the mind has an indispensable part to play.

Third, a proper use of the mind strengthens our witness in the world. I am still convinced that one of the major reasons why people reject the gospel in the West today is not because they perceive it to be false but because they perceive it to be trivial. They think it is inadequate for the complexities and challenges of the world today. We know, of course, that in evangelism, in conversion, and in regeneration, the Holy Spirit has an indispensable part to play. Only he can lead a sinner to Christ. But when he leads us to Christ, he does not do it in spite of the evidence but because of the evidence, when he opens our minds to attend to it. To sum up, anti-intellectualism insults God, impoverishes us, and weakens our testimony in the world. A proper use of the mind glorifies God, enriches us, and strengthens our witness in the world.

For reflection and discussion

- We often hear of knowledge leading to pride and corruption, but with proper humility and grace, might not the use of the mind be a great gift? How might greater knowledge of God and his world lead us to greater love and service?
- Is there such a thing as "good power"?

According to the Rev. John C. Rankin, president of the Theological Education Institute ("The Six Pillars of Honest Politics," *www.teipublishinghouse .com*):

Apart from Jesus as Son of God and Son of Man, the three most powerful men in the Bible are Moses, Daniel and Paul. In each case, they a) knew the Hebrew Scriptures inside out, b) they knew the pagan political cultures in which they lived inside out, c) they knew the pagan religions in those cultures inside out, and d) they were followed by signs and wonders. These were robust men, compromising nothing in the pursuit of wisdom and character, loving the Lord their God with heart, soul, mind and strength. And Jesus their Messiah fulfilled and transcended all they pursued.

- Are people of God always to be on the margins, creating only subcultures or parallel culture?
- Or are we to be salt and light in every sphere, *in* but not *of* the world?
- What do you think of the relationship between loving God with the whole self and leadership? Who today follows God in this way?

Modern Science, a Child of Christianity

By **Charles Thaxton**, PhD, chemist, biologist, historian, and coauthor of *Mystery of Life's Origins*, *The Soul of Science*, and a contributor to *Finding God at Harvard*. He survived two bouts of cancer that left him with one leg and one lung. Charles and his wife are on the faculty for homeschooled teens at Konos Academy near Atlanta.

The dominant view of reality in medieval Europe was essentially Greek as posited by Aristotle and others. This cosmology offered no motivation to investigate nature by observation and experiment. To the Greeks, reality consisted of forms and essences, not material things; therefore, observing "what is" was less important than reasoning "what ought to be." To the Greeks, nature was eternal and self-existent, not created. It was also imbued with attributes of divinity and not to be tested or acted upon.

Late medieval Christianity's greater familiarity with Scripture began to emphasize the doctrine of creation. Through the advent of the printing press, the ideas of Scripture were widely disseminated. People discovered that both Testaments regarded the material world as substantial, real, and good. Scripture valued sensory experience. The Hebrews had an empirical test for identifying a false prophet. Saint John introduced his first epistle with an empirical emphasis describing their reports of Jesus: "We have heard," "We have seen with our eyes," "Our hands have touched." Jesus said to the doubting ones after his resurrection, "Touch me and see."

A created world is contingent upon the will of the Creator and need not necessarily conform to *a priori* reasoning. Thus scientists began to emphasize observation using the five senses and experiment in order to gain new knowledge. Philosopher Francis Bacon (1561 – 1626) set out to reformulate scientific method to give the empirical, inductive process a more central place. (Not until the end of the seventeenth century would Isaac Newton reach a new understanding of physical reality.)

The voyages of discovery in the fifteenth century not only opened up New World trade routes, they gave further proof that ancient knowledge was both incomplete and often wrong. Explorers like Magellan contradicted the ancients by experience. They, for example, did not fall off the edge of the earth when sailing uncharted waters.

In 1572, a new star appeared in the skies over Europe that remained visible for a year and a half, even in the daytime, hovering above the moon. Because the Greek system viewed the heavens as changeless, some of the learned professors refused to acknowledge the new star, calling it an optical illusion. But for everyone else it was clear evidence the old system was in trouble.

Copernicus had taken the first bold step, refashioning the cosmic picture. He put the sun at the center in his system, thus making Earth one of the planets. Later Kepler would discover that the orbits were elliptical.

By the end of the seventeenth century, Newton had synthesized the work of Copernicus, Tycho Brahe, Kepler, and Galileo by achieving a unity of heaven and earth, with the same substances in the heavens and earth, all equally subject to mathematical analysis. Newton banished the Aristotelian terrestrial/celestial dichotomy that had dominated intellectual thought for nearly two thousand years.

The modern scientific enterprise was now ready to explore by the senses, combined with mathematics as well as the structure and operation of the universe. The Christian belief in a loving and brilliant Creator, and marvelous creation, inspired this new form of inquiry. As for my own study, I concur with physicist C. F. Von Weizsacker's conclusion that modern science is a "legacy," I might even have said "a child, of Christianity."

For reflection and discussion

- In what sense do you think of, or experience, God as beyond us or "transcendent"?
- What evidence is persuasive to you that God is also "immanent"?
- What prayer comes to mind in response to the reading?

The Bible and Its Influence on Culture

By Kelly Monroe Kullberg

Biblical knowledge unlocks for us the meaning of a large body of literature, art, history, and even news.[1] Consider the following newspaper headlines:

Molecular Biologist Traces a Mitochondrial Adam
Championship Game a David Versus Goliath Battle
Good Samaritans Honored for Aiding Victims
Arms Race Could Trigger Armageddon
Wildlife Refuge a New Noah's Ark

You're not alone if you've failed to be your "brother's keeper" or been banished "east of Eden." You're in good company if you've been "thrown into a lion's den," treated as a "scapegoat," "fallen on your sword," or seen "the writing on the wall."

But these specific references to Scripture are only small-scale instances of the Bible's influence on the English language. Whole volumes exist just to list the great books inspired by the gospel. We've mentioned Shakespeare and Tolstoy. There is also Steinbeck's *Grapes of Wrath*, and Alan Paton's *Cry, the Beloved Country*. Lew Wallace's *Ben Hur* was the bestselling novel of the nineteenth century, surpassing *Uncle Tom's Cabin* and only being surpassed eighty-four years later by *Gone with the Wind*. *Ben Hur* is historical fiction set in the times of the New Testament. It is a revenge-tragedy turning to redemption and explores the person of Christ and the nature of his kingdom.

The Bible has also inspired and generated many great works of art. Scripture gives us a glorious story from which innumerable writers, painters, sculptors, musicians, and scientists have borrowed through the ages. Think of the youthful power of Michelangelo's *David*. The pathos of Bach's *Saint Matthew Passion* and *Saint John Passion*.

We find such allusions in the titles, and often the content, of films like *Chariots of Fire* and *The Matrix*. In Ernest Hemingway's novel *The Old Man and the Sea*, the old man stretches himself on the mast as Jesus was stretched on a cross. In Charles Dickens's *A Tale of Two Cities*, Sidney Carton walks through the garden, an allusion to Gethsemane, before he chooses to take another man's place at the guillotine. William Faulkner based the title of his 1936 novel *Absalom, Absalom!* on the tragic story of King David and his eldest son.

We pick up inklings of Eden in Joni Mitchell's milestone song "Woodstock," "We are stardust, we are golden, / ... / And we got to get ourselves back to the garden."[2] Of course scriptural allusions echo throughout the lyrics of Emmylou Harris, Bruce Cockburn, Bob Dylan, and U2. James Taylor's "New Hymn" is a gorgeous, articulate longing for God, whoever or whatever the seeker feels that may be. The singer-seeker casts his bread upon the water: "We hunt your face and long to trust that your hid mouth will say again / 'let there be light,' a clear new day."[3]

For reflection and discussion

Authors once relied on the reader's biblical knowledge, but many today were not raised with biblical stories and teaching, and therefore the allusions are missed. Realizing this, a growing number of communities are beginning to offer biblical literacy in public education once again, not to preach but to teach, and to unlock the richness of much of our heritage, culture, and hope.

- Are there films that you've understood because you're biblically literate? Which?
- Do you feel a bit daunted by the thought of reading some of "the great books"?
- Is it hard to find the time to get through a novel? Do you read new books, old ones, or both?
- What music "echoes" the Bible in the beauty of creation? A tragic fall? Hope?

Picasso: Art as Entertainment

By Kelly Monroe Kullberg and Lael Arrington

One of the most recognized painters in twentieth-century art, Pablo Picasso (1881 – 1973), is best known as the cofounder of Cubism, along with Georges Braque. By disassembling parts of a figure and reassembling them from multiple perspectives, he showed the fragmentation of modern life as well as the artist's radical autonomy from traditional ideas about form. His painting is heralded as the beginning of modern art. Inadvertently, Picasso rendered onto canvas the biblical theme of sin's power to shatter and disfigure in ways never before explored.

Picasso is probably the most prolific artist on record, having produced over ten thousand paintings and one hundred thousand prints. What may be less familiar is the question that arises from the whole of Picasso's life: Is "art" about paint on a canvas or the living of life?

As a young man, Picasso spent most of his time in Barcelona and Paris, where he featured his lovers in his Rose period and Cubist paintings. His growing wealth and fame gave him entry into affluent society. In 1918, he married ballerina Olga Khokhlova. However, conflict ensued over his bohemian tendencies and numerous affairs, including one with a seventeen-year-old by whom he fathered a daughter.

Politically, Picasso remained neutral during the Spanish Civil War, and during World Wars I and II he refused to fight. Braque and others suspected him of cowardice more than pacifism. But a sense of his revulsion at war's suffering and brutality assaults the viewer in perhaps his greatest work, "Guernica." After the liberation of Paris in 1944, Picasso began an affair with a young art student, Françoise Gilot. They had two children, but Gilot left Picasso after nine years, accusing him not only of infidelity but also of physical abuse. He soon married Jacqueline Roque. In painting his new wife (and Olga and his young children) Picasso reverted to a more representational and sensitive portrayal. Perhaps love could not bear to dismember and disfigure the beloved.

Picasso, in his seventies, began to sense that he was no longer attractive, but rather grotesque, to women. In this realization, and perhaps in a season of soul-searching, he shared with the world at least one humble confession:

> In art the mass of the people no longer seek consolation and exaltation, but those who are refined, rich, unoccupied ... seek what is new, strange, original, extravagant, scandalous.
>
> I myself, since Cubism and before, have satisfied these masters and critics with all the changing oddities which have passed through my head, and the less they understood me, the more they admired me.
>
> By amusing myself with all these games, with all these absurdities, puzzles, rebuses, arabesques, I became famous and that very quickly. And fame for a painter means sales, gains, fortunes, riches. And today, as you know, I am celebrated, I am rich. But when I am alone with myself, I have not the courage to think of myself as an artist in the great and ancient sense of the term. Giotto, Titian, Rembrandt were great painters. I am only a public entertainer who has understood his times and exploited them as best he could. . . .
>
> Mine is a bitter confession, more painful than it may appear, but it has the merit of being sincere.[4]

Usually an artist's recognizable style expresses his core identity. But Picasso took no sides in wars, kept no faith with the women he loved, and continually changed styles, colors, and perspectives. The artist who tried to paint every possibility, even mutually exclusive ones, ultimately didn't stand behind any of them, even his own style.

For reflection and discussion

Imagine the internal confusion of a person with gifts, lusts, wealth, and fame, but without a true north to guide him. Integrity would be unlikely. Dis-integrity, and ultimate disintegration, would be the natural course.

- How do you respond to Picasso's constantly changing style?
- What kind of legacy does the world seem to think he has left? Does that seem at variance with his own frank assessment?
- Where are you inclined to follow your desires rather than God's calling to a kingdom kind of life of integration and commitment?
- If God is the Artist and your life the canvas, what kind of painting is God making of you? How do you want to respond to him about that?

Life as Entertainment

By Lael Arrington, with information primarily from *Life: The Movie* by Neal Gabler.

Perhaps the most significant cultural shift as we move forward in the new millennium is how life is becoming entertainment. Our presidential campaign candidates submit to the rule of YouTube, questioned by cartoon characters and Confederate rebels holding assault rifles. Our criminals perform real chase scenes on police shows. Our professors introduce their newest book decked in leather and flanked by buff and inscrutable bodyguards. As Neal Gabler has documented in *Life: The Movie*, "The deliberate application of the techniques of theater to politics, religion, education, literature, commerce, warfare, crime, *everything*, has converted them into branches of show business, where the overriding objective is getting and satisfying an audience."[5]

The finest art has always offered transcendence — inviting us to stand outside ourselves and gain perspective. Artistic images, music, and stories engage our rational faculties, which mediate and critique our emotional and visceral responses. Entertainment makes an end run around the intellect, stimulating the nervous system in much the same way as drugs do.

If art is sublime, then entertainment, according to Gabler, "is primarily about fun. It pulls us in, holding us captive, taking us both deeper into the work itself and deeper into ourselves, or at least into our own emotions and senses, before releasing us. All one has to do is watch people filing silently out of a movie theater, their eyes vacant, their faces slack, to see how one must reemerge after being submerged this way in a film. Entertainment is Plato's worst nightmare.

"If the primary effect of the media has been to turn nearly everything into entertainment, the secondary and ultimately more significant effect has been to force nearly everything to turn itself into entertainment in order to attract media attention."

Including people.

In the entertainment culture, the gold standard of personal value is no longer moral virtue or even significant accomplishment, but whether a person can grab and then hold the public's attention. And since what grabs and holds attention is fear and pleasure, those elite few who learn how to manipulate fear and pleasure attain the status of dreams: celebrity. To quote Daniel Boorstin, "The celebrity is a person who is known for his well-knownness."[6]

Gabler writes, "Not only are celebrities the protagonists of our news, the subjects of our daily discourse and the repositories of our values, but they have also embedded themselves so deeply in our consciousness that many individuals profess feeling closer to, and more passionate about, them than their own primary relationships."

When Princess Diana died suddenly and violently, the outpouring of grief dumbfounded the royal family but confirmed *People* magazine editor Richard Stoley's set of rules for a successful cover:

> Young is better than old. Pretty is better than ugly.
> Rich is better than poor. TV is better than music.
> Music is better than movies. Movies are better than sports.
> Anything is better than politics.
> And nothing is better than a celebrity who just died.[7]

For reflection and discussion

- In light of the glut of messages clamoring for attention, how do you respond to entertainment as a means of communication? Do you find it morally neutral?
- If you blog or put videos on YouTube or put yourself out there in our entertainment culture, what is your motivation? If you follow celebrities, why?

Pablo Picasso became well-known for his ability to confound and even shock the public. So did Ezekiel with his outrageous visions and dramas.

- Perhaps you would like to read Ezekiel 24 and 34 and consider how God uses fear and pleasure to grab the attention of his people. What does he desire in response?
- How might you want to respond to God about your engagement with entertainment?

General Revelation

By Sarah Sumner, PhD, professor of theology and ministry at Haggard School of Theology, Azusa Pacific University. She holds both an MBA and a PhD in systematic theology and writes books on leadership and relationships; *www.leadershipabovethe line.com.*

The word *theology* literally means "the study of God." But if you think about it, no one can study God per se. We can study God's words. We can study God's actions. But we can't study God himself. All we can study is God's revelation of himself. So a better definition of theology would be "the study of the revelation of God."

The marvel is that we can know God personally even though we cannot study him. We can pray to him and listen to him speak. We can praise him and apprehend his joy. We can sense the promptings of his Spirit. We can also experience his comfort. Yet we would never know him if he did not reveal himself to us.

Divine revelation is simply that which God has revealed and there are two main types: general revelation (that which God has revealed to all people everywhere at all times) and special revelation (that which God specially revealed to particular people at particular times). The incarnation and Scripture constitute God's special revelation; the universe, by contrast, is God's general revelation.

If we take seriously the notion that all of nature and all of history are aspects of divine revelation, then it's logical to conclude that *all there is to study is revelation!* The heavens are revelation (they declare the glory of God, see Psalm 19:1); people are revelation (we bear God's image, see Genesis 1:26–27); and God's Word is revelation (it is God-breathed, see 2 Timothy 3:16–17).

Granted, not everything that exists has been revealed. "The secret things belong to the LORD our God, but the things revealed belong to us and to our children forever" (Deuteronomy 29:29). We will never know, for instance, the fullness of the mind of God. As the apostle Paul said, "How unsearchable his judgments, and his paths beyond tracing out! 'Who has known the mind

WEEK 3

of the LORD?' ... For from him and through him and to him are all things" (Romans 11:33 – 36).

As Christians, we know that Scripture and the incarnation are both "from him and through him and to him." In other words, we know that special revelation is from God. But sometimes we forget that general revelation is also from God. The universe itself is "from him and through him and to him," even though it's passing away (1 John 2:17). Though it is not the same thing to study Scripture as it is to study the world (and everything in it), it simply isn't true that studying God's general revelation is a "secular" activity, as many have mistakenly claimed.

The proper work of a Christian is to seek God everywhere — in Scripture, in prayer, in music, in math, in drama, in pain, in nature, in work, and in relationships with people — both in special *and* general revelation. To me, it's fantastic that we can praise the Lord and feel moved to adoration, not only by the words of a hymn that recall God's special revelation but also by the melody itself that generally reveals God's beauty and creativity and brilliance.

Praise the Lord for sweet melodies that soothe us! Praise him for the marvel of lyrics and language and words! Praise him also for our ability to communicate with each other and share in the experience of being human! Praise him for his love! Praise him for his presence here on earth! Praise him for his greatness in Christ Jesus! Praise him! Praise him because the revelation of God is so vast and expansive that it's possible for us to think theologically all throughout each day. Oh, may today be a glorious day of wondering at the Great Revealer and trusting in his wisdom and love.

For reflection and discussion

- Sumner suggests ways that God is revealed through a hymn. What are some ways God is revealed through your favorite poem, through a pendulum clock, through a baseball game, through an integrated circuit, or through an ant?
- Can you think of ways that your home or your marriage or your family is a finger pointing to the glory of God?
- If "all there is to study is revelation," be mindful of ways to enjoy God today, and consider what you may want to say to God in response.

Note: *Throughout this day and the rest of the week's devotionals, look for the recurring theme of wonder in response to God's revelation.*

Ancient Empires and the Struggle for Babylon

By Kelly Monroe Kullberg and David Kullberg

Through the eyes of faith and study, history is the story of a sovereign God who trumps evil as he establishes his kingdom in the world. One intriguing starting place for a sweeping overview of ancient history is the book of Daniel, the young Hebrew prophet forced into the service of Nebuchadnezzar, the king of the Neo-Babylonian Empire (605 – 562 BC).[1]

The book of Daniel tells of the years of Israel's exile and influence on King Nebuchadnezzar. Taken nine hundred miles from his home, into captivity, Daniel would never again see his beloved Jerusalem, but he brought the God of Israel with him, into Babylon.

Babylon was a magnificent capital of the ancient world, regarded as the holy city of earlier Babylonia (circa 2300 BC) and the center of the Neo-Babylonian Empire from 612 BC. Its ruins can be found in present-day Iraq, fifty miles south of Baghdad. (Some believe this location to be at or near the site of the garden of Eden.)

The king of Babylon had a disturbing dream of an enormous statue. Daniel, known for integrity, academic stature, and faith in God, was the only man in Babylon who could accurately describe and interpret the King's dream. Daniel told Nebuchadnezzar:

> The head of the statue was made of pure gold, its chest and arms of silver, its belly and thighs of bronze, its legs of iron, its feet partly of iron and partly of baked clay.
>
> DANIEL 2:32 – 33

Daniel explained to the king the symbolic meaning of the dazzling statue, describing what historical theologians generally agree would become four of the great kingdoms of antiquity:

1. Babylon (head of gold)

Daniel said to King Nebuchadnezzar: "The God of heaven has given you dominion.... You are that head of gold" (Daniel 2:37 – 38).

WEEK 3

59

Babylon, the center of empire and culture, was more than a once-great city. Its name still remains a proud symbol for the City of Man. Built on the Euphrates River, where it grew in size and influence, Babylon was famous for extravagant palaces for kings, hanging gardens, temples to various gods, gold shrines, and ornate beds for temple prostitutes. The new Babylon of Daniel's day erected a 650-foot "glimmering enamel ziggurat eerily reminiscent of the former tower of Babel," writes Bible scholar Beth Moore, with a timely warning, "Few could resist Babylon's charms."[2]

2. Medo-Persia (silver) 539 BC

Daniel: "After you, another kingdom will arise, inferior to yours" (Daniel 2:39).

In 539 BC, Babylon fell to Cyrus the Great, king of Persia. Babylon's fifty-six miles of walls were impenetrable, so Cyrus's troops awaited the evening of a Babylonian feast before diverting the Euphrates River upstream. The Persians then marched under the walls through shallow water. Cyrus claimed the city by walking through the gates, with little resistance from the drunken Babylonians.

An unlikely hero to the Jews, Cyrus later issued a decree permitting the exiled Jews to return to their homeland and, under the leadership of Ezra and Nehemiah, rebuild the temple.

Under Cyrus and, later, King Darius, the ancient Babylonian arts of astronomy and mathematics were renewed. The city remained under Persian rule for two centuries, until Alexander the Great's entrance in 331 BC.

3. Greece (bronze) 331 BC

Daniel: "Next, a third kingdom, one of bronze, will rule over the whole earth" (Daniel 2:39).

In 331 BC, the Persians were defeated by Alexander the Great, and Babylon fell to the young Greek conqueror. Greece's cultural contributions in law, philosophy, art, and architecture are legendary in shaping Western civilization. In curious alignment with Daniel's interpretation of the statue's bronze belly and thighs, historians today refer to "Aegean civilization" as a term for the Bronze Age civilizations of Greece and the Aegean.

In 323 BC, following Alexander's death in the palace of Nebuchadnezzar, political factions soon emptied the city, and Babylon's empire virtually came to a close, though more than a century later, sacrifices were still being performed in its old sanctuary.

4. Rome (iron) 146 BC

Daniel: "Finally, there will be a fourth kingdom, strong as iron ... and as iron breaks things to pieces, so it will crush and break all the others" (Daniel 2:40).

In the Battle of Corinth in 146 BC, Rome defeated Greece and incorporated it into the Roman Empire. By the 140s BC, when the Roman Empire conquered the region, Babylon had declined to complete desolation and obscurity.

The future and eternal kingdom foreseen

Daniel to Nebuchadnezzar: "While you were watching, a rock was cut out, but not by human hands. It struck the statue on its feet of iron and clay and smashed them.... But the rock that struck the statue became a huge mountain and filled the whole earth" (Daniel 2:34 – 35).

Daniel: "In the time of those kings, the God of heaven will set up a kingdom that will never be destroyed, nor will it be left to another people. It will crush all those kingdoms and bring them to an end, but it will itself endure forever" (Daniel 2:44).

Further, some scholars see in Daniel chapter 9 a clear calculation, accurate to the year of Jesus' birth, predicting the coming of the Messiah within the time of the Roman Empire.

WEEK 3

For reflection and discussion

- What are some historical events which raise concerns for you about God's role?
- Where have you seen evidence of God's activity on the world scene?
- How does Daniel's point of view speak to yours?
- What would you like to bring to God in prayer around this Scripture?
- How does Daniel's revelation of God's providential hand directing history affect your confidence in the future?

Note on the recent fate of Babylon: *Reconstruction was started in 1985 by Iraq's Saddam Hussein, building on top of the old ruins of Babylon. Many bricks used were inscribed with: "Built by Saddam Hussein, son of Nebuchadnezzar, to glorify Iraq." At the city entrance, Saddam installed a huge portrait of himself alongside Nebuchadnezzar.*

Plato: Lover of Truth, Beauty, and the Good

By **John Mark Reynolds**, PhD, professor of philosophy, Biola University. Reynolds makes frequent "study" trips to Disneyland with his students at the Torrey Honors Institute, of which he is founder and director; *www.johnmarkreynolds.com*.

Plato (ca 428 – 348/7 BC) was the philosopher of love. He wrote to cajole the thoughtless into falling in love with wisdom. His dialogues are both art and philosophy, containing some of the greatest stories ever written (such as the Atlantis myth from *Timaeus*) and ideas that still intrigue even the most analytic of modern thinkers. His influence on the church has been remarkable and ranges from Saint Augustine to The Inklings, the Oxford literary discussion group that included J. R. R. Tolkien and C. S. Lewis.

It is no accident that in *The Last Battle*, Narnia's Professor Kirk "added under his breath, 'It's all in Plato, all in Plato: bless me, what do they teach them in these schools.'"[3] Professor Kirk was right. There is no understanding Christendom without considering the writings of that noblest of pagans, Plato.

Plato lived in a dark time that was dominated by the polytheistic religion of Homer and Hesiod. The love of a god in this twisted system was a prelude to destruction or rape, not to a beatific vision.

The cultural establishment killed his great teacher Socrates to defend itself from reason, and Plato waged a clever war against it using both reason *and* beauty.

He used the yearning of the human heart for something *more* to challenge the powerful. There is a desire for justice in every human, from the decadent aristocrat to members of the mob, but justice is hard to find. There is a hunger for truth, but if the truth is out there, then it is difficult to uncover. This longing for something "other" Plato calls "love."

Plato knows love is dangerous. So many men in his culture, as in our own, limit love to physical passion. Dangerously few see it as the quest for a soul mate. Only a remnant recognize reality and love the physical, the soul, and ideas on their way to a greater love for the Good.

In the *Symposium*, Plato examines this unsatisfactory state of affairs. In a brief dialogue at the very center of the book, he has his master, Socrates, discover a great truth:

> "Now tell me about love," he [Socrates] said, "Is Love the love of nothing or of something?"
> "Of something, surely!" he said.

Plato realizes that love is of *something*. He cannot believe that any common and natural desire is ultimately incapable of finding its proper fulfillment. The deep longing for justice, beauty, and truth must have an end. Contrary to the religion of Homer, the cosmos is not fundamentally chaotic but contains a great and good order.

Plato believed, based on best reason and best human experience, that there was more to the cosmos than empty desire and death.

This great Good is unknown to Socrates in *Symposium*. It is known to exist, but its nature is unknown. The vision of this known Unknown is the proper end of the philosophical life.

At the end of his life, Plato would defend the idea of a Creator God, the mysterious known Unknown, but he did not discern the name of that God.

The truth Plato could not see, Saint Paul revealed to the Greeks in his great sermon of Acts 17 in Plato's city of Athens. The ancient world finally received the good news its brightest and best had longed to hear.

In space and time, not just in the world of ideas, the known Unknown took flesh and dwelt among us. The incarnation was the mystery that even Plato's great vision could not penetrate.

Plato desperately wanted knowledge of the judgment beyond death. In *Republic* X, he invented a story of a man who died and came back to life again. He told a story about justice in the afterlife, and Socrates said:

> His story wasn't lost but preserved, and it would save us, if we were persuaded by it, for we would then make a good crossing of the River of Forgetfulness, and our souls wouldn't be defiled.
>
> REPUBLIC X, LINE 621

We stand on the other side of the incarnation where a God-Man died and came to life again. He came not just to tell us of the far country but also to live within us. The simplest Christian knows what Plato could not know. This is sufficient reason for both profound humility and great joy.

God did not stand beyond us. There was no reason to think he would love us and good reason to think he would not, but love needs no reason. God condescended to love humanity. This love is not merely mental but put on flesh so that we could behold "his glory, the glory of the one and only [Son], who came from the Father, full of grace and truth" (John 1:14).

We are driven by love to God, who is good, truth, and beauty, a love that is not just an abstraction but which, as Dante said, "moves the sun and the other stars."

For reflection and discussion

- What do the good, the true, and the beautiful look like today? How do you experience your longings for this?
- Are these longings just wishful thinking? How may God be speaking to you through your desires?
- How can our longings take us to God and his Word? What would that look like?
- Is it possible that you love God's truth — the precepts, the poetry, the prophecy — more than you love God as a person? Would you rather read books about God than spend face time with him?

The Big Bang and the Bible

By **Hugh Ross**, PhD, an astronomer and astrophysicist, founder and president of Reasons to Believe (a science-faith think tank). Ross has authored or contributed to over fifteen books, including *Creation as Science*. Adapted from a paper by Ross and professor emeritus John Rea, Old Testament, Regent University. The original (Issue 3, 2000, Facts for Faith) is at *www.reasons.org*.

Most physical science textbooks credit Arno Penzias and Robert Wilson with the discovery that the universe arose from a hot big bang. While it is true that they were the first (1965) to detect the radiation left over from that event, they were not the first scientists to recognize that the universe expanded from an extremely hot and compact beginning. In 1946 George Gamow calculated that the present abundance of elements in the universe could only be accounted for by cosmic expansion from a near infinitely hot condition. In 1929 Edwin Hubble showed that the velocities of galaxies result from a general expansion of the universe. As early as 1925 Abbé Georges Lemaître, an astrophysicist and a Jesuit priest, was the first scientist to promote a big bang creation event.

The first direct scientific evidence for a big bang universe dates back to 1916. Albert Einstein noted that the field equations of general relativity predicted an expanding universe. Unwilling to accept the idea of a cosmic beginning implied by such expansion, Einstein altered his theory to conform with the "preference" of his day — an eternally existent universe.

All these scientists, however, were upstaged by Job, Moses, David, Isaiah, Jeremiah, and other Bible authors writing as much as 2,500 years ago or more. The Bible's prophets and apostles explicitly described the two most fundamental features of the big bang: a transcendent cosmic beginning in the finite past and a general, ongoing expansion. "This is what God the LORD says — he who created the heavens and stretched them out ..." (Isaiah 42:5). They also implied the progressive cooling of the cosmos.

The Hebrew verb translated "created" in Isaiah 42:5 (as in Genesis 1:1 and similar passages) is *bara*. One of its primary definitions is "to bring into existence something new, that which did not previously exist."

Other Scriptures comment on the stretching out of the heavens. The Hebrew verb forms indicate this stretching is both "finished" and "ongoing."

WEEK 3

Isaiah 40:22 depicts both actions in the same verse. The simultaneously finished and ongoing property of stretching is identical to the big bang concept of cosmic expansion: All the physics (specifically, the laws, constants, and equations of physics) are instantly created, designed, and "finished" so as to guarantee an ongoing, continual expansion of the universe at exactly the right rates with respect to time so that physical life will be possible.

Jeremiah argues implicitly for a big bang universe when he declares, "The laws of the heavens [thermodynamics, gravity, and electromagnetism] are fixed." These constants have not changed since the creation event itself.

Continual cosmic expansion under fixed physical laws means that radiation from the creation event will get colder as the cosmos gets older, which is exactly what scientists can now measure. Furthermore, if the physical laws had changed, we would not be here to discover or discuss them. Changes in the laws of gravity or electromagnetism would make stars impossible. Gravity, electromagnetism, and thermodynamics yield stable orbits of planets around stars and of electrons around the nuclei of atoms, stabilities on which life depends. Most importantly, the constancy of these laws means we can trust what we observe and measure. We can trust it to reveal the truth, not an illusion. And that fits God's stated purpose — to reveal himself and his attributes in what he has made (Romans 1). His Word and his world yield a consistent picture of our Creator and Savior.

For reflection and discussion

Many people are unaware of the Bible's specific detail regarding the origins, constants, and expansion of the universe.

- What new aspect of creation might you want to further explore?
- If Scripture is accurate about such large questions, what smaller, personal matters might be illuminated with "insider information" from the same Bible?
- What aspect of God's world, and Word, are you most thankful for today?

C. S. Lewis, J. R. R. Tolkien, and the Quest for Joy

By **Martha D. Linder**, former teacher of English, Collège du Léman, Versoix, Switzerland. An Anglophile living in Florida and a lifelong enthusiast of C. S. Lewis, Linder teaches Bible studies and serves on various civic and ministry boards in her community. Linder encourages truth, beauty, and goodness in the lives of many younger friends.

It was at a faculty meeting in Oxford on May 11, 1926, that Clives Staples Lewis and John Ronald Reuel Tolkien spoke for the first time, little realizing that they would form one of the greatest literary friendships of the twentieth century. Although Tolkien had been born in South Africa, and Lewis in Northern Ireland, their backgrounds were similar: they had both lost their mothers in childhood, been wounded in bitter battles in France in World War I, and were currently professors of English literature at Oxford. More importantly, Tolkien and Lewis both had childhoods dominated by their imaginations. It was their love of "northernness," however, that sparked the flame of excitement, inducing Tolkien to invite Lewis to "Coalbiters," a society Tolkien had founded, where members read Icelandic sagas and myths in their original languages.

Lewis's love of what he called "northernness" had begun as a child. Reading Longfellow's *Saga of King Olaf*, he was caught up in an "indescribable intensity of heart-breaking longing" and a desire for something that he could only call "joy." He sought to recapture that sensation in northern myths, beautiful music, and the splendors of nature — but joy proved elusive.

An atheist at the time of their meeting, Lewis accepted Tolkien's invitation with gusto, never dreaming where their association would eventually lead.

As these two men grew to know one another, Tolkien asked Lewis if he would listen to and critique a major myth he was writing, *Silmarillion*. They began meeting weekly and were soon joined by Lewis's brother "Warnie" and kindred spirits such as Hugo Dyson, Robert Havard, Charles Williams, and Owen Barfield. Gathering at Lewis's rooms at Magdalen College or at the "Eagle and Child" pub, they dubbed themselves "The Inklings." They brought their manuscripts to read to each other, encouraging each other onward, and

WEEK 3

read together the works of literary lights such as Dorothy Sayers and George MacDonald. Readings would end in great spirited conversation and uproarious laughter.

Much later on, Lewis's *Chronicles of Narnia* and Tolkien's *Lord of the Rings* were first heard at gatherings of The Inklings. In fact, Tolkien quite frankly stated that were it not for Lewis's encouragement, he would never have completed writing the *Lord of the Rings* trilogy.

As The Inklings forged deep bonds of friendship, Lewis began to realize that these were "good" men but, alas, Christians. This was perplexing to Lewis. How could these brilliant scholars believe in a myth? Appreciate myth? Yes. Revel in myth? Yes. Compose myth? Yes. But to *believe* in a real but supernatural God, who came to earth to forgive sins and reconcile man to himself? Incomprehensible. He preferred the worldviews of George Bernard Shaw, Bertrand Russell, and their ilk.

It was Tolkien, however, a lifelong Roman Catholic, who finally put the pieces together for Lewis. On September 19, 1931, after dinner together, Lewis, Tolkien, and Dyson walked and talked in the college gardens until four o'clock in the morning.[4] As Lewis wrote to his boyhood friend Arthur Greeves,

> Now what Dyson and Tolkien showed me was this: that if I met the idea of sacrifice in a Pagan story I didn't mind at all.... I like [liked] it very much and was mysteriously moved by it.... Now the story of Christ is simply a true myth, a myth working on us in the same way as the others but with this tremendous difference that it *really happened*, remembering that it is God's myth, whereas, the others are men's myths.[5]

That night Lewis "gave in, admitted that God was God, and knelt and prayed." His belief and love of Christ was to follow and possess him with lasting and no longer elusive joy.

Later, Lewis tells us in the preface to his perennial bestseller, *Mere Christianity*, "Ever since I became a Christian I have thought that the best, perhaps the only, service I could do for my unbelieving neighbors was to explain and defend the belief that has been common to nearly all Christians at all times."[6] This book and those which followed were an outpouring of his brilliant mind, blending imagination and logic, and continue to capture readers today. As a result, Lewis is considered the greatest and most often quoted Christian writer of the twentieth century. Lewis and Tolkien could not have anticipated that multiple millions of their books, products of a God-forged friendship, would find eager readers.

Did Lewis marry? Not until he was an old bachelor of fifty-eight. Curiously, her name was Joy. But that's another story.

For reflection and discussion

Lewis and Tolkien stood strong against the "culture of death" in their own time. They fought for the race of men and women and did not let the Devil steal their joy despite the horrors each experienced in the trenches of World War I and in the ivory towers of modernity and nihilism. They bore much of God's image in their humanity: love and scholarship, conscience and courage, art and imagination.

- Has your life been touched by the writings of these two friends, whether in books, films, mythology, or conversations about faith? How so?
- What specifically touches you in some way as you think of *Narnia* or the *Lord of the Rings*?
- What have you always wanted to create? Thank God for small beginnings. And a few creative friends.

The Hudson River School of Painting: A Brush with Glory

By **Terry Glaspey**, a student of art, theology, and intellectual history with an MA in history. An essayist, Glaspey is the author of several books, including *Book Lover's Guide to Great Reading*.

There is a tradition, going back at least as far as King David, of recognizing in nature the fingerprints of God, a manifestation of his glory. In Psalm 19, David sings out, "The heavens declare the glory of God; the skies proclaim the work of his hands." Such recognition of God's majesty in nature is what fueled the imaginations of one of America's most important schools of painting.

The Hudson River School was a mid-nineteenth-century American art movement of loosely affiliated landscape painters. Their earliest works were primarily of the Hudson River Valley in upstate New York, though many of them traveled throughout the United States and even abroad, looking for vistas of beauty and grandeur. Their aesthetic vision was fueled by the influence of romanticism and by their Christian vision of the created world. They saw the unspoiled landscape of the Americas as an expression of the majesty and glory of the God who had created it.

Their paintings were highly detailed and realistic, with an emphasis on wide untamed vistas and subtle symbols and effects that evoked a sense of their spiritual vision: the dramatic effects of light illuminating a landscape or a cross visible among the foliage. Human beings and their civilization are usually absent from their work or, if present, dwarfed by the mountains and trees.

Nature, wrote Thomas Cole (1801 – 1848), the founder of the Hudson River School, provides the soul "a sweet foretaste of heaven." The influence of Cole's strong evangelical faith and his conservative values can be seen most clearly in his two famous series of allegorical paintings: the five-part "The Course of Empire" (which depicted the rise and fall of human civilization) and the four-part "Voyage of Life" (which focused on the stages of a human life, from birth to eternity).

Cole's prize student, Frederic Edwin Church (1826 – 1900) carried on the tradition of infusing breathtaking landscapes with a distinctly spiritual aura. An expedition to South America in search of exotic scenery resulted in one of his most famous paintings, "The Heart of the Andes." It made him an instant celebrity. This massive painting (over five feet high and nearly ten feet wide) was installed in a specially lit and decorated room in New York City, where he charged admission for the public to view it. For weeks it was the talk of the town and drew large crowds of spectators. Other unforgettable paintings by Church include "Niagara" and "Cotopaxi."

Other important painters of this school, including Asher Brown Durand and Albert Bierstadt, are united in their depiction of majestic landscapes unspoiled by the intrusion of humanity. Their spiritual vision of a beauty beyond words calls to something deep within. Such paintings perform perhaps the highest service that art can offer up to us — they create a moment of transcendence.

For reflection and discussion

In Thomas Cole's "The Course of Empire," we see what has been called his "wonderfully tragic vision" of the rise and fall of civilization, played out over centuries against a particular scenic backdrop — a distinctive rocky outcropping overlooking gently rolling hills that stretch down to an inlet of the sea. In the first painting a small circle of teepees marks the beginning of civilization. The second shows agrarian development. A young shepherd tends his animals. A woman does her chores by the brook. In the third painting the rocky acropolis looks down upon a sweeping empire. Lavishly adorned buildings swathe the hills and shoreline. A colossal statue of a great man welcomes ships to the harbor. In the fourth, Viking-style ships fill the shoreline. Buildings burn. The invading army slaughters homeland troops and ravishes their wives and daughters. In the final painting, "Desolation" (at *http://web .sbu.edu/theology/bychkov/cole.html*) vines encircle the crumbling pillars and shrubbery sprouts amid weathered blocks of stone. The cityscape reverts to landscape.

Why would a landscape painter who delights in God's majesty in nature paint such a series? I (Lael) think of the summer I traveled from Orlando to Colorado. On the cog railway to the summit of Pike's Peak, as we gained altitude and ever-grander vistas, what hit me was not culture shock but creation shock. I was shaking off the all-about-you-ness of Orlando's thrill rides and five-star resorts — designed to enchant and cater to our every whim — and instead I was feeling like a small speck on a gigantic mountain.

Cole's series packs the same power. Not that we are supposed to feel inconsequential before God's mountains or shorelines, but rather that the sweeping vistas and crashing waves take us to the greatness and majesty of God. And the resorts and empires "grow strangely dim in the light of his glory and grace."

- Can you recall a scene or painting that aroused a sense of transcendence? Give some details of what made it seem vivid and meaningful to you.

Christian counselor Leighton Ogg has asked, "Of what did Job repent?" His answer: "His wonder was too small."

- How can you nurture and acknowledge your wonder for God today?
- Look at the entire series of "The Course of Empire" paintings at the website mentioned on the previous page. What do you find sobering? Hopeful?

Sex, Intimacy, and Worship

By Bruce Herman, a painter and Lothlórien Distinguished Chair in Fine Arts at Gordon College in Wenham, Mass., whose work has been exhibited in eleven major cities. This entry germinated at a Harvard Veritas forum with Herman, Bill Edgar, Elisabeth Overmann Bauman, and Drew Trotter speaking on "Media and Image, Veritas or Vanitas?" *www.brucehermanonline.com.*

I don't think it's a mistake that Jesus referred to himself as a bridegroom and the church as his bride. Romantic love gestures toward divine love. Genuine erotic love is a powerful and beautiful reflection in this world of the world above — hallowed human love, not its cheap imitation. Promiscuous sex is a game, a lie, because you can't possibly mean it: I give myself to you and take it back. It's the same with religion — which can also be promiscuous, a pose.

In art and in popular culture, there has been a gradual slide away from any sense of what is taboo. Without taboos, there is no meaning. Taboos fence in a particular experience — and what is fenced in also fences other things out. Case in point: sexuality. The fence around sexuality is there to protect something that is very vulnerable and precious. If you knock the fence down, you no longer have the sense of preciousness, and eventually all sensitivity is lost.

What is sex? At its core, sex is letting your guard down. It's saying, "I trust you enough that I don't have to protect myself in your presence. I can take off my clothes as well as all my pretenses. I can let down the fence with you because I trust you. It's safe to give myself to you, and you belong to me and I to you." And this is possible only when there is lifelong commitment to honor that gift of self.

No one can entrust themselves to another person who has no intention of keeping that trust. That's the heart of sex. The physical aspect of sex is not irrelevant, but it's actually more a symbolic enactment of the spiritual reality taking place. I entrust myself to you and give myself wholly into your care by becoming utterly transparent, utterly vulnerable.

Sex at its best is trust. Why have a fence around it? Because it is so precious, so vulnerable, and so subject to corruption. That which is most precious is most rare.

WEEK 3

And authentic intimacy is especially rare these days.

It is the same with prayer and communion with God, which is the ultimate form of intimacy. Bride and Bridegroom. "I can let my guard down with you, God, because I trust you." Genuine prayer is not some kind of performance. Jesus said, "Lock the door before you pray." This is your relationship with God. Don't violate it by inviting the whole world in to see how great you are at praying. We have problems in our culture with images that violate our sense of what's true, what's beautiful, what's good, what's holy because we have lost the habit of mind which says there is something in my life which must be protected that doesn't belong to just anybody. We have radically democratized the spiritual life and invited the whole world in as if this were a spectator sport.

Though congregating to worship together is a great joy, we need to avoid the subtle temptation of a performance-like prayer and song, profaning what — who — is most sacred. The hyped phenomenon of "worship style" or "worship experience" as self-conscious performance can be like the performance-oriented pop culture — and can subvert the genuineness of our encounter with the Lord.

Worship *is* encounter with God, not an ecstatic experience that can be televised or broadcast or prompted by a technique. You can't have it both ways. You can't have intimacy and also have your sex life or your religious life publicized as a spectator sport. Either you'll have the public display of communion/sex or you'll have authentic intimacy — one or the other, but not both.

Communion is true communication, and it means entering into, knowing the other person intimately. You cannot know another person or know God until you can let down your guard, and no one lets down their guard as a public event — that is, unless they are lying or acting on stage. The authentic article can only be encountered in privacy. Hence the taboo.

We are told that one day believers will join "thousands upon thousands," from every race and nation, encircling the throne of God and singing "Worthy is the Lamb who was slain ... to receive glory!" Mysteriously we will have total intimacy with God and with those thousands of fellow worshipers, singing with the hosts of heaven in that great congregation at the end of time, "Holy, Holy, Holy" — entering fully into what we so deeply desire — perfect communion of bride and Bridegroom.

For reflection and discussion

Place me like a seal over your heart, like a seal on your arm; for love is as strong as death, its jealousy unyielding as the grave. It burns like blazing fire, like a mighty flame. Many waters cannot quench love; rivers cannot sweep it away. If one were to give all the wealth of one's house for love, it would be utterly scorned.

SONG OF SONGS 8:6 – 7

These feelings are universal — and sexual feelings are protected only under God's sovereign covenant with us — in lifelong marriage.

- How do these passages in the Song of Songs make you feel?
- Can you see the passion and beauty in the romantic love described by King Solomon's poem?
- If you are married, how might you build more sacred privacy, thus intimacy, into your life?
- If you are single, how are other forms of intimacy between single friends guarded by God? How are they achieved, and what sorts of "fences" are needed?
- Why do you think the Song of Songs, a poem about sexual intimacy, has been traditionally associated with Christ and the church? Read Paul's stunning assertions in Ephesians chapter 5, where he says that mutual submission and self-forgetfulness is the paradigm of marriage and our life as the bride of Christ (vv. 21 – 33).

WEEK 3

God's Second Word: The Bible

By Kelly Monroe Kullberg, adapted from her book *Finding God Beyond Harvard*.

To have proper knowledge about reality, and therefore proper confidence in the living of life, it helps to begin by humbly, quietly, carefully — paying attention. Is there a true north by which or by whom to navigate? Is truth knowable? How? This is the discipline in philosophy called "epistemology." Many believe that truth is knowable because truth is *self*-revealing. We're given senses and a mind, spirit, and conscience to respond. Truth speaks our language. Christians believe that truth is a person who has revealed himself in three words: First, the creation of the universe; second, a book, the Bible; third, a person, Jesus Christ, "the Word become flesh."

Here we will pay attention to the second Word of truth, the Bible.

Second Word: The Bible

If there is a God who can create a universe, it would follow that he could manage to write and oversee the printing of a book. He could even care for its translation into many languages and cultures. Unique among sacred texts, the Bible claims to be God's Word in print, preserved over millennia, yet always fresh.

The Author-God of the Bible opens the book, and himself, to our investigation, inviting the reader to experience the Word as either false or true, leading to death or life. It is full of guidance for living as well as useful information for archaeologists, historians, scientists, healers, artists, lovers, parents, students, and leaders.

Astrophysicist Hugh Ross was a skeptic who used history and science to test each of the world's "holy books." To his surprise, he found the Bible noticeably different from the other religious texts — simple, direct, and specific. "I determined there were over 300 statements with no contradictions. As a scientist, I had to figure the probability of such accuracy; it was less than 1 in 10 to the 300th ($1/10^{300}$). Why such accuracy? Because the Bible and the universe have the same Creator."[1]

The book — or rather the collection of sixty-six books, once called "the divine library" and canonized as the Bible — is compelling at various levels:

WEEK 4

77

its consistency with scientific discovery; the accuracy of journalistic details; the fidelity of its transmission over time; the *coherence* and *symphony* of its many books though written over 1,600 years, in three languages (Hebrew, Greek, Aramaic), on three continents (Europe, Asia, Africa), by forty writers spanning the spectrum of rich and poor, nobility and commoner, in times of wartime and peace; and, finally, the clear fulfillment of many specific prophecies (e.g., Daniel's prophecy of empires and the many Old Testament details of the birth, death, and resurrection of the Messiah).

This Word is a hitchhiker's guide to the whole cosmos — especially life on one amazing blue planet. The text seems true to our human nature and our desires for love, mercy, connection, meaning, and glory. In its pages we find three-dimensional people like ourselves, with wavering faith, mixed motives, pride and jealousy, at times humility and regret. The stories are gritty, honest, surprisingly unedited, and filled with real-life detail. It's full of the stuff we're full of.

The Bible. Examined for lifetimes by scholars. Cherished by children. Read as the only hope for the dying. Studied in its layers of depth, coherence, and wisdom. On a good day we'll even do what the Author says. (The best evidence for the truth of Scripture, naturally, comes with the fruit of living it.)

With regard to fashionable and recycled "controversy" regarding the authority of Scripture and "the historical Jesus," I recommend the prodigious scholarship of scholars like F. F. Bruce, N. T. Wright, and Bruce Metzger. And I cannot help but offer here the common sense perspective of eminent philosopher and epistemologist Dallas Willard, in his helpful statement, "My Assumptions about the Bible":

> On its human side, I assume that [the Bible] was produced and preserved by competent human beings who were at least as intelligent and devout as we are today. I assume that they were quite capable of accurately interpreting their own experience and of objectively presenting what they heard and experienced in the language of their historical community, which we today can understand with due diligence.
>
> On the divine side, I assume that God has been willing and competent to arrange for the Bible, including its record of Jesus, to emerge and be preserved in ways that will secure his purposes for it among human beings worldwide. Those who actually believe in God will be untroubled by this. I assume that he did not and would not leave his message to humankind in a form that can only be understood by a handful of late-twentieth-century professional scholars,

who cannot even agree among themselves on the theories that they assume to determine what the message is.

The Bible is, after all, God's gift to the world through his Church, not to the scholars. It comes through the life of his people and nourishes that life. Its purpose is practical, not academic. An intelligent, careful, intensive but straightforward reading — that is, one not governed by obscure and faddish theories or by a mindless orthodoxy — is what it requires to direct us into life in God's kingdom.[2]

For reflection and discussion

The Bible's Author refines our vision of himself, and thus of ourselves. Not only does he reveal himself as the Maker of the heavens and earth but, all the more so, as the Lover of our souls, with a plan to redeem all creation.

Many come to love this Word like we love treasure maps and treasures, like we love opening a love letter. It is a story worth living in. And a Word that is alive. More than anything, many love the Bible because we find in it the Author's *heart*, seen most clearly in his word made flesh — the person of Jesus.

- What has been your experience of reading the Bible? Challenges? Satisfactions? Goals?

The Genius of Jesus

By **Lael Arrington**, adapted from *The Divine Conspiracy* by Dallas Willard, who teaches philosophy at the University of Southern California, *www.dwillard.org*; and from *Finding God Beyond Harvard* by Kelly Monroe Kullberg.

"Jesus is not just nice, he is brilliant," writes Dallas Willard in *The Divine Conspiracy*. "He is the smartest man who ever lived.... He always has the best information on everything and certainly also on the things that matter most in human life. In our culture Jesus Christ is automatically dis-associated from brilliance or intellectual capacity. Not one in a thousand will spontaneously think of him in conjunction with words such as *well-informed*, *brilliant*, or *smart*. Einstein, Bill Gates, and the obligatory rocket scientists will stand out.

"What lies at the heart of the astonishing disregard of Jesus found in the moment-to-moment existence of multitudes of professing Christians is a simple lack of respect for him. He is not seriously considered or presented as a person of great ability. We all know that action must be based on knowledge, and we grant the right to lead and teach only to those we believe to know what is real and what is best.

"Jesus knew how to suspend gravity and eliminate unfruitful fruit trees without saw or axe. He only needed a word. Surely he must be amused at what Nobel prizes are awarded for today. He knew how to transform the tissues of the human body from sickness to health and from death to life. In fact he knew how to enter physical death, actually to die, and then live on beyond death. Forget cryonics!"

Jesus' contribution to human knowledge extended widely. In *Finding God Beyond Harvard*, Kelly Kullberg writes, "Jesus taught a culture how to value women and children. He understood ancient empires, Rome, agriculture and the natural world, ethics and human relations. He taught how a life of gratitude yields the fruit of health, joy, and purposefulness. He was a skilled carpenter. He even taught Peter a few things about fishing.

"He also lived with authority. He didn't teach chemistry; he turned water into wine. He didn't teach weather patterns; he calmed a storm. He didn't teach medicine; he healed hurting people and instructed his followers to heal in his name. He didn't teach moral philosophy; he forgave and enabled us to forgive. He didn't teach a course on world hunger; he fed the multitudes and commanded his followers to feed them also. Jesus fired on all pistons.

"I love how Jesus saved the woman about to be stoned to death. How he saw people who were hiding or ashamed. I love his humility to empty himself of power and self-defense, his confidence in God's love even while dying on the cross. I'm grateful for his eyewitness knowledge of the Father and his promise to prepare a place for us with him in heaven forever.

"When Dallas Willard spoke with professors and graduate students at the faculty club on 'The University and the Brilliance of Jesus,' a humanities professor said, 'I'm confused. You, one of the world's prominent philosophers, believe in Jesus Christ as the hope of the world?'

"To which Willard responded, 'Who else did you have in mind?'"

For reflection and discussion

- In what areas of life do you recognize Jesus' brilliance and wisdom — faith, relationships, work, education, ethics, sexuality, showing compassion to the needy? Are there areas where you tend to overlook Jesus' teaching?
- What kind of authority do you recognize in Jesus?
- Do you believe that he is competent to direct the totality of your life in the twenty-first century? Why or why not?
- How do you want to respond to him in light of this reading?

WEEK 4

Moral and Ethical Relativism

By **Kerby Anderson**, national director, Probe Ministries. Anderson is a national radio host, author of ten books, including *Christian Ethics in Plain Language*, and has taught worldview issues to students in Eastern Europe; *www.probe.org.*

A view of relative ethics holds that if there is no absolute truth, then there is no absolute standard for ethical behavior. And if truth is merely personal preference, then certainly ethics is personal and situational.

Moral relativism is the belief that morality is relative to the group or person. In other words, there is no set of rules that universally applies to everyone. In a sense, moral relativism can be summed up with the phrase: It all depends. Is murder always wrong? Relativists would say, "It depends on the circumstances."

Moral relativism is self-defeating. People who say they believe in relativism cannot live consistently within their ethical system because moral relativists make moral judgments all the time. They speak out against racism, exploitation, genocide, greed, and much more, demonstrating that moral relativism is self-defeating.

There are two other problems with moral relativism. First, one cannot critique morality from the outside. If ethics are relative to each culture, then anyone outside the culture loses the right to critique it. Essentially that was the argument of the Nazi leaders during the Nuremberg Trials. What right do you have to criticize what we did within Nazi Germany? We had our own system of morality. Fortunately, the judges and Western society rejected such a notion.

Second, one cannot critique morality from the inside. Cultural relativism leaves no place for social reformers. The abolition movement, the suffrage movement, and the civil rights movement are all examples of social movements that ran counter to the social circumstances of the culture. Reformers like William Wilberforce and Martin Luther King Jr. stood up in the midst of society and pointed out immoral practices and called society to a moral solution. Abolishing slavery and fighting for civil rights were good things even if they were opposed by many people within society.

Not only is moral relativism self-defeating, moral relativism leads to moral anarchy. It is based upon the assumption that every person should be allowed to live according to his or her own moral standards. Consider how dangerous that would be in a society with such vastly different moral standards.

Some people think stealing is perfectly moral, at least in certain circumstances. Some people think murder can be justified. Society simply cannot allow everyone to do what they think is right in their own eyes.

Obviously, society allows a certain amount of moral anarchy when there is no threat to life, liberty, or property. Each year when I go to the state fair, I see lots of anarchy when I watch the people using the bumper cars. In that situation, we allow people to "do their own thing." But if those same people started acting like that on the highway, we simply could not allow them to "do their own thing." There would be a threat to life, liberty, and property.

The character of God — his love and righteousness, justice and mercy, etc. — is an unchanging north star by which to find our way through a world of moral complexity. Whether outside our own culture, calling Nazi war criminals to account, or inside our own culture, challenging racial discrimination and abortion, Christians have a consistent foundation from which to speak out against social evils based upon God's revelation. God's commands provide a fence of protection that guards against the anarchy of everyone "doing what is right in his own eyes." Looking at the chaos and cruelty of surrounding nations, King David was able to say,

> The law from your mouth is more precious to me
> than thousands of pieces of silver and gold.
>
> PSALM 119:72

For reflection and discussion

- How have you experienced the appeal of moral relativism? The dangers?
- When you read Jesus' moral requirements of us in his Word (Matthew 5), how would you compare or contrast your response with that of King David as cited in Psalm 119 above?
- How do you see God's love for you expressed in his moral law? How do you want to respond to him about this reading?

WEEK 4

The Bethlehem Star

By Frederick Larson, JD, attorney, former professor of law, Texas A&M University. Often voted Professor of the Year, Larson is founder of The Star Project. A presentation is available at *www.bethelehemstar.net*.

The star of Bethlehem is second only to the cross as an icon of Christianity. In chapter 2 of Matthew's gospel we read of this celestial portent announcing the birth of Jesus. Matthew's star fairly dances in the sky. From a naturalistic perspective, it does impossible things.

But the harder we push the historical record, the closer we examine the astronomical facts and the better we understand the math that drives the universe — the brighter the star shines. We have ample evidence to conclude that the star was real — an astronomical sign that the ancients actually saw and that we moderns can fully embrace.

Solving an ancient mystery begins with marshaling the clues from all sources, both within the Bible and without. Matthew's text reveals many characteristics of the biblical star: It signified birth and kingship. It had a connection with the Jewish nation. It was associated with precise timing. It rose in the east, like other stars. It endured over time and stopped over Bethlehem. We know from histories outside the Bible that this mysterious star wasn't a mere perception of believers or an invention of later church clerics. In fact, the Romans saw the star too. They minted coins that celebrate it.

We now know the universe moves according to mathematical laws, like the movements of a great clock. These laws, puzzled out by Kepler and refined by Newton, allow us to reassemble the skies of the ancient world. Modern software star maps can display the precise appearance of the night sky as seen from anywhere on Earth at any time in history. We can mathematically wind back the hands of time. We can see what so excited the Magi, first-century Jerusalem, and the Romans. And we find that real astrophysical events of that time dovetail precisely with Matthew's many points — a triple conjunction, Jupiter, the planet of Kings crowning the star of Kings (Regulus), Jupiter's dance through the constellations of Virgo (the virgin) and kingly Leo (the lion), Jupiter and Venus blazing together nine months later — signs that, when explained by the visiting experts, would have amazed and alarmed Herod enough for him to order, "Kill the babies."

Take one of Matthew's most troubling clues. His text states that Christ's star stopped. But the laws of physics prevent stars from simply stopping. Stars have mass. Inertia must be obeyed. So, what can Matthew have meant? It turns out that the ancients called planets "wandering stars," and planets do stop in their travels through the field of fixed stars — an observational effect called "retrograde motion." Viewed on a time scale of weeks and months, not only do they stop, they appear to backtrack. So, retrograde motion is the key to this problem. But there is so much more. In fact, each of Matthew's many points yields to scientific inquiry. Each could and did occur in the night sky over Jerusalem in the first century. Few matters bearing on the spiritual realm can be stated with such mathematical certainty.

But a huge issue looms. If science explains the star, isn't the miracle destroyed? Emphatically no! If the star was part of our great mathematically precise clockwork universe, then it was a clockwork star. God placed Christ's star into his precision celestial machine at the beginning of time, perfectly arrayed to announce the arrival of our Messiah. A breathtaking demonstration of his power and beauty.

For reflection and discussion

- If the star was an obvious supernatural phenomenon, why do you think Herod and his counselors were unaware of it?
- Do you think this explanation diminishes or enlarges the glory of God at work in announcing his Son's arrival on planet Earth? Why?
- If, from the instant God flung the universe into existence, he programmed the very stars themselves, as Larson proposes, what can this mean for the events and circumstances of your life? For world events?
- What do you want to tell God about this picture of his power and brilliance?

Dr. Faustus:
The Vanity of the Easy Button

By Lael Arrington

Christopher Marlowe's Elizabethan play *The Tragical History of Dr. Faustus* begins where Ecclesiastes leaves off: "Of making many books there is no end, and much study wearies the body."[3] Dr. Faustus, doctor of divinity at Wittenburg and "glutted now with learning's golden gifts," surveys his books and wonders, Why study logic? To dispute well? He reasons, "Then read no more; [I have] already attained that end." Research medicine? Why, he has cured "a thousand desperate maladies." Law is only fitting for "a mercenary drudge." And so Faustus comes back round to divinity as "best" but "hard": "We must sin, and consequently die ... an everlasting death." And so he bids Divinity good-bye.

Knowledge, even knowledge about divinity, does not satisfy. Faustus closes his Bible and opens books of spells and conjurings. "These are those that Faustus most desires.... All things that move between the quiet poles / Shall be at my command." Faustus aches to "gain a deity." Become a god. To live "in all voluptuousness" and bid the demon Mephistopheles perform his every whim. "That Faustus's name ... May be admir'd throughout the land."

And so Dr. Faustus makes his deal with the devil: twenty-four years of "profit and delight ... honour and omnipotence" in exchange for his soul, signed in blood. The all-time "easy button." Chant this chant. Summon this spirit. No struggle. No trusting an unpredictable God. No waiting. No courage needed to risk or fight. "You shall be like god," the ancient invitation still beckons. Speak and make it so.

Like Esau despising his birthright, Faustus waves off any concern for his soul, even when Mephistopheles assures him that hell and its torments are unspeakably real. Faustus shrugs, "I think hell's a fable."

Good and evil angels joust for his soul: "Faustus, repent; yet God will pity thee." "God cannot pity thee." His mind wavers, but he finds his heart is hardened and cannot repent.

In grand irony, Faustus, who relinquishes eternal joy in exchange for demonic power, fritters his prowess away on cheap frat-boy tricks: whacking the pope in the head while staying invisible and making horns sprout from the head of a young knight. Like a rush captain showing up at the keg party with Beyoncé, Faustus impresses his scholar-friends at dinner by conjuring up Helen of Troy.

Later, in response to Faustus's request, Mephistopheles delivers Helen to be his lover. But Helen's kiss conjures up a magic of its own ...

> Come, Helen ... I will be Paris, and for love of thee,
> Instead of Troy, shall Wittenberg be sack'd;
> And I will combat with weak Menelaus,
> And wear thy colours on my plumed crest;
> Yea, I will wound Achilles in the heel,
> And then return to Helen for a kiss.[4]

Is Marlowe merely penning pretty words or hinting at the vanity of magic's ease? Helen's beauty arouses Faustus's longings for a strength which could only have been won in the very struggles he has foregone. His disdain for the bare-knuckled conflict between good and evil ends in weakness, ennui, and longings for the laurels without the war.

Midnight approaches and Lucifer, Beelzebub, and Mephistopheles — the unholy trinity — come to claim their man. On stage, hell yawns and roars, and the horrific reality brings Faustus to his long-lost senses:

> The devil will come, and Faustus must be damn'd.
> O, I'll leap up to my God ... see, where Christ's blood
>   streams in the firmament!
> One drop would save my soul —
>   half a drop! ah, my Christ!

But his last grasp at control and pleasure is in vain. With a clap of thunder, the devils set upon him.

> Ugly hell, gape not! come not, Lucifer!
> I'll burn my books! — O Mephistopheles!

For reflection and discussion

Perhaps you'd like to read the final scene (*www.gutenberg.org*) where Faustus enters with his scholar friends and then counts the clock down to his final reckoning.

- In what ways do you relate to Faustus's love of books and life of study? What do you think is the blessing and danger of books?
- How do you respond to the serious and dreadful tone Marlowe evokes as Faustus faces the fires of hell? Do you think Jesus took hell and Satan seriously (Matthew 25:41)?
- In the wilderness, Satan offered Christ an "easy" way to accomplish his mission: "Just turn these stones into bread. Make a soft landing from the pinnacle" (see Matthew 4). How did Christ respond? How do you think God's way of redemption compares to American dreams of the "good life"? How is God calling you to hard choices?

Buddhist and Christian Ideals in Art

By Lael Arrington, adapted from *Orthodoxy* by G. K. Chesterton, author and journalist.

Pilgrims flock to the temples of Nepal and northern India to follow the traditional footsteps of Buddha, from his birthplace in Lumbini to the forest near Kushinigar where he died and, they believe, attained nirvana at the age of eighty. At Bodh Gaya, called "the navel of the world," they pay homage at the temple and Bodhi tree on the spot where, 2,500 years ago, Siddhartha Gautama sat in meditation under the original Bodhi tree and became the Buddha, "the enlightened one." Pilgrims visit the golden Buddha at Sarnath, in a temple that commemorates the site where he gave his first teachings on the Middle Way, the Four Noble Truths, and the Eightfold Path to five fellow seekers who became the first monks of the new order.

As G. K. Chesterton pointed out in *Orthodoxy*, no two ideals could be more opposite than a Christian saint in a European cathedral and a Buddhist saint in an oriental temple.

"The opposition exists at every point; but perhaps the shortest statement of it is that the Buddhist saint always has his eyes shut while the Christian saint always has them very wide open. The Buddhist saint has a sleek and harmonious body, but his eyes are heavy and sealed with sleep. The medieval saint's body is wasted to its crazy bones, but his eyes are frightfully alive. Granted that both images are extravagances, are perversions of the pure creed; it must be a real divergence which could produce such opposite extravagances. The Buddhist is looking with a peculiar intentness inwards. The Christian is staring with a frantic intentness outwards. If we follow that clue steadily, we shall find some interesting things."

Buddhism posits that individual personality is an illusion. "Christianity," Chesterton continues, "is on the side of humanity and liberty and love. Love desires personality; therefore love desires division. This is the abyss between Buddhism and Christianity; that for the Buddhist personality is the fall of man, that for the Christian it is the purpose of God, the whole point of his cosmic idea.

WEEK 4

89

"Certainly the most sagacious creeds may suggest that we should pursue God into deeper and deeper rings of the labyrinth of our own ego. But only we of Christendom have said that we should hunt God like an eagle upon the mountains: and we have killed all monsters in the chase.

"By insisting especially on the immanence of God we get introspection, self-isolation, quietism, social indifference — Tibet. By insisting especially on the transcendence of God we get wonder, curiosity, moral and political adventure, righteous indignation — Christendom."[5]

For reflection and discussion

- If you've ever made your own "pilgrimage" to a favorite painting or sculpture that connects to your faith, how did you find it meaningful?
- How do you see the pro-autonomy demonstrations in Tibet — might they expose Chesterton's early twentieth-century values and style at work in this piece? Might they reveal an internal tension between the Buddhist commitment to abandonment of desire and the validity of desire? Or both?
- Chesterton says that "love desires personality." How do you see this in your own relationships?

The Future of China, and Jesus in Beijing

By **Richard W. Ohman**, a former president and trustee of The Trinity Forum. He lives in New Hampshire and travels regularly to China.

China — what to make of it? Response to this question will undoubtedly consume an ever-increasing amount of time, energy, and analysis as our new century unfolds. The context for discussing this question is becoming clear and involves at least three major themes: economic potential, political rigidity, and the nation's soul. David Aikman's book *Jesus in Beijing*[6] addresses the least-discussed of these today — the nation's soul — which may well be the most important in answering the questions about China and its future.

Today China has apparently discarded both its ancient (Confucian) and modern (Communist) ideological and moral bases in its pursuit of growth and wealth. What fills this moral vacuum will be decisive in determining the future course of China, whether it be a world tyrant or a cooperating member within an increasingly globalized world.

When China's economic growth falters, the moral legitimacy of the current political regime will be tested, and the world will get to see the real banner under which China marches. This test may come sooner than we think. China's present economic growth is driven by a huge energetic population, market reforms, global liquidity, and a managed currency. This combination over the past decade has propelled China forward at an unprecedented rate of growth. But this growth has also generated huge global financial imbalances that suggest turbulence ahead, perhaps severe.

Jesus in Beijing introduces a wild card into traditional analyses of China: the growth of its Christian church. Most people outside church circles would consider this topic incidental to the "main" events of economics and politics. Yet growth of the church, particularly in urban areas among highly educated people, is reaching the point where it could begin to influence the tilt of government decisions in the future. This is significant because the institutions that form the bedrock of our global world — democracy, capitalism, free trade, and global financial markets — are in and of themselves morally neutral. They are organizing principles that derive their present moral force from the faith and beliefs of Western civilization. China and the rest of the non-Western world have generally accepted these institutions and their moral anchors because of the dominance of the West. They are playing by the current rules, but they are not necessarily following their own moral beliefs.

China is emerging as a new economic colossus and thus positioning itself to increasingly project its own moral values. China's soul, or moral core, will thus have influence well beyond the narrow categories of church and missions. The success of the Christian church in China could well define the parameters of China's future, and perhaps ours.

Aikman does a masterful job in tracing the long and convoluted history of Christianity in China in a concise and clear way. He tells the story using its key personalities, thus making it come alive. As he recounts the past, it is interesting to observe how each of the three major streams of Christianity (Eastern Orthodox, Catholic, and Protestant) have had their day in China over the past fourteen hundred years. Each in turn was banished for different reasons. The recent resurgence of Christianity in China, after the Communist takeover in 1949, is much different from the three previous beachheads in that its key leadership is uniquely Chinese.

Aikman's book clearly catalogs the background and development of this Chinese leadership and their stressful relationship with the Communist government. Persecution and imprisonment have been ever-present backdrops to the church's growth. Ironically, as church leaders point out, this pressure has only made them stronger. The government's interference with the church also includes interference with outside Christian organizations operating in China. Indeed, some believe that Aikman's book has exacerbated their already difficult situation. China has always resisted encroachments from the outside world. Perhaps this period will be different because of China's need for world markets to keep its economy growing and because of the strength and indigenous nature of its Christian church.

The future of the Christian church in China will be the subject of much debate, speculation, and fundraising. In the end, its future will not be determined by prognostications, methodologies, or anyone's will, because it is not ours to determine. In reading *Jesus in Beijing*, one gets the clear sense that a far greater story is unfolding than can be reduced to a logical, pragmatic story line. The Christian church in China seems to be driven by a historical imperative that is spontaneous in nature and far greater than the sum of its individual personalities or specific events. Many would see in this story a divine hand. If this be true, then the current size of the church in China and its rate of growth, which some critics believe are overstated by Aikman, are subordinated to the larger force of God's sovereign working.

For reflection and discussion

Beyond the economic and political development of China, *Jesus in Beijing* describes the third rail of *faith* on which China might be traveling into the future — and also a new moral base essential to the stability of government. Aikman's insights present a counterpoint to many Western notions as to how churches grow and prosper. In any country, including perhaps the most dynamic country in today's world, China, fidelity to the gospel truth, not circumstances, dictates the church's health and growth.

- What are some of your impressions and interactions with China and Chinese people?
- How do you respond when you learn that the Christian church is growing around the world, whether in China, Africa, or Latin America (whether or not it makes the news)?
- How might you be led to pray for countries where faith in Christ is wavering?

Worship: The Red Barn Run

By Kelly Monroe Kullberg

After a decade in Cambridge, I moved to a pine cabin, in the woods, on Boston's North Shore. In a vast expanse of estuary and ocean, summers were full of wildflowers, beaches, and tidal currents that challenged my sea-kayaking skills. During fiery autumns and frozen winters, hikes, books, and the scent of wood smoke spoke to me, "Breathe and rest."

Life on that boundary of land and water began for me as an escape — from exhaustion and from the city with its omnipresent reminders of a lost love in the Age of the Almost-Marriage. Though much in love for several years, we became distracted, frustrated, and called it quits. When I returned home from a long trip, I saw his car not in my driveway but in the driveway of my neighbor. They eventually married. And so it was in this cabin that I questioned, often with anguish, my past choices and failures. I faced the fact of wasted time: I had postponed marriage and children while caring for the children of others and trying to change the world. I questioned my frail faith in God's sovereignty.

In that season of doubt and bitterness, I often went for hikes in the snowy salt marsh at low tide. One day the sunlight was getting away from me, and I thought I'd catch the last of it. I threw on some Gore-Tex and hiking boots and was off on what I remember as "the red barn run." I had a routine for these outings: put some wood in the stove for heat that night, go down through the woods, pass the neighbor's chicken barn, greet the sheep, skirt the big red barn, hike into the marsh to the tide's edge, and be back home in under an hour.

Tonight was different. A shining planet rose like a jewel beneath the crescent moon. Stars slowly emerged as members in the choir. Songbirds in their snowy pine trees became a timbered chorus of complex and lilting harmonies. The ocean tide slowly rose to the occasion. Earth and sky became the colors of bread and wine, flesh and blood. The setting sun turned the barn to orange and, later, to crimson.

Something about it seemed too good to be false.

I felt inklings of a symphony behind which might be a score and a conductor.

I sensed a story with a wooing author. I felt something like Tolkien's enchanted vision, but here the rightful owner of the one ring was the lord of light, not of darkness. The bearer of that ring to rule the spheres was some sort of wild and relentless lover who could find me anywhere.

Moon and tides danced together. Creatures were changing shifts. Some were off to sleep, and others waking. It struck me that, in fact, this happens everywhere, every day, every year. We live on a life-giving planet, in a vast solar system, which is just one member of a still more vast and finely tuned universe. And we have minds and hearts that are free to reject or to receive the gift and the giver of it all — to join the dance or to wait it out.

In that hour there was too much beauty to be comfortable, to pay the weak compliment of aesthetic pleasure. It all seemed too orchestrated and conspicuous for me to do anything but be still and silent. I felt it all as con-spir-acy — a breathing together — inviting me.

But without me. What stopped and then sickened me that night, beneath that starry host, was the feeling that I could not participate. All creation, except for me, seemed to be joining in a cosmic chorus. The more I listened and watched, the more it seemed like *worship*. And yet of all God's creatures, I was on the outside, wanting in, and yet standing against it in rebellion.

Beauty can be painful to bear alone. But I was the one who had chosen aloneness, the one who had run away after a great loss. The universe could sing and dance the night away for all I cared. My own story seemed flat and cold, the midwinter indeed bleak and unending.

How could I enter back into God's presence with this enchanted symphony of the creation around me? How could I trust the One behind it all? The answer came unbidden and clear: I was to choose life, to join the dance, by *forgiving*. Only by doing so could I enter into that abundant reality which I really did desire.

I had been dismembered from life by my unwillingness to forgive. I was now invited to be re-membered to life by choosing forgiveness.

Whether I bent my knees, or my legs were broken for me, I don't know. I fell to the wet earth, forehead down in mud and snow, fighting nausea, reminding myself to breathe. I was my own inquisitor: In what story had I been living? Was it the story of life in the garden before the fall or after? Was it a story which accepted, even expected, the epic movements of creation, fall, and redemption? Was it a story with time depth and future hope, or was I stuck in the minuscule cell of self and moment?

I began by asking for mercy for myself. And then I began to forgive a betrayal that felt like a primal wound.

Bitterness is like saltwater at high tide, forcing us to shrink back, to retreat into safe places and sorrow, but that evening on the ocean, someone changed the tides in me. He welcomed me back in. I slowly rose and joined that symphony of worship, of gratitude, of life.

When his light and love floods us, it shifts the boundaries of our being. Our hearts get bigger. Our minds begin to heal. I was grafted into the Tree of Life, brought into the land of the living.

Sometimes, when the sun sinks low enough, when the glow of crimson captures my attention, I behold its light, its glory — if you will — its face. On the hike out to the tide that night, I saw the world in the warm light of the sun setting behind me. On the way home, I saw the sun itself.

Soggy and content, before entering the dark woods and then the warm cabin, I looked back across that sanctuary. And the red barn was lit from within.

For reflection and discussion

- Can you relate to this sense of loss and bitterness in any way? If so, how does it affect you?
- Does anything block you from "joining the chorus" worshiping God?
- Do you ever feel like an outsider, looking in, when it comes to worship?
- God longs to draw us in. What one or two motions could you make to join the dance?

The Council of Nicaea:
The Voice Beneath the Altar

By **Frederica Mathewes-Green**, MA, columnist and author of nine books, including *The Illumined Heart: The Ancient Christian Path of Transformation*. Since 1997, she has recorded books for the blind with the Radio Reading Network of Maryland.

When he opened the fifth seal, I saw under the altar the souls of those who had been slain because of the word of God and the testimony they had maintained. They called out in a loud voice, "How long, Sovereign Lord, holy and true, until you judge the inhabitants of the earth and avenge our blood?"

REVELATION 6:9 – 10

During the first centuries of Christianity, the church was battered within and without. Pseudo-Christians distorted the faith and misled the faithful, while the powerful Roman Empire persecuted Christians with torture and death. When local church members were able to gather the remains of their fellow believers (often, this was forbidden), they lovingly interred these broken bodies beneath their altars, a reminder that the blessed departed are invisibly present to join us in worship. John writes that, in his vision, he heard the voice of the martyrs crying out from under the altar. The persecutions ended when, by God's mercy, the Roman Emperor Constantine had a miraculous conversion in 312 AD. However, a new distortion of the faith was about to arise. A priest named Arius proposed that, if Christ is the Son of the Father, he can't be the same age as the Father. Christ must have been created by God, at some point before the universe was made. This would mean that Jesus is not *really* God, not in the way God the Father is.

That theory may sound familiar to you; throughout the centuries, there have been many who find it more appealing to see Jesus as an exalted man than to recognize him as fully God. The teachings of Arius provoked great controversy, and Emperor Constantine summoned church leaders from around the known world to come to Nicaea, a suburb of Constantinople, to settle the matter (not to reconfigure the canon and burn the banished books, as many have claimed). The Council of Nicaea rejected Arianism and affirmed that Jesus is truly God — "begotten, not made, being of one substance with the Father."

The Syrian writer Marutha of Maiperqat is credited as author of a description of how the council convened. When the 318 church leaders assembled, it was obvious that many of them had endured persecution. Virtually all of them, Marutha says, "were more or less maimed.... Some had the nails of their fingers or toes torn out; some were otherwise mutilated." Thomas of Marash, he says, had been imprisoned for twenty-two years, and each year his captors had cut off a finger, put out an eye, or wounded him some other way in an attempt to make him deny Christ.

The emperor was astounded by the suffering evident in the faces and bodies of these men. Marutha says that Constantine went from one man to the next, bowing his head and humbly kissing "the marks of Christ in their bodies," the scars that bore witness to their faith. When Constantine came to Thomas of Marash, he was overcome. As a peasant would bow to a king, the Emperor bowed to the wrecked body and shining soul of this Christian conqueror. He said, "I honor thee, O martyr of Christ, who art adorned with many crowns!"

For almost two hundred years, Roman emperors had brought persecutions upon Christians, but God knew there would come a time when an emperor would bow to a martyr of Christ.

For reflection and discussion

- What form does martyrdom take today? (For current stories see *www.prisoneralert.com*.) Have you ever been harassed or persecuted for your faith? How did you respond?
- What does this reading tell us about the end of time, when "every knee should bow,... and every tongue acknowledge that Jesus Christ is Lord" (Philippians 2:10 – 11)?
- How does this motivate you to pray? To act? To give?

The Irony of Intolerance

By Greg Koukl, president of Stand to Reason. With master's degrees in philosophy of religion and ethics as well as Christian apologetics, Koukl is adjunct professor of Christian apologetics at Biola University, host of a radio talk show, and author of *Tactics: A Game Plan for Discussing Your Christian Convictions*; *www.str.org*.

In today's world, one word is invoked as the No. 1 rule of civil behavior and conversation: "tolerance." And while most people think they understand what it means, a recent discussion I had with high school students exposed some fuzzy thinking on the subject.

I began the discussion by writing two sentences on the board. The first, "All views are equally valid," expressed a popular understanding of tolerance. All heads nodded in agreement. Nothing controversial here.

Then I wrote the second sentence: "Jesus is the Messiah and Jews are wrong for rejecting him." "You can't say that," a student challenged, clearly annoyed. "That's intolerant," she said, noting that the second statement violated the first. What she didn't see was that the first statement violated itself.

I pointed to the first statement and asked, "Is this a view, the idea that all views have equal merit?" The students all agreed. Then I pointed to the second statement — the "intolerant" one — and asked the same question: "Is *this* a view?" Slowly my point began to dawn on them.

If all views are equally valid, then the view that Christians are right about Jesus and Jews are wrong is *just as valid* as the idea that Jews are right and Christians are wrong. But this is hopelessly contradictory. They can't both be true.

"Would you like to know how to escape this trap?" I asked. They nodded. "Reject the popular misunderstanding of tolerance and return to the classical view." I turned to the board and wrote two principles I learned from Peter Kreeft of Boston College:

> Be egalitarian regarding persons.
> Be elitist regarding ideas.

"Treat *people* as equally valuable, but treat *ideas* as if some are better than others," I said, "because they are. Some ideas are true, some are false. Some are brilliant, others are dangerous. And some are just plain silly." To say so does not violate any meaningful standard of tolerance.

Real tolerance, I explained, is about how we treat people, not ideas. Classic tolerance requires that every person be free to express his ideas without fear of abuse or reprisal, not that all views have equal validity, merit, or truth.

By contrast, the popular definition of tolerance turns the classical formula on its head:

> Be egalitarian regarding ideas.
> Be elitist regarding persons.

If you reject another's *ideas*, you're automatically accused of disrespecting the *person* (as the student did with me). On this view, no idea can be opposed — even if done graciously — without inviting the charge of incivility. The offender can then be personally maligned, publicly marginalized, and verbally abused as bigoted, disrespectful, ignorant, and — ironically — intolerant.

This view of tolerance has gone topsy-turvy: Tolerate most beliefs, but don't tolerate (show respect for) those who take exception with those beliefs, especially politically correct ones. Contrary opinions are labeled as "imposing your view on others" and quickly silenced. "Tolerance" becomes intolerance.

Whenever you are charged with intolerance, *always ask for a definition*. If tolerance means neutrality, then no one is ever tolerant because no one is ever neutral about his own opinions. This kind of tolerance is a myth.

Jesus had no need for this kind of manipulation and no interest in it. He took the confrontations as they came and engaged them with intelligence, confidence, and grace. He answered his critics with truth, not with empty charges of intolerance. And he was willing to pay the price for his convictions in what was then a truly intolerant world.

Jesus understands real intolerance better than any of us, not as its perpetrator but as its prey. In the end, though, he was victor, not victim, defeating all intolerance by an act of sacrificial love.

For reflection and discussion

- Have you been on the giving or receiving end of intolerance? How did you respond?
- Can you offer a specific example of where Jesus' example can help you extend genuine tolerance and mercy? Of how Jesus' example can help you respond to intolerance with sacrificial love?
- What do you want to say to God in response to this reading? To your own attitudes? To your relationships?

The Copernican Principle

By **Guillermo Gonzalez**, PhD, associate professor of physics at Grove City College and a recognized expert on the astrophysical requirements for habitability. Gonzalez is cofounder of the Galactic Habitable Zone and coauthor of *The Privileged Planet: How Our Place in the Cosmos Is Designed for Discovery*; www.privilegedplanet.com.

In a memorable passage from the 1994 book *Pale Blue Dot*, the late astronomer Carl Sagan reflects on an image of Earth taken by Voyager 1 from four billion miles away:

> Earth seems to be sitting in a beam of light, as if there were some special significance to this small world. But it's just an accident of geometry and optics.... Our posturings, our imagined self-importance, the delusion that we have some privileged position in the universe, are challenged by this point of pale light. Our planet is a lonely speck in the great enveloping cosmic dark.[1]

The idea that we are insignificant in the cosmic scheme, fashionable among modern scientists, is known as the Copernican Principle, named after astronomer Nicolaus Copernicus (1473 – 1543). According to the popular story, Copernicus demoted us from our place of importance by showing that our universe was not Earth-centered, but rather sun-centered, Earth revolving around the sun like all the other planets. Or so the story goes. That story has a single, decisive problem: it's false.

The real story is more subtle. The pre-Copernican cosmology envisioned by Aristotle, Ptolemy, and other ancients was a set of nested, concentric spheres that encircled our Earth. The "center" of the universe was considered no place of honor any more than we think of the center of the Earth as being somehow exalted. It was seen as the corruptible, base, and heavy portion of the cosmos. Things were thought to fall to Earth because of their heaviness. The Earth in pre-Copernican cosmology was the "bottom" of the universe rather than its "center."

When Christian theology was added to the mix in the Middle Ages, the bottom of the universe became, quite literally, *hell*. Dante's *Divine Comedy* immortalized this vision, taking the reader from the Earth's surface through the nine circles of hell, which mirror the nine celestial spheres above.

WEEK 5

The "official story" gives the false impression that Copernicus relegated us to an insignificant backwater and scientifically established the unimportance of our "pale blue dot." But far from demoting the status of Earth, Copernicus, Galileo, and Kepler saw the new scheme as exalting it. They thought the Earth's new position removed it from its place of dishonor.

Let's fast-forward four centuries and see whether recent astronomical discoveries confirm these early astronomers' convictions about Earth's significance.

If you were a cosmic chef, your recipe for "cooking" up a habitable planet would *need* many ingredients. In order to maintain a stable, moderate climate and produce an atmosphere that would sustain sentient, intelligent life, you would need a rocky planet large enough to hold on to a substantial atmosphere and oceans of water. You would need a large moon to stabilize the tilt of the planet's rotation axis. You would need the planet to have a nearly circular orbit around a main sequence star similar to our sun. In order to avoid excessive asteroid and comet impacts, you would need to give that planet the right kind of planetary neighbors within its star system and put that system far from the center, edges, and spiral arms of a galaxy like the Milky Way. And, you would need to "cook" it during a narrow window of time in the history of the universe.

The probability of having all these ingredients come together is small. Earth-like planets are rare. While this fact contradicts the Copernican Principle, rarity alone does not make the Earth and its inhabitants truly privileged.

Consider what it takes for scientific discovery. Read any book on the history of scientific discovery, and you'll find magnificent tales of human ingenuity, persistence, and dumb luck. What you probably won't see is any discussion of the conditions necessary for such feats. A discovery requires a person to do the discovering and a set of circumstances that makes it possible. Without both, nothing gets discovered.

Although scientists don't often discuss it, the degree to which we can "measure" the wider universe from our Earthly home is surprising. Few have considered what science would have been like in, say, a different planetary environment.

Think of the following features of our Earthly home: the transparency of its atmosphere in the visual region of the spectrum, a large moon (just large enough to perfectly cover the sun during a total solar eclipse), and its particular location in the Milky Way Galaxy. Without each of these assets, we would have a very hard time learning about the universe. For example, scientists were able to test Einstein's General Theory of Relativity by observing light "bending" around the sun during a total eclipse.

It is not idle speculation to ask how our view of the universe would be impaired if, for example, our home world were perpetually covered by thick clouds. After all, our Solar System contains several examples of such worlds: Venus, Jupiter, Saturn, and Saturn's moon, Titan. These would be crummy places to do astronomy.

The central argument, the central wonder of our research is this: If a planet satisfies all the requirements for habitability, it also satisfies the requirements for making a wide range of important scientific discoveries. In other words, the best places for observers are also the best places for observing. It is the connection between life and discovery that makes our home a truly "Privileged Planet."

For reflection and discussion

- What new scientific discoveries have seemed to challenge your faith?
- How have you responded? How might you use the Internet or resources in this book to answer any questions?
- If we are not at the center of the Universe, but rather on a terrifically positioned observation platform, what does that suggest about God? And about us?

Leo Tolstoy

By Philip Yancey, bestselling author. Reprinted from *Soul Survivor: How Thirteen Unlikely Mentors Helped My Faith Survive the Church*. Yancey, a writer who enjoys exploring the deepest mysteries of his faith, is also editor at large of *Christianity Today*.

As a writer and as a pilgrim, Tolstoy (1828 – 1910) struggled with the tension between the world as it is and as it should be. At the time he wrote, almost half the Russian population lived as virtual slaves. Tolstoy inherited hundreds of such peasants. The differences between their ordinary lives and the self-indulgent lives of rich people like himself began to eat away at Tolstoy, paralyzing his ability to write.

After reading the straightforward commands of Jesus ("Sell everything you have and give to the poor, and you will have treasure in heaven"), Tolstoy freed his serfs, gave away his copyrights, and began to dispose of his immense estate. To identify with the common people, he put on peasant clothes, made his own shoes, and began working in the fields.

His desire to reach perfection led him to devise ever new lists of rules. He gave up hunting, tobacco, alcohol, and meat. He determined to sell or give away everything superfluous — the piano, furniture, carriages. He drafted rules for developing the emotional will, rules for developing lofty feelings and eliminating base ones, rules for subordinating the will to the feeling of love.

Tolstoy's quest for holiness ended in disappointment. In her diary, his wife wrote:

> There is so little genuine warmth about him; his kindness does not come from his heart, but merely from his principles.... no one will ever know that he never gave his wife a rest and never — in all these 32 years — gave his child a drink of water or spent five minutes by his bedside.

Like a spawning salmon, Tolstoy fought upstream all his life, in the end collapsing from moral exhaustion. He thought that his own will would suffice to chase away evil, and it failed him. Up to the moment of his death, the diaries and letters kept circling back to the rueful theme of failure, exposing the gap between gospel ideals and the contradictions of his own life. Leo Tolstoy was a deeply unhappy man.

In view of such failures, what can I possibly learn from the tragic life of Leo Tolstoy? I come away inspired by his reverence for God's absolute ideal. Tolstoy reminds us that, contrary to those who say the Gospels solve our problems, in many areas — justice issues, money issues, race issues, personal issues of pride and ambition — the gospel actually adds to our burdens.

Tolstoy's fictional portrayal of life contained within it the heart of the gospel that had always eluded his rational search. Tolstoy was far better at painting a picture of redemption than explaining it. *Anna Karenina* chronicles the spiritual awakening of Levin, a major character.

> Knowledge unattainable by reasoning has been revealed to me personally, to my heart ... and I am obstinately trying to express that knowledge in words and by my reason.
>
> I shall still get angry with my coachman Ivan. ... There will still be a wall between the holy of holies of my soul and other people, even my wife, and I shall still blame her for my own fears and shall regret it ... but my life, my whole life, independently of anything that may happen to me, every moment of it, is no longer meaningless but has an uncontestable meaning of goodness, with which I have the power to invest it.

Sadly, Tolstoy never allowed that gospel to bring comfort to his own life. With crystalline clarity, Tolstoy could see his own inadequacy in the light of God's ideal. But he could not take the further step of trusting God's grace to overcome the inadequacy.

For reflection and discussion

Perhaps you'd like to sample Tolstoy's work at *www.sparknotes.com*.

- How does this reading offer fresh insight into the tension between longing to live a Christlike life, on the one hand, and needing to receive God's love and mercy, on the other? How do you experience this tension in your own life?
- How do you respond to God's perfection? Do you find it a source of discomfort? Comfort? Both?
- How does God's mercy and grace comfort you?
- How do you want to respond to God's heart of mercy and goodness? To others who may struggle with their own failings?

Rembrandt van Rijn:
The Return of the Prodigal Son

By Kelly Monroe Kullberg and David Kullberg

Rembrandt van Rijn (1606 – 1669) wrote to a patron that he sought to achieve through his art "the greatest and most natural movement." The original Dutch may be better translated as "most natural emotion, or motive."

This great painter is considered to have achieved in his faces and scenes a merger of earth and heaven unlike any artist in the tradition of Western art. But that interiority, light, and depth of emotion within his paintings was forged in a life, a fire, of redemptive sorrow. Like the prodigal son whose homecoming would be the subject of Rembrandt's final painting, Rembrandt would also shed his vanity and pride as he came to know the heart of God.

According to authors Mark Galli and Ted Olsen, "The Dutch artists of Rembrandt's day gained respect painting landscapes, still lifes."[2] But Rembrandt was captivated by the moving Bible stories his mother used to read to him. After leaving his home of Leyden for Amsterdam, "he developed his affinity both for depicting dramatic personal reactions and for using chiaroscuro (painting in light and dark). In most of his paintings, light emerges from darkness, creating a timeless, emotional movement that draws the viewer into the scene."[3]

By the late 1620s, Rembrandt was already a renowned artist, convinced of his own genius and "lustful for everything the world had to offer."[4] But his short period of early success was followed by grief and disaster. During his sixty-three years, not only did his dear wife, Saskia, die, but he also lost three sons, two daughters, and the two women with whom he lived. His popularity plummeted and, having wasted his fortune, he was forced to sell his home and art collection.

One of Rembrandt's most famous works was *The Return of the Prodigal Son*, which he painted shortly before his death. The masterpiece is now displayed at the Hermitage museum in St. Petersburg, Russia. There the museum guides do not refer to the painting as "the prodigal son," but rather "the compassionate father." Jesus told the story (Luke 15:11 – 32):

"There was a man who had two sons. The younger one said to his father, 'Father, give me my share of the estate.' ... The younger son got together all he had, set off for a distant country and there squandered his wealth in wild living....

"When he came to his senses, he said,... 'I will set out and go back to my father.'...

"While he was still a long way off, his father saw him and was filled with compassion for him; he ran to his son, threw his arms around him and kissed him.... 'Bring the best robe and put it on him.... Let's have a feast and celebrate. For this son of mine was dead and is alive again; he was lost and is found.'"

Referring to this painting in his book *Return of the Prodigal Son*, author Henri Nouwen wrote, "As I look at the prodigal son kneeling before his father and pressing his face against his chest, I cannot but see there the once so confident artist who has come to the painful realization that all the glory he had gathered for himself proved to be vain. Instead of the rich garments ... he now wears only a torn under-garment covering his emaciated body.

"Moving my eyes from the repentant son to the compassionate father, I see ... glory that is hidden in the human soul and surpasses death." Nouwen saw in the face of the father "an inner light, deeply hidden, but radiating an all-pervasive tender beauty."[5] He saw the expression of God's tender heart for us.

As in several other Rembrandt paintings, the father of the prodigal son is a self-portrait, but not in the usual sense. Nouwen believed, "Here it is not Rembrandt's face that is reflected, but his soul, the soul of a father who had suffered so many a death.

"Created in the image of God, Rembrandt had come to discover through his long, painful struggle the true nature of that image ... the father crying tenderly, blessing his deeply wounded son, as if the father is saying, 'You are my Beloved, on you my favor rests.'

"Everything comes together here: Rembrandt's story, humanity's story, and God's story. Time and eternity intersect; approaching death and everlasting life touch each other."[6] Sin and forgiveness embrace.

The young Rembrandt had been a proud and prodigal son. Through suffering, he became the loving father.

For reflection and discussion

- Have you ever visited a Rembrandt painting? Perhaps you could offer a reflection on how it impacted you.
- If you can locate a larger image of *The Return of the Prodigal Son* (see *www.artresourceinc.com*), what do you think Rembrandt may be trying to show about the Father's compassionate love for his returning son? How might you have experienced that sort of love from the Father?

Henri Nouwen saw in himself aspects of the foolish but repentant younger son. And then a friend surprised him by telling him that he thought Nouwen was called to become the father.

- Where do you see qualities of the wayward son in yourself? Or the older brother?
- What are your challenges in returning to the father's love?
- In what way can you grow toward becoming more like the compassionate parent yourself?
- Picture yourself in that strong and tender embrace of your loving Father. What prayer comes to mind?

PostSecret: Extraordinary Confessions from Ordinary Lives

By Lael Arrington

> I'm a Southern Baptist Pastor's wife.
> No one knows I don't believe in God.
> *PostSecret* CONTRIBUTOR

This pastor's wife found one of Frank Warren's postcards. All across America, Warren left them in train stations, supermarkets, even tucked in library books, inviting people to anonymously reveal a secret on a postcard and mail it to him to be displayed as part of a community art project.

Confessors were urged to use words, images, string, business forms — anything that would make their secrets as visually arresting as possible. The only stipulations: It must be true; you must not ever have told anyone.

From the astonishing seventy thousand responses, Warren's project has become a book (actually a series) and website, *PostSecret* (*http://postsecret .blogspot.com*). Cleverly marketed in a brown paper wrapper, hundreds of long-suppressed dreams and desires, laments and agonies spill out of this postmodern confessional. What is spoken in secret exposes contemporary sensibilities in conflict: So many dreams and ideals to confound the cynics. Raw authenticity, yet still masked to protect terrible wounds. Barbs of blame and judgment that never convey open intolerance. Virtual humility — gut-wrenching regret and apologies that protect radical autonomy and elude accountability.

Each week Warren mounts another twenty postcards on his website. At one point ranked by *New York* magazine as the third most popular blog on the Internet, his website continues to attract millions of visitors a month.

Loneliness is a major theme: "I feel so lonely I could die." "I hope drugs will take me before the loneliness does." So is lostness: "I feel blank inside." The Baptist pastor's wife wasn't the only one struggling with God: "Finding God is proving difficult." "I tell people that I don't believe in God, when really, I just refuse to worship a God that would let my grandfather hurt me like he did." "I don't know what to say to God anymore."

We may not talk much about hell in America, but the prospect makes some card-writers sweat. "I'm terrified of not existing." "I tell people I'm an atheist. But I believe I'm going to hell." And on the next page, one word scrawled so large it covers both pages, the script suspended over yellow and orange flames: "shoplift."

Warren has inadvertently created a nameless community of fellow travelers, baring their souls to no one and everyone. "The things that make us feel so abnormal are actually the things that make us all the same," he writes in his introduction. "A secret shared is the beginning of a journey of healing."

> I have, at times, knowingly allowed my child to bear the brunt of her father's wrath in order to save myself from it.
> I hope she can forgive me someday. Even if I never can.

The book and website offer an achingly real R-rated catalog of deep longings, secret sins and consequences, and raise the question: How do we find relief from true moral guilt? Publicly naming the thing that aches can bring a measure of peace. But one secret-bearer confesses he has mailed all his secrets in and they are still "killing me every day."

For reflection and discussion

- Do you find this phenomenon intriguing? Why or why not?
- What are the benefits and dangers of accountability? Of making things right in community?

As I read all the snapshots of sorrow and rage, joy and hope, I see people who need a touch. I catch glimpses of all the individual stories folded into God's larger story. I'm reminded that "Christ plays in 10,000 places," always pursuing us with love and forgiveness, grace and mercy. The miracle of the cross — that Christ became all our shameful secrets and bore our guilt, that we have forgiveness for the asking — shines even more brightly against the true moral guilt of our worst secrets. "The blood of Christ, who ... offered himself unblemished to God, [will] cleanse our consciences from acts that lead to death, so that we may serve the living God!" (Hebrews 9:14).

- How do you want to respond to God about his peace and mercies, new every morning? About seeking the help you need to deal with your secrets? About his compassion for those who are hurting? About extending that compassion to others?

Jesus' Resurrection:
When Truth Confronts Our Worst Suffering

By Gary R. Habermas, PhD, chair of philosophy and theology, Liberty University. Habermas, an acknowledged world expert on the resurrection of Jesus, has written sixteen of his thirty-two books on the resurrection, including *The Risen Jesus & Future Hope*. His study took on a very personal dimension in 1995 when his wife died.

Good theology is indispensable. Having strong reasons for these beliefs is even better. But being able to apply both to the worst suffering we will ever face may be the toughest task of all.

My wife and I visited a hospital in 1995 for what were described as fairly routine tests. Within minutes, my world changed forever. Debbie might have cancer, and I was unprepared for the final verdict: terminal stomach cancer. There was no remedy. I measured my life by the severity of the shocking news that arrived repeatedly in the days ahead. Sometimes I was unsure how to place one foot in front of the other.

I remember those days very clearly, along with the daunting questions. Debbie was only forty-three years old. We had four children still at home. Four months later she died. We had celebrated our twenty-third anniversary while she was in bed. My dearest friend was gone. Irrevocably. The pain failed to subside. What could I tell our children? I said this was the worst pain I could experience.

During our ordeal, a graduate student asked me, "Where would you be now if Jesus hadn't been raised from the dead?" I have spent forty years researching Jesus' resurrection and it was obviously relevant to my wife's sickness. But my investigation was devoted chiefly to the historical, theoretical aspects. God had to teach me how to apply resurrection truth to my daily life.

During my own skeptical years, I had developed a strategy called the "minimal facts method." Basically, I argued in many books and debates that the New Testament was at least a book of ancient literature. But even on this basis alone, we still have plenty of facts to show that Jesus truly had been resurrected. I even took the historical data that skeptics had good reasons to admit and used their own basis to argue the resurrection.

A quick summary shows that critical scholars seldom ever questioned

Jesus' death by crucifixion. Virtually no one doubts that, afterward, Jesus' followers at least thought they had seen the risen Jesus. Accordingly, they were willing to die, and many of them did. Further, skeptics like Jesus' brother James and Saul of Tarsus were even converted by their own experiences with the risen Jesus. And almost all scholars acknowledge that the resurrection message was proclaimed very early — immediately after the crucifixion. Moreover, Jesus' tomb was found empty.

Let's look in more detail at just a couple of categories of evidence for the resurrection and the early testimony to seeing the risen Jesus. Nearly all scholars think that after Jesus' death, the disciples had real experiences which they reported were appearances of their Master. This is a critical starting point. The most important text is 1 Corinthians 15:3 – 8, which is taken by scholars to be the strongest indication of the historical resurrection appearances. Most think that this testimony constituted the oral teaching of the earliest church and actually predates Paul's conversion or the New Testament.

There is little dispute that Paul is passing on this tradition that he received, probably from the apostles Peter and James, the brother of Jesus, during his first visit to Jerusalem, just three years after his conversion (Galatians 1:18 – 24). Scholars generally place Paul's reception of this material in the mid-30s AD. Years later, Paul confirmed the nature of this gospel proclamation with Peter, James, and John (Galatians 2:1 – 10 NIV). A stronger substantiation from these four best-known, earliest eyewitnesses could hardly be hoped for from an ancient historical text.

Further, the empty tomb is strongly attested. According to all four gospel accounts, women are cited as the key witnesses. But due to the strong Jewish disinclination to recognize female testimony in decisive issues, these texts probably would not have agreed in citing the women unless they were actually the principal witnesses. Further, the location of the tomb in Jerusalem meant it could be observed by either friend or foe. Critical scholars agree that the empty tomb report is attested in several of the gospel sources.

I had concluded that the best explanation for these events was that Jesus had truly been raised from the dead and appeared to his followers. Critics seemed strangely unable to offer a more convincing explanation.

But here the facts of history touch our lives. Jesus suffered arguably the most painful death imaginable. Nothing altered his pain — it raged hour after hour. He cried out to his Father but without any physical relief. Even the Son of God learned through his suffering (Hebrews 5:8).

Then it hit home: Why should I expect less suffering? If God did not stop his Son's pain, on what grounds could I demand better treatment?

But Jesus' prayer was answered *after* his suffering ended, on the first Easter morning. In a similar manner, Debbie's resurrection would also be God's answer. I still do not know why she died, but I know the One who raised his Son. The fact of Jesus' resurrection trumps even our greatest suffering. As Paul states, Christians mourn for their loved ones too, but we mourn with resurrection hope (1 Thessalonians 4:13 – 14). Death has lost its biggest sting (1 Corinthians 15:53 – 57).

For reflection and discussion

- What aspects of the gospel accounts of the resurrection seem most persuasive to you? Least persuasive?
- What does the resurrection reveal about God's inclination toward struggle? About his often bewildering pathway to joy?
- What questions do you have about death? The afterlife? Resurrection? How do you want to bring these questions to God in prayer? In Scripture study? In conversation with others who have experienced such losses?

Rome: From Glory to Apathy

Note: *The fall of Rome precipitated a rise of cynicism, fear, and apocalyptic predictions. You'll find these themes woven through the rest of the readings for this week.*

By Lael Arrington. For a virtual tour of ancient Rome, visit *www.romereborn .virginia.edu.*

Like no empire before it, the Roman Empire united the ancient world and enforced its peace. The Romans developed an unprecedented political unity of mankind under a universal law. Every modern Western nation still bears the mark of Roman law and ideas.

At the height of imperial rule, Caesar Augustus ushered in the Pax Romana — two hundred years of peaceful prosperity. The Pax provided historically unique conditions for the spread of Christianity. The apostle Paul wrote of Jesus, "But when the set time had fully come, God sent his Son, born of a woman." The time was right in part because of the Pax. Often called "the Americans of antiquity," Romans were builders, and Roman engineers had linked Asia, Africa, and Europe with an astonishing network of roads and bridges. Roman soldiers had made travel safer than it had ever been. Pompey the Great had cleared the seas of pirates. The good news of Jesus Christ swiftly advanced over Roman roads made safe by Roman security. Roman admiration for and assimilation of all things Greek had provided a common language, Koine Greek, in which the New Testament was written and could be read throughout the empire.

However, as Roman historian Livy wrote: "An empire remains powerful so long as its subjects rejoice in it." The Pax Romana ultimately crumbled and Rome declined as people lost confidence that their worldview offered hope, especially for the vast majority living in brutal poverty.

Increasing numbers of people gave lip service to the scheming, drinking, womanizing gods they privately held in contempt. The gods provided no answers and less hope. The Greek philosophers that had destroyed the old mythologies had raised the right questions but had not provided soul-satisfying answers. Desperate for answers and searching for hope, people felt a deep spiritual hunger. In Christ the early church provided the answers to the big questions of life and offered forgiveness and hope. Still, at the time of Constantine's conversion, only about 20 percent of the population was Christian.

Without a sufficient ethical base, society was degenerating to the point where even the pagan writers cried out against the morals of the day. When we think of the names of first-century emperors like Caligula, Claudius, and Nero, we generally think of the moral decay associated with them.

In *How Should We Then Live?* Francis Schaeffer wrote, "The decadent Romans were given to a thirst for violence and a gratification of the senses. This is especially evident in their rampant sexuality. For example, in Pompeii, the phallus cult was strong. Not all the art in Pompeii was like this, but the sexual representations were unabashedly blatant. [From doorknockers to decorative mosaics, the phallic symbol was prominently displayed in homes of the affluent.]

"Apathy was the chief mark of the late Empire. The elite abandoned their intellectual pursuits for social life. Officially sponsored art was decadent, and music was increasingly bombastic. Even the portraits on the coins became of poor quality. [The population declined severely as people in desperate poverty resorted to infanticide, and men of wealth and education married later and had fewer children.]

"As the Roman economy slumped lower and lower, burdened with an aggravated inflation and a costly government, authoritarianism increased to counter the apathy. Since work was no longer done voluntarily, it was brought increasingly under the authority of the state, and freedoms were lost. For example, laws were passed binding small farmers to their land. So, because of the general apathy and its results, and because of oppressive control, few thought the old civilization worth saving.

"Rome did not fall because of external forces such as the invasion by the barbarians. Rome had no sufficient inward base; the barbarians only completed the breakdown — and Rome gradually became a ruin."[1]

For reflection and discussion

In his book *Are We Rome?* Cullen Murphy writes, "Rome and America are the most powerful actors in their worlds, by many orders of magnitude. Their power includes both military might and the 'soft power' of language, culture, commerce, technology, and ideas."[2] Like Thomas Cole's *Course of Empire* paintings, Murphy's book challenges us to wonder whether America is launching our own Pax or hastening the day when vines creep up the crumbling columns of the Lincoln Memorial. We're reminded that what looks impossible in the present reality looks inevitable in hindsight. You might enjoy googling Murphy's book and reading a review as you reflect on the following questions:

- How do you think Jesus as "the Life" connects to the problems of ancient Rome and the modern world?
- In light of your own tendency to apathy, what do you think it means that Jesus Christ is "the Life"?
- How do you want to talk to God about this reading? About our country? About the temptation to apathy or cynicism?

Seeing Through Cynicism

By **Dick Keyes**, director of L'Abri Fellowship, Massachusetts. Adapted from his book *Seeing Through Cynicism*. Keyes is adjunct professor at Gordon-Conwell Seminary and Westminster Theological Seminary.

Cynicism has to do with the seeing through and unmasking positive appearances to reveal more basic underlying motivations of greed, power, lust, and selfishness. In a world saturated in artificiality, spin, and banality, it's hard to be sincere about life. Philosopher Peter Sloterdijk writes that cynicism "is the universally widespread way in which enlightened people see to it that they are not taken for suckers."

On a scale with cynicism at one end and sentimental optimism at the other, I have always been much closer to the cynicism pole. My internal voices have always gravitated toward suspicion, but faith in Christ challenged my cynicism. There was something too facile about its tidy and convenient dismissal of virtue. I realized that the cynical judgments I made were overconfident suspicion, overreaching what I could actually know.

If we turn our suspicion to cynicism itself, we find that cynics are unable to reject all ideals. If they did, they would live in silent resignation. Every rock thrower needs something to stand on to have any accuracy or do any damage with the rocks. Cynics will hold at least one ideal against ideas and practices of conventional society. So, modern cynicism stands on platforms of honesty, freedom, or authenticity to throw rocks at perceived dishonesty, oppression, and hypocrisy.

The film *M*A*S*H*, a story of surgeons in a field medical unit in the Korean War, was seen as an archetypal cynical film — mocking everything, especially the military, rules, and religion. But it didn't mock everything. The cynicism was coming from the platform ideals of personal freedom, friendship, and coolness, which were presented as highly attractive but not stated, recognized, or defended, and certainly never mocked.

I question the honesty of cynicism itself. Where do these ideals come from? How are they justified? Aren't they naive? Sentimental? The cynic, in mocking the hypocrite, makes an *implicit* appeal to a moral order in the universe (by which people *ought not* to be hypocritical). Where does this moral order come from?

The genius of cynicism is that it is a voice in your ear which does not usually hang around long enough to be interviewed. It is usually expressed in innuendos, passing remarks, moods, cartoons, hints, insinuations, unacknowledged assumptions, and jokes. I want to push cynicism to come out of the closet, to be honest about both its ideals and its overconfident claims to see through people, institutions, and God.

Cynicism links itself with the unreliability of all human knowing. But cynicism is a great act of trust in our own critical thinking. How does the cynic know enough to be able to see through all that he claims to see through? To justify the cynical judgment, we must be virtually omniscient or at least know a great deal more than we can know about the motivations of other people. God, who really is omniscient, is not a cynic.

When Jesus confronted people who were locked into a deep cynicism about him, he did not argue; he told them stories and asked questions: "What good will it be for you to gain the whole world, yet forfeit your soul?" (Matthew 16:26). In this way he helped them understand their own beliefs, their position before God, and their need for his mercy.

Jesus looked behind cynical challengers, pointing out their less-than-honest motives for rejecting him. "How can you believe since you accept glory from one another but do not seek the glory that comes from the only God?" (John 5:44). He also challenged them to look at the evidence that he presented: "You can believe."

For reflection and discussion

- Do you tend to be more of a cynic or a sentimental optimist?
- How does God enable us to see the brokenness that the cynic sees — but without losing the hope that the cynic rejects?
- How does God enable us to recognize the glory in the world that the cynic cannot see — but without the sentimentality that the cynic fears?
- How do you want to respond to God about this reading?

The End of the World

By **William Lane Craig**, PhD, ThD, professor of philosophy at Talbot School of Theology. Author of *Reasonable Faith*, Craig is an acclaimed expert on the existence of God and a debater who draws standing-room-only crowds in Europe, the US, and Canada; *www.reasonablefaith.org*.

Doubtless, one of the chief difficulties presented by Christian eschatology is that it just seems incredible that next year, say, or next Tuesday the universe is going to be obliterated by the return of Christ and judgment day.

Even New Testament Christians faced scoffers saying, "Where is this 'coming' he promised? Ever since our ancestors died, everything goes on as it has since the beginning of creation" (2 Peter 3:4).

What these scoffers could not realize is that a purely physical approach to eschatology itself involves an apocalyptic scenario of impending worldwide destruction. If the universe is currently suspended in a high energy, false vacuum state, then at some point in the future it will inevitably slide into a lower energy state, bringing with it a complete metamorphosis of nature. Because this is an indeterminate quantum phase transition, it is unpredictable and could happen at virtually any time, as soon as tomorrow. In such a transition, bubbles of true vacuum will begin to form at places throughout the universe and propel themselves across the universe at fantastic speed. In *The Five Ages of the Universe*, cosmologists Fred Adams and Gregory Laughlin describe such an apocalypse:

> Silently, and without warning of any kind, it came....
>
> The shock wave began at a particular but rather undistinguished point of space-time and then traveled outward at blinding speed, rapidly approaching the speed of light. The expanding bubble then enveloped an ever larger portion of the universe. Because of its phenomenal velocity, the shock wave impinged upon regions of space with no advance warning. No light signals, radio waves, or causal communication of any kind could outrun the advancing front and forewarn of the impending doom. Preparation was as impossible as it was futile.
>
> Inside the bubble, the laws of physics and hence the very character of the universe were completely changed. The values of the physical constants, the strengths of the fundamental forces, and the masses of the elementary particles were all different. New physical laws ruled in this Alice-in-

Wonderland setting. The old universe, with its old version of the laws of physics, simply ceased to exist.

One could view this death and destruction of the old universe as a cause for concern ... [or] as a reason for celebration. Inside the bubble, with its new physical laws and the accompanying new possibilities for complexity and structure, the universe has achieved a new beginning.[3]

The parallels between this scenario and the apocalypse described in 2 Peter 3:8 – 13 are striking and unmistakable: a complete metamorphosis of nature, sudden, without warning, like a thief in the night, unavoidable, issuing in a new heaven and a new earth, a renovated universe.

Unlike our cosmologists, however, the author of 2 Peter does suggest that we do something to prepare:

Since everything will be destroyed in this way, what kind of people ought you to be? You ought to live holy and godly lives as you look forward to the day of God and speed its coming.

2 PETER 3:11 – 12

Now please do not misunderstand me: I am in no wise suggesting that what we read in 2 Peter is a poetic description of an impending quantum phase transition of the universe. Rather I am making the more modest point that if physical eschatology involves apocalyptic doomsday predictions that could be realized tomorrow, then we should not balk at similar forecasts made by the Bible simply on the grounds of its unexpectedness and mind-boggling otherness.

The difference between believers and unbelievers, then, lies not in the belief in the possibility of the world's imminent end but rather in the anticipation of that "blessed hope" for which the church yearns.

For reflection and discussion

- What aspect of this reading do you find new or surprising?
- Christians have been accused of not caring for this world, not engaging in its redemption because they are waiting for a scenario like this to bring in God's physical kingdom on earth. In the light of Genesis 1:28 teaching us to be good and fruitful stewards of this earth, and Jesus' life and commands to bless and love the world, how do you respond?
- What do you think "speeds" the day of the Lord (2 Peter 3:12)? How can we be the kind of person who "looks forward to and speeds" this day?

Augustine's *City of God*:
Two Cities, Two Loves

By **William Edgar**, ThD, professor of cultural apologetics, Westminster Theological Seminary, and author of *Reasons of the Heart: Recovering Christian Persuasion*. Edgar is a popular speaker and jazz pianist in North America and France.

When we are properly communing and conversing with the living God, we will do a great deal of good on this earth. When we love God as we should, we will love our neighbors as well. Paradoxically, those who are most devoted to God are often the most productive in this world.

Perhaps no better illustration of this paradox exists than the apologetics of St. Augustine (396 – 430). As Bishop of Hippo in North Africa, Augustine lived at a time when the Roman Empire was in sharp decline. Citizens were looking for a scapegoat and blamed the Christians for the deterioration of the empire.

When the "Eternal City" was sacked by the Goths in 410 AD, the church was said to be the cause; because Christians believed in only one God, it was argued, the church was corrupting the city. The pagan gods of Rome were older and could be trusted to protect the people from its enemies, but the Christian faith intruded by declaring that there is only one God. Because this "new" religion accepted no synthesis with other religions and its God refused to belong to the Roman pantheon of gods, the pagan gods no longer protected the city. Rome's downfall was thus blamed on the uncooperative believers in an uncooperative God.

Augustine's answer to this attack was his extraordinary treatise against paganism, *The City of God*. In it he argues that whether one begins with Greek philosophy, Roman life, or biblical prophecy, there can only be one truth because only one God fits the aspirations of all people. Continuing, he says that the church is not at fault for Rome's troubles, and Rome would be a better place — far better than the gods could create — if this single truth were confessed.

Against this charge of disloyalty, Augustine states that the hope of heaven actually makes life on this earth more productive, not less. Far from being uncooperative, Christians are better citizens, more generous to the poor, and greater peacemakers than the pagans. The parallels between the fifth century and our own are obvious.

The charge is often made today that the world is in trouble because of widespread intolerance. Religious people are especially intolerant because they believe in one truth, it is said. Sadly, as we have seen, there are fanatics who do embrace wrongheaded strategies. But if we follow Paul's discussion in Romans 12, we should reach a very different outlook. Love for the "City of God" means more involvement, not less, with the "City of Man." The worship of God means a better apologetic, not a weaker one.

We could use apologetic answers like Augustine's in our own day. His approach was twofold, being negative in the sense that he dismantled the case against the church with careful scholarly investigation of the facts. But more fundamentally it was positive: Augustine answered the charges made against the gospel by constructing a Christian worldview.

The *City of God* was nothing less than the beginnings of a new philosophy of history. Instead of the ancients' cyclical view, it puts forth a linear approach in which history is moving from a beginning to an end. However complex and contradictory the various trends, history is relentlessly moving toward the grand climax when God will judge the world and establish a new order. This apologetic, in other words, is global and all-encompassing.

When we rightly understand both the obstacles and the opportunities of our world, we can be both realistic and hopeful — realism with hope or, better, realism because of hope. Thus the impact we make will be deeply authentic.

For reflection and discussion

- What parallels do you see between the fifth century and our own?
- Where do you see these issues in the foreground today?
- Consider the attacks on the value of organized religion. Are they fair? Does Christianity contribute to the decline or the upbuilding of humanity?
- Where do you observe this in your own church and community?
- What part is God inviting you to take?

Vincent van Gogh and Seeing

By **Catherine Claire Larson**, staff writer, Prison Fellowship, and author of *As We Forgive: Stories of Reconciliation from Rwanda.*

> There are no ordinary people. You have never talked to a mere mortal.... Next to the Blessed Sacrament itself, your neighbor is the holiest object presented to your senses.
>
> C. S. Lewis, *The Weight of Glory*

When I finished seminary, my next destination would be prison. I write for Prison Fellowship, whose goal is to share the gospel with prisoners. Yet in interviewing many of the incarcerated, they have given the gospel to me.

Grace has put on prison garb and strode before my eyes in the form of former prostitutes and addicts and violent criminals who now claim Jesus as their only hope. There's no question in their minds about their sin problem; a pounding gavel, a clanging door, and an aching ampleness of time have brought that home. Perhaps because of this, when Jesus grabs them, they radiate God's light with a brightness that hurts unaccustomed eyes.

Like these friends, I want to know Jesus like the woman who washed Jesus' feet with her tears, worshiping in reckless abandon, lost to self, scandalous in love.

The trouble is — my vision. I don't see my past or present as worthy of the judge's gavel. And so I miss out on the Savior, till the reflected light from redeemed eyes exposes my darkness. If I am to see rightly, I need new eyes. I need the eyes of an artist.

Vincent van Gogh (1853 – 1890) has taught me how to see better. The great and later very troubled artist spent the early years of his life as an evangelist. After seminary, his fervor led him to the dreary mines of Borinage, Belgium, where he so wished to reach and identify with the poor coal miners that he gave away his food, clothing, and possessions as he did good works and shared the gospel. He writes, "Those who walk in the darkness, in the centre of the earth, like the miners," are more "impressed by the words of the Gospel" than those who do not face such dark conditions.

Although relational pain, depression, and severe epileptic seizures later debilitated him, what strikes me about Van Gogh was the way he *saw* people. He did not see people as they were but rather as they *might* be. He said, "I prefer painting people's eyes rather than cathedrals, for there is something in the eyes that is not in the cathedral — a human soul, be that of a poor beggar or of a street walker."

Artists see possibilities in the ordinary, everyday things many people overlook. We too are called to be artists of the soul — to see in every human being, no matter how ruined and desolate, the glorious possibility of restoration through Christ's love. Total restoration will not be complete (in us or others) until we see Christ. But the beautiful beginnings of a masterpiece are evident in every believer. I hope others see it in me.

As Van Gogh once said, "Christ is more of an artist than the artists; he works in the living spirit and the living flesh, he makes men instead of statues."

We can join in his work if we will let him be our vision, both in how we see ourselves and others.

For reflection and discussion

- Has art ever given you the experience of seeing Christ?
- Have you met a person whose eyes reveal Christ to you?
- How do you think your own life experience might limit your ability to see him?
- What do you really want? How does this come into your prayer?
- What friend(s) come to mind when you consider Van Gogh's words that Christ "works in the living spirit and the living flesh, he makes men instead of statues"? Who might you pray this for today?

Attention Deficit Culture:
Practicing the Presence of People

By Fred Harburg, a senior fellow of The Trinity Forum (*www.ttf.org*) and director of strategy for PathNorth (*www.pathnorth.com*), who has served as an organizational architect and consultant for companies, including IBM, General Motors, Disney, AT&T, Motorola, and Fidelity Investments.

Increasingly common stories of traffic accidents involving people "texting" while driving add poignancy to the epidemic of fractured attention in our world. There is a presumption that multitasking is a necessary, even admirable skill in our hyper-speed age, but nothing could be further from the truth.

As an Air Force instructor pilot, one of the first myths I had to dispel for aspiring young pilot candidates was the idea that good pilots are multitaskers. Research supports a different conclusion. The best pilots are excellent at rapid sequencing. They give full and complete attention to a visual indication, an aural signal, or a kinesthetic sensation, interpret it accurately, act on it effectively, and then move to the next appropriate point of focus. Scientists from the NASA Ames Research Center conclude that attempting to split attention is deadly for a pilot.

What is true for pilots and drivers is also true for those who have the privilege and the personal or professional responsibility for dealing with other human beings. The blinding pace of our world makes it tempting to split the signal rather than to give our full attention to the people with whom we are engaged at any given moment, but the consequence of doing so can wreck a relationship just as it does a car or a plane.

In *The Practice of the Presence of God*, a seventeenth-century monk named Lawrence describes the idea of giving full attention to his relationship with God. Brother Lawrence explains that he "decided to give all to gain all ... adoring God as often as I could, keeping my mind in his holy presence and recalling it as often as it wandered. I had no little difficulty in this exercise, but I kept on despite all difficulties and was not worried or distressed when I was involuntarily distracted.... The effect of repeating these acts is that they become more habitual and the presence of God becomes, as it were, more natural." He summarized this mindfulness of God as being "an interior gaze on God which should always be quiet, humble, and loving."

Michael Mason acknowledged the deep wisdom of Lawrence and extrapolated it to relationships between people. In his book *Practicing the Presence of People*, Mason encourages us to honor others by giving them our full attention and turning our interior gaze on God's handiwork in them. He asks us to tune out the noisy chatter of our distractions, preoccupations, and personal anxieties and tune in to a consuming appreciation for the full value of those with whom we are engaged.

This is the antithesis of paying lip service to one conversation while simultaneously answering a text message or email on a mobile device. Lest we think this is merely a generational divide, the research shows that while younger people may be more accustomed to and technically adept at multitasking, they are no better at simultaneously handling two neural stimuli than their less tech-savvy elders. Yet this split-signal behavior is now so pervasive in the business world that many do not even see it as the enormously rude act which it is.

Most of us confuse "busy" with "important" and fail to see that we find our own significance most powerfully when we recognize the infinite value that God places in those around us. I'm an amateur at being fully present for others and letting them have the spotlight, but I have experienced enough of it to taste its rich reward and to be convinced that when I split the signal, we both lose.

For reflection and discussion

It's getting harder to focus. We are bombarded with noise and images. The Matrix is a vortex. We no longer opt in. We must develop the disciplines to opt out. The web, WiFi, cell phones, TV, radio, iPods, credit cards, airplanes — we are the first generation that can be everywhere and nowhere at the same time. Going home to everyone — and to no one.

- Do you long for a focused life? And a life of excellence?
- Are you loving well the *people* whom God has placed in your life?
- Long ago the writer of the Proverbs observed, "Folly brings joy to those who have no sense, but those who have understanding keep a straight course" (15:21). But how?

• Do you long to know the overriding passion and purity of heart of willing one thing?

In his book *The Call*, in a chapter called "The Focused Life," Os Guinness explores the result of endless choice. It is not only overload but also a profound loss of unity, solidity, and coherence in life. "But ultimately only one thing can conquer choice — being chosen. 'I have chosen you,' Jesus said, 'you have not chosen me.' We are not our own; we have been bought with a price." Guinness also writes that this sense of calling "provides the story line for our lives and thus a sense of continuity and coherence in the midst of a fragmented and confusing modern world."[4] Calling is a "yes" to God that carries a "no" to the chaos of modern demands.

Are you able to unplug from the world in order to abide in the True Vine? Ask God for help. Meditate on Jesus' words in John 15:5, 9, 11:

> I am the vine; you are the branches. If you remain in me and I in you, you will bear much fruit; apart from me you can do nothing.... Now remain in my love.... I have told you this so that my joy may be in you and that your joy may be complete.

• Consider it a challenge: Spend a day *alone* with the Lord in his creation. Unwired. Read Marva Dawn's *Keeping the Sabbath Wholly* and begin practicing the Jewish and Christian joy of Sabbath-keeping — it's a great place to begin.

The Secret Gospels

By Darrell Bock, PhD, professor of New Testament, Dallas Theological Seminary. Bock is a *New York Times* bestselling author and major network adviser. In both the US and Germany, he has researched the Gnostic gospels to write *The Missing Gospels* and *Dethroning Jesus*. His blog is at *http://blog.bible.org/bock/*.

WEEK 7

In 1946, ancient texts emerged from the Egyptian desert. These "Nag Hammadi texts" included fifty-two different nonbiblical books. Among them were several gospels and other works that claimed to give Jesus' teaching, mostly after his resurrection. Such a discovery may well have gone unnoticed, except at universities, had not some scholars and *Da Vinci Code* author Dan Brown begun to claim that these "secret gospels" told us much about the earliest Christianity.

Popularized in books, TV documentaries, and movies, the gospels of Thomas and Judas and other Gnostic texts have left many with historical uncertainty regarding Jesus. Tapping into the suspicion that history is rewritten by the winners, some scholars are finding an audience for claims that what we really see in the first few centuries AD is a "kaleidoscope of Christianities" — many alternative messages to the simple message the church preached for centuries, that Jesus is the Son of God and the Savior who died for sin and gives God's Spirit (Titus 2:11 – 14).

Other scholars have been surprised that these new challenges gained so much traction because we actually have known about these "secret" gospels for centuries. The most copied Nag Hammadi text, *The Apocryphon of John*, is a gospel that church father Irenaeus described as heresy in AD 180. Even more, what these gospels teach make it unlikely that they were truly reflective of Jesus. Why?

These gospels come from a second-century movement known as Gnostic Christianity. Gnostics believed that creation was not the product of one God, but a team product of several underling gods. So the original creation was so flawed that it will never be redeemed. This contrasts with the sacred Old Testament Scripture Christianity embraced from the very beginning, where the one God of Israel creates a good creation and the matter that is a part of it is good, not inherently evil as in Gnosticism. So any work that taught an evil creation from the beginning would never have been considered a serious candidate to reflect the theology of Jesus and his followers, who were Jewish and accepted the idea of creation from one God.

The roots of these writings are also problematic. The New Testament gospels were written by those who walked with Jesus or spent significant time with those who did. None of the Gnostic gospels, with the possible exception of portions of the *Gospel of Thomas*, have any likelihood of reaching back to the apostles. That exception, *Thomas*, is a "hybrid" gospel, mixing a few sayings that may draw on the earliest tradition with others that do not. This is why *Thomas* was excluded. The early third-century church father Origen told us that *Thomas* was not read in the churches, an indication that it was not Scripture.

In contrast, the apostles or those taught by them wrote the four gospels. For example, Mark and Luke were colleagues of Peter and Paul, respectively. The early church tradition is clear about such a close connection for these middle two gospels.

The case for Luke is interesting. From reading Luke and Acts, if you tried to guess the author, which is what those who deny an apostolic connection claim the early church did, all you could determine is that the author of the gospel of Luke was a companion of Paul. So many other candidates existed: Timothy, Silas, Titus, Barnabas, Epaphras, just to name a few. Yet the tradition is unanimous that Luke, hardly the most prominent of the candidates, wrote the third gospel and Acts. In other words, you would not name him as the likely author if you were guessing who it might be.

The same kind of argument applies to Mark and Peter, as Mark is not among the best known of Peter's companions either. *The point is that the church was not afraid to name non-apostles as authors because they knew the authors' connection to the apostles.* The secret gospels lacked such roots and so were rejected.

As fascinating as these texts are, they lack the pedigree and accuracy of the Bible's four gospels. Sometimes history is written by the winners because the winners deserve to win. The content of these gospels is not so much a secret as it (1) represents teaching distinct from the Jewish roots that fed Christianity and (2) reflects instruction separated from Jesus' teaching rooted in apostolic sources.

The unique Christian message about Jesus is precisely that, a unique claim of a unique role in the plan of God for all of humanity. The invitation to restore the broken relationship with the one and only Creator comes through the One that God has shown to be Savior. And our understanding of history and ancient texts points to the fact that those around Jesus preached this uniqueness.

For reflection and discussion

The Gnostics' goal was transcendence — to rise above this evil world through secret "insider" knowledge. In this view, death takes one back to immaterial light, rendering this world and life in it mostly irrelevant. The Christian view of redemption claims life in this world matters, and the power that raised Jesus from the dead is available to bring God's kingdom into a good but fallen world.

- Transcendence or redemption: What difference do you think it makes in your life with God and others which view you take?
- What encourages or challenges you about the unique message of Jesus?
- How do you want to respond to Jesus in light of this reading?

The Middle Ages and the Second Great Schism

By Jerry MacGregor, a bestselling author and Talbot Seminary graduate who did post-doctoral work at Oxford University. He has worked in publishing for years as a writer, editor, and literary agent and is a former publisher for Time-Warner.

After the fall of the Roman Empire in the fifth century, western Europe was divided by various kingdoms, families, landowners, and barbarian armies. Trading and manufacturing disappeared as travel by both land and sea became unsafe, leading to a breakdown in economies. Civic infrastructures failed, so there were few schools, libraries, or civic centers. Art, culture, architecture, and government projects came to a stop almost overnight.

In the midst of civil chaos, the Christian church rose as the lone pillar of stability. When barbarian leaders renounced paganism and embraced Christianity, the church became the dominant force in medieval society. Monks and monasteries became the repositories of knowledge, and priests served as educators and advisers to political leaders. Under Charlemagne, a medieval empire of sorts was created, only to break up under the force of new invasions from Vikings from the north and Muslim Saracens from the east.

The response was not just to wage war but also to evangelize the barbarians, bringing peace to the region. Though still a patchwork of kingdoms and city-states, intellectual life revived, roads and bridges were constructed, and numerous scientific and technological breakthroughs occurred. Above all, cities flourished. The center of the known world moved from the shores of the Mediterranean to the urban areas of Europe, and Pope Innocent III declared himself monarch of the entire Christian world.

But with stability came lust for power. The Crusades led to the arming of many, and the rise of political leaders brought about a resurgence of states. The Hundred Years' War (basically an argument among English kings over the throne of France) caused people to view themselves as French or English citizens. The length and brutality of that conflict, the creation of standing armies, and the resulting drain on European society caused many to doubt the church, which repeatedly failed to resolve the situation.

By the middle of the fourteenth century, European society was in uproar. The aristocracy was unable to defend their lands, monarchies continually involved their subjects in brutal and pointless conflicts, and the middle class faced an economic crisis. Revolts in England and France revealed discontent with the political systems, and the Black Death brought not only physical miseries but economic chaos. In the midst of such turmoil, the masses lost faith in a just God.

Instead of providing spiritual and moral leadership, the church allied itself with the upper classes and entangled itself in power struggles. Instead of providing hope and guidance, many priests were corrupted by money and power and failed to provide the most basic social services — particularly that of caring for the dying. The Pope was living in France and was viewed as a puppet of the French government focused on raising money for his lavish lifestyle.

Reformers demanded the church give up its wealth and began arguing for the priesthood of every believer. In response, the papacy energetically attacked, accused critics of heresy, denied them the sacraments, and used the Inquisition to silence them. In the eyes of many, the church lost its moral authority.

Upon the death of Pope Gregory XI, a Roman mob threatened the French-dominated cardinals to elect an Italian. They elected a simple, uneducated priest, thinking they could control him. But the new pope surprised everyone by exercising his leadership. The Frenchmen fled Rome, reassembled in Avignon, declared the election invalid, and chose a new French pope. That meant two popes, two feuding administrations — both competing for followers, patronage, and money. Both declared the followers of the other to be heretics, worthy of excommunication.

Politicians and scholars tried to resolve the situation. The theological faculty at the University of Paris was asked to decide the issue, but no one had the leadership, the ability, or the will to make enemies of either side. A church council was called with the intent of deposing both popes and declaring one new leader, but that merely led to the creation of a *third* pope. Making the situation worse, governments in conflict tended to support different popes so as to gain political advantage over their neighbors.

This went on for three decades, leading reformers such as John Wycliffe and Jan Huss to declare the existence of a pope unnecessary, since the true church is simply a gathering of Christ-followers. Others preached apostolic poverty and insisted civil authority was superior to that of the pope, since governments had the responsibility of overseeing the church. The Pietistic movement emerged, placing priestly powers in the hands of individuals and encouraging people to view their walk with God as a personal responsibility rather than an organized institution.

By the time the papal schism was finally resolved through an all-church council in 1414, church authority had waned, civil leaders had begun to stand up to the church, and reformers had started gathering followers. Alternate voices gained strength, as people began reexamining the role and teachings of the church. The events of this difficult era led directly to the Reformation that would usher in the modern world. From the ashes of this disastrous century rose the foundation of the Protestant church — a church not aligned with power or government but with an emphasis on personal holiness, hands-on ministry, and the primacy of Scripture.

> In my distress I called to the LORD;... From his temple he heard my voice; my cry came to his ears. The earth trembled and quaked ... because he was angry.
>
> 2 SAMUEL 22:7 – 8

For reflection and discussion

- What did you find encouraging or discouraging about the church of Jesus Christ?
- How have you personally experienced a failure of godly leadership or been inspired by leaders of vision and risk?
- How is God calling you to be a person of influence for him?

The Fact/Value Divide

By Nancy Pearcey, PhD, former Francis A. Schaeffer scholar at the World Journalism Institute and now scholar of worldview studies at Philadelphia Biblical University. Adapted from her book *Total Truth: Liberating Christianity from Its Cultural Captivity*. Pearcey is editor at large of *The Pearcey Report, www.pearceyreport.com.*

WEEK 7

The most potent way Christianity is marginalized in modern society is through the division of life into two separate spheres: a sacred realm of prayer, worship, and personal morality against a secular realm of politics, business, academia, and so on.

The institutions of public life claim to operate by principles that are objective, scientific, and "value-free." But what does that mean for values? They have been relegated to the private sphere of personal choice. Thus, this division is sometimes called the fact/value split. Split off from objective truth, values have been defined literally as *whatever a person values*. "The individual is left to his own devices," explains sociologist Peter Berger, in everything "from expressing his religious preference to settling on a sexual lifestyle." Notice that telling phrase, "religious preference." When religion is redefined as a value, it is no longer considered an objective truth to which we *submit*, but only a matter of personal taste which we *choose*.

Clearly, this is a far cry from the way [we who believe the gospel] use the term *values*. To communicate effectively today, we must understand that the concept of truth itself has been divided — a process that scholars often illustrate using the image of a two-story building. In the lower story are science and reason, which are considered public truth, binding on everyone. Over against it is an upper story of noncognitive experience, which is the locus of personal meaning. It is the realm of private truth, where we hear people say, "That may be true for you but not for me." We can diagram the division like this:

VALUES
private, subjective, relative

FACTS
public, objective, universally valid

This is not merely an intellectual distinction but can be a soul-wrenching dilemma. Ever since the Enlightenment, the realm of "facts" has been identified with a materialist philosophy that pictures the universe as a vast machine, with no place for things like spirit or soul or moral choice. This has produced an inner division between what people think science teaches (that we are machines in a deterministic universe) and what they desperately want to believe (that our lives have purpose and meaning).

The dilemma was illustrated dramatically in the life of the well-loved writer C. S. Lewis. As a young man Lewis abandoned his childhood Anglican faith to adopt atheism and materialism. These fashionable philosophies tantalized his intellect but left his imagination hungry. As he later wrote, "Nearly all that I loved [poetry, beauty, mythology] I believed to be imaginary; nearly all that I believed to be real [mechanistic materialism] I thought grim and meaningless."[1] It was this agonizing inner conflict that drove Lewis's spiritual search for a truth large enough to satisfy the whole person.

What a joy it was when Lewis finally discovered that the gospel *was* that all-encompassing truth. In his own punchy phrase, Christ's resurrection was the "myth [that] became fact." He did not mean *myth* in the sense of *false* but in the sense that it meets humanity's deepest need for contact with the transcendent realm. On one hand, the gospel was the fulfillment of the ancient myths he had always loved. And yet — wonder of wonders! — it had actually happened in time, space, and history.

In short, Christianity rests on historical events that are confirmable by hard-nosed historical and empirical evidence while at the same time expressing the most exalted spiritual meanings. God's truth is a unified whole — and thus it has the power to bring healing and wholeness to our fractured world.

For reflection and discussion

- How have you seen this fact/value divide in the public square? Perhaps in your own life? What creates connections between them?
- How do you respond to Pearcey's point that God has given us truth about total reality, not just about religious things?
- What difference might living in "total truth" make in your participation in business? Academics? Politics? In your personal relationships? In your relationship with God?

Darkness

By **Hugh Ross**, an astrophysicist and astronomer, founder and president of Reasons to Believe, a science-faith think tank. Ross has authored or contributed to over fifteen books, including *Creation as Science*, and has addressed students and faculty on more than three hundred college campuses; *www.reasons.org*.

WEEK 7

When an up-and-coming heavy-metal band recruited our son to play drums, I wondered what David had gotten himself into. The word *darkness* featured in the band's name gave me chills.

For better or worse, our home became the practice site. Soon some of the band members expressed curiosity about my work, about how I link astrophysics with my faith. One evening they listened for over an hour as I explained how twenty-first-century discoveries about cosmic darkness have yielded the most impressive scientific evidence to date for a supernatural, super-intelligent Creator, the God of the Bible.

They were stunned to learn that Scripture foreshadowed these cutting-edge discoveries. In Job 38, God asked, "Where does darkness reside? Can you take [it] to [its] places? Do you know the paths to [its] dwellings?" For over three thousand years, no human could answer. But, astronomers now know that darkness makes up 99.73 percent of all the stuff of the universe. They know that dark stuff comes in three forms. They've even determined *where* these different forms of cosmic darkness reside:

Ordinary dark matter (comprised of protons, neutrons, and electrons) resides in halos closely surrounding galaxies of all types.

Exotic dark matter (composed of particles that do not strongly interact with photons) resides in halos distantly surrounding large galaxies and galaxy clusters.

Dark energy (the self-stretching property of the cosmic space surface) resides everywhere, evenly distributed. (Note: All the universe's matter and energy reside on the three-dimensional surface of our four-dimensional cosmos — height, width, depth, and time.)

The precise locations and amounts of this exotic and ordinary dark matter provide exactly what's needed for a stable spiral galaxy, and advanced life is possible *only* in a stable spiral galaxy.

The measured quantities and specific locations of the three kinds of darkness offer spectacular evidence for supernatural, super-intelligent design. The level of fine-tuning in the dark-energy component alone is astounding. If it varied by as little as one part in 10^{120} (that's 10 with another 119 zeros after it), life in the universe could not exist. Just how astounding is this number? It's as if the tiniest imaginable variation in Earth's mass — the addition or subtraction of a quintillionth of a quadrillionth of a quadrillionth of a quadrillionth the mass of an electron — would make Earth uninhabitable. What explanation, other than the God of the Bible, can anyone give for this level of design? Within the realm of reason, none.

Do answers to these questions about darkness make the light of Scripture shine more brilliantly? I believe they do, particularly for twenty-first-century skeptics. Job 38 includes nearly fifty questions about nature that underscore the incomparable wisdom and power of God. Scientists today can answer just ten — an indication of how much we still have to learn. And yet each of the answers, like those about darkness, shows the intricacy of God's plan, the steadfastness of God's purpose, and the magnitude of God's care for his creation, including living creatures. Not one person could be alive without God's attention to detail in crafting the universe.

What's more, each answer researchers find yields powerful new evidence for believers and doubters alike that God exists and that his Word can be trusted. Both our hearts and our minds can embrace His provision for our redemption and our eternal life with him.

As for David's band, after digging into my books on how the cosmos reveals God, they composed a new song, "Intelligent Redesign." Through it God's light penetrates many more dark places.

For reflection and discussion

- What do you think is the strongest evidence for the existence of God — evidence from the physical universe? Evidence from your experience with him? Both?
- In Isaiah 45:7 God says, "I form the light and create darkness." What do you think might be God's good purpose in creating darkness?
- How do you see the Father of Lights' steadfast love in the darkness he's allowing in your life?

Tyndale:
The Bible into English

By Kelly Monroe Kullberg

How did the Bible itself come to be? The sixty-six books of the Bible were originally written in Hebrew, Aramaic, or Greek. Most of the Jewish Bible, or Christian Old Testament, was written in Hebrew. The New Testament was originally written in Greek.[2]

In the early decades and centuries of the Church, skilled scribes meticulously hand-copied texts onto scrolls made of leather. Other copies were written on papyrus, a form of paper made from reeds. By the fourth century, books were being produced on separate parchment pages held together with hinged wooden covers. Such a book was called a *codex*, from the Latin word for "wood block." During the fourth century, Saint Jerome's translation of the Bible into commonplace Latin was known as the *Vulgate*.

The journey the Bible made from its original languages to English was a difficult one.

In the fourth century the Bible, in Latin, arrived in England. By the seventh century, a monk named Caedmon made an English hymn with biblical allusions, and translations from the Latin Bible were made into Old English for teaching purposes. By the tenth century, selected passages from both the Old and the New Testament were translated into English.

In the fourteenth century, the priest John Wycliffe was the first to translate the entire Bible into English — the Middle English of Chaucer — from the Vulgate. A group of Wycliffe's fellow priests began copying and distributing this translation. They drew their authority for doing this from the Bible itself and not the church and, as a result, became a clear threat to church authority.

Wycliffe and his friends were soon under attack, and Wycliffe was charged with heresy. He lost his teaching position and was called to Rome to answer charges. He died before he could do this. Nonetheless, the church's Council of Constance (1414 – 1418) condemned his work. English translations of the

Bible were outlawed. The winds of the Reformation were blowing strong in the church.

Onto the scene came an Oxford linguist named William Tyndale (1494 – 1536), skilled in eight languages — Hebrew, Greek, Latin, Spanish, French, Italian, English, and German.

He sought to translate the Bible so even "the boy that drives the plow" could learn it. And so he left England for Germany where it was safe to work and where he probably met and received support from Martin Luther, who was then translating the Bible into German. Tyndale translated the New Testament by 1526 and the first five books of Hebrew Scriptures, or "Pentateuch," by 1530.

Johannes Gutenberg had already invented a system of movable type around 1450, making it possible to mass-produce books. The very first book printed on Gutenberg's press was two hundred copies of Saint Jerome's *Vulgate*. Twenty-one of those copies still exist today.

Tyndale's English New Testaments were soon smuggled into England. Though he tried to work in secret, he was betrayed, brought to trial, and condemned to death. He was led to the stake on October 6, 1536. There he was strangled and his body burned. His last words were, "Lord, open the King of England's eyes." Within a year, Henry VIII allowed English Bibles to be distributed. Within seventy-five years, two million English Bibles were distributed throughout a country of six million people.

Biblical literacy catalyzed the arts, literature, medicine, education, and social service. William Shakespeare, for example, was thoroughly educated in the English Bible. Scholars have claimed that without Tyndale, we wouldn't know the name Shakespeare; nor would the English language have evolved with Shakespeare's own catalytic influence.

Tyndale's influence on the English language was solidified in the publication in 1611 of the King James Bible. Its committee relied heavily on existing translations and foundationally on Tyndale's. The KJV was designed for public reading from English pulpits and became the English Word of God for many generations. Alistair McGrath, a renowned Oxford scholar on the literature of the Bible, notes, "Without the King James Bible, there would have been no *Paradise Lost*, no *Pilgrim's Progress*, no Handel's *Messiah*, no Negro spiritual, and no Gettysburg Address." Let's thank God for Tyndale, burned at the stake for giving us the Bible in English.

For reflection and discussion

Try to imagine the value of a Bible if only twenty existed in the world. If you have your own Bible, former generations would have thought you a very privileged person.

- Do you know people who've never taken an opportunity to read some of the Bible?
- What books, or passages of books, in the Bible do you feel closest to?
- What work of art — song, book, poem, speech, or film — might you most miss if not for the Bible's translation into English?

Michelangelo:
The Image of Renaissance Humanism

By Francis Schaeffer, DD. Excerpted from *How Should We Then Live?* With his wife, Edith, Schaeffer founded L'Abri Fellowship, a study center in Switzerland where individuals pursue questions of faith, meaning, and purpose in community; *www .labri.org*.

In the Academy in Florence is Michelangelo's (1475 – 1564) great room. Here we see, on either side, Michelangelo's statues of men "tearing themselves out of the rock." These were sculpted between 1519 and 1536. They make a real humanistic statement: Man will make himself great. Man as man is tearing himself out of the rock. Man will be victorious.

As the room in the academy is arranged, it strikingly sets forth [Renaissance] humanistic thought. As we go past these men tearing themselves out of the rock, we come finally, at the focal point of the room, to the magnificent statue of David (1504). As a work of art, it has few equals in the world. Michelangelo took a piece of marble so flawed that no one thought it could be used and out of it he carved this overwhelming statue. But let us notice that the *David* was not the Jewish David of the Bible. *David* was simply a title. Michelangelo knew his Judaism, and in the statue the figure is not circumcised. We're not to think of this as the biblical David but as the humanistic ideal. Man is great!

The *David* was the statement of what the humanistic man saw himself as being tomorrow! In this statue we have man waiting with confidence in his own strength for the future. Even the disproportionate size of the hands says that man is powerful. This statue is idealistic and romantic. There was and is no man like the *David*. If a girl fell in love with the statue and waited until she found such a man, she would never marry. Humanism was standing in its proud self and the *David* stood as a representation of that.

But there are signs that by the end of his life, Michelangelo saw that humanism was not enough. Michelangelo in his later years was in close touch with Vittoria Colonna, a woman who had been influenced by Reformation thought. Some people feel they see some of that influence in Michelangelo's life and work. However that may be, it is true that his later work did change.

Many of his early works show his humanism, as does his *David*. In contrast stand two later *Pietàs* (statues of mourning over the dead body of Jesus), in the cathedral in Florence and in the castle in Milan. Neither was completed. In the *Pietà* in the cathedral of Florence, Michelangelo put his own face on Nicodemus (or Joseph of Arimathea — whichever the man is), and in both of these *Pietàs*, humanistic pride seems lessened if not absent.

The humanists had been sure that man starting from himself could solve every problem. There was a complete faith in Man. Man starting from himself, tearing himself out of the rock, out of nature, could solve all. The humanistic cry was, "I can do what I will; just give me until tomorrow."

But the end result was not Michelangelo's *David*, but [1960s filmmaker] Michelangelo Antonioni's nonhero. All there is in the film is the camera that goes "click-click-click" and the human has disappeared. The main character snaps pictures of individual things, particulars. One might point out, for example, the models he snaps. All their humanity and meaning are gone.

After a scene in which clowns play tennis without a ball, there is at the end of the film a reverse zoom shot in which the man who is the central character disappears entirely, and all that remains is the grass. Man is gone. Modern people, on their basis of reason, see themselves only as machines. But as they move into the area of non-reason and look for their optimism, they find themselves separated from reason and without any human or moral values.

On the basis of revelation — the Bible and the revelation of God through Christ — there are certainties of human values and moral values. And there is a reason why man is man. But not for these people with a humanist position.

Modern people are in trouble indeed. People function based on their worldview. Therefore, society has changed radically. This is the reason — and not a less basic one — that it is unsafe to walk at night through the streets of many of today's cities. As a man thinketh so is he.

For reflection and discussion

- In what ways does Michelangelo's *David* move you? And the historical David who inspired the artist (1 Samuel 17), how do you see him in comparison to the statue?
- Modernists' confident expectation that man will be able to fulfill his potential and solve his problems through education and technology has met

with a great deal of postmodern skepticism. How do you respond to the modernist optimism? The postmodern skepticism?

- In what ways do you feel optimistic about your potential? Pessimistic?
- What do you think is the bedrock of human value? What ultimately gives you a sense of dignity?
- How do you want to respond to God about this reading?

The Gospel of Self-Esteem

By **Archibald D. Hart**, PhD, professor of psychology and dean emeritus of the Graduate School of Psychology, Fuller Theological Seminary, and author of more than twenty-four books, including *Thrilled to Death: How the Endless Pursuit of Pleasure Is Leaving Us Numb*; *www.hartinstitute.com*.

Is high self-esteem all it's cracked up to be? If you suffer from low self-esteem, are you doomed to failure? What new picture of self-esteem is emerging from the science of psychology, and how does it agree with God's Word on the subject?

In the upheaval of the late '60s and early '70s, the concept of self-esteem took off. "If only we can help people to feel better about themselves, we will solve many social problems and mental illnesses" became the driving force that sent teachers, parents, and even the states of California and New York in the 1980s scurrying to set up commissions and task forces on self-esteem. It became a national preoccupation that has now ended as a hopeless quest. Research now conclusively shows that such efforts do little to improve social problems, academic performance, success in the workplace, or even to enhance our happiness.

The bottom line is that while everyone intuitively recognizes the reality of "self-esteem," there is no evidence that by boosting these self-feelings one can accomplish more in life. Research psychologists have now clearly demonstrated that self-esteem is the *consequence* of accomplishing something significant in life, *not* the *cause* of accomplishments or failures.

In his 1994 presidential address to the American Psychological Association, Martin Seligman, a significant leader in the new "positive psychology" movement, denounced several "sacred cows" of psychotherapy, one being that in order to reduce mental illness we should try to increase the self-esteem of our children. He stated: "Undeniably, depressed people have low self-esteem. But bolstering self-esteem without changing hopelessness ... accomplishes nothing." He received a standing ovation! His research shows that teens from the ghettos have the highest self-esteem ratings of any group, *not* the lowest! The problem is that their self-esteem is "unwarranted."

As we teach and counsel others, we must caution one another to identify and address the myths that have penetrated the whole concept of self-esteem. Sermons abound on how one is to "love oneself," but we need to carefully interpret Matthew 19:19. We must be mindful that our participation in newly emerging worship styles is radically God-centered and not unduly influenced by the self-esteem movement's emphasis on my needs and my feelings. Perhaps we need to pay more attention to the wisdom that Paul expresses in Romans 12:3 which tells us all we need to know about the self-esteem problem even though its focus is not on low self-esteem, but rather on an inflated and distorted sense of self.

> For by the grace given me I say to every one of you: Do not think of yourself more highly than you ought, but rather think of yourself with sober judgment, in accordance with the faith God has distributed to each of you.
>
> ROMANS 12:3

Paul outlines the essential ingredients for building a Christian understanding of what I call "authentic self-esteem," an understanding and acceptance of yourself for who you really are. There is nothing wrong with being imperfect. Sometimes feeling bad acts as a stimulus to do better or try something different. It can prompt confession, change, and courage. One of the biggest mistakes you can make as a parent is to always protect your children from pain and failure. By cushioning feeling bad, the self-esteem movement has made it harder for us to feel good. It has encouraged cheap success.

From the words of Paul, I deduce that the essence of a healthy self-attitude must be based, first, on an honest and truthful self-understanding and image ("think ... with sober [honest] judgment"); then, second, on a willingness to accept that you are who you are, created in God's image ("in accordance with the faith God has distributed to each of you"). All other self-feelings lead to self-hate. Your attitude to yourself (which is what self-esteem is really all about) must be based plainly and simply on thinking about yourself with complete honesty. You must own your flaws *and* your strengths.

It must never be dishonest ("Do not think of yourself more highly than you ought"), not exaggerated or distorted. Many psychologists have pointed out that the struggle often is with an "internal filter system" we develop early in life that tends to deny our successes and hoards the memories of failures. Self-honesty requires one to be diligent in challenging these denials. After all, in God's kingdom there is always forgiveness and restoration. No matter how inadequate you may feel about yourself or how insignificant your life may appear to be on the outside, you should always remember that the grace of God covers every shortcoming. You will always be precious to him, however you feel about yourself. One can never go beyond the reach of his grace and forgiveness.

Here lies the key to how you should feel about yourself: your self needs to become more and more transparent to itself as you become less and less self-conscious. This is authentic self-esteem. You know who you are, how you have been redeemed, and how precious you are to God — not because you are wonderful but because he has made you his child.

For reflection and discussion

- Has the question of self-esteem caused confusion or problems for you or for others?
- What could help you become more honest? To get closer to being "more transparent to yourself as you become less and less self-conscious"?
- Consider reflecting on Jesus' attributes (bold, lowly in heart, joyful ...) and abilities (to create, comfort, rule ...) as a goal for your life. How do you respond to 2 Corinthians 3:18: "And we all, who with unveiled faces contemplate the Lord's glory, are being transformed into his image with ever-increasing glory"?

Major and Minor Themes

Note: *This week you will notice a theme: how we can see the justice and goodness of God in the midst of pain and evil.*

By **John Eldredge**, bestselling author. Adapted from *Major and Minor Themes* CD. Eldredge is author of *Waking the Dead* and *Walking with God* and founder of Ransomed Heart Ministries, which hosts conferences that provide personal interaction with his message; *www.ransomedheart.com.*

Jesus says, "I have come that they may have life, and have it to the full" (John 10:10). But frankly, that fullness seems pretty rare. Life can break your heart. So how do we find the breakthrough that Scriptures talk so much about?

Years ago I read in one of Francis Schaeffer's works that there are two themes to the gospel: a major theme of hope, love, and life triumphant, and a minor theme of suffering, sorrow, and loss. How are we to understand this, especially the minor theme, in the context of the gospel? There is the cross, there is suffering. It may be internal things (shame or fear) or external things (physical suffering, difficulty in a marriage or a relationship, loss of a career, a church that falls apart), just wherever and however life is hard. That's what we mean by the minor theme.

I think the hardest thing I ever went through was the death of my friend Brent Curtis in a climbing accident. To lose someone immediately, violently, with two boys and a wife that he loved and left behind and with all our shared dreams of ministry together (our book, *The Sacred Romance*, had only been out a year) was an absolutely awful experience. But from before it happened, God was in it.

I really enjoy arranging for great vacations, great parties, great dinners. And God, over several years, had thwarted nearly every one of them. Vacations shut down by freak snowstorms. Special parties spoiled when somebody got sick. Event after event, something went wrong. And finally, on a flight home from one of those absolute disasters, I asked God what he was doing.

He said, "John, you are not an eternal person. Your hope is fixed entirely in this life."

WEEK 8

And I had to admit that he was right. I mean, I didn't think about heaven much. I was trying to make life happen now.

Brent was killed two weeks after that conversation. And what his death exposed in me was the intensity of this incredible, fierce commitment to find life now. To arrange for as much pleasure and happiness as I could. Like nothing else, suffering disrupts us. It exposes all sorts of things beneath the surface of our lives. God is in that.

Having said that, however, I think a terrible theology has taken root in the church: I believe we have made the minor theme the major theme.

Most churches talk in depth about the cross, the sufferings of Christ, and the crosses we need to carry. Look, life's just hard, so let's just live with it. It's either the theology that says the fall is everything and all you can hope for now is heaven, or it's become cool and edgy to talk about the minor theme. Recently many pastors who focus on the minor theme are seeing their congregations growing because people are saying, "Wow, he's so real." And honesty is good. We don't want to fake a good marriage. We don't want to fake a maturity we don't have.

But from the music, to the songs, even the way of dress, it's the minor theme. In fact, if you acknowledge some breakthrough, you can be viewed as living the cliché, a less than honest Christianity.

Here's what has happened: In the modern era the church talked about the major theme, and in some ways, only the major theme. "We're just walking in the victory of Jesus!" And people responded, "That isn't my life. I can't relate to that. I'm out of here."

And now in the postmodern era, what's become cool is to major in the minor theme. I heard on Christian radio just the other day a well-known artist singing about how you don't really hear the voice of God. God's kind of elusive, but that's what faith is — hanging on even though you really don't get much in this life. And I wanted to throw a chair through the window. I mean, that is not the gospel.

Yes, the gospel has a minor theme. And I want to be very honest about what it's like to live in this world. The Christianity that talks only about hope, joy, and overcoming would be hollow, syrupy, shallow. In the young and emerging church there is an honesty that I respect, and that is very good.

But the world is well acquainted with darkness and confusion and, for the most part, many believe that is all there is. If all we offer people is just realness and we all just sit in the minor theme, then what are we offering? Where's the breakthrough? Where's the resurrection of Christ, the ascension of Christ? And where is the rest of Scripture that talks about how he does heal the brokenhearted? That we reign in life with Christ? That in all these things we are more than conquerors? I want to talk about that major theme as well, as Schaeffer warned so many years ago, and make it the major theme. We must be honest about the minor theme, but we must keep it the minor theme.

For reflection and discussion

- What have been your own experiences with "the minor theme" of suffering, loss, disappointment? How have they challenged or encouraged your ideas about "the major theme"?
- Do you agree that overcoming *is* the major theme? Do you think we get only glimpses of it? Or do you believe that we can expect "hope, love, and life triumphant" in *this* life (see Romans 5:17; 8:36 – 39)?
- What can overcoming look like even when pain and suffering goes on unresolved and there is no deliverance?
- Do you see God's activity and character in specific experiences, both the major and minor themes? How do you wish to respond to him?

The Renaissance and Reformation

By **James Emery White**, PhD, professor of theology and culture at Gordon-Conwell Theological Seminary. He is founding and senior pastor of Mecklenburg Community Church in Charlotte, N.C. He is the author of more than a dozen books. Adapted from his book *Serious Times: Making Your Life Matter in an Urgent Day*; *www.serious times.com.*

The Renaissance (fourteenth to sixteenth centuries) was birthed in Italy but gradually spread throughout Europe. As the word means, the Renaissance was a "rebirth" of culture inspired by the rediscovery of ancient Greece and Rome and their spirit of learning. It was a turn from the medieval focus on the world-to-come to a fascination with the world-at-hand.

Many forces produced the Renaissance, most importantly the rediscovery of ancient texts and languages. The rebirth was tied to a recovery of those disciplines, from art to science, which had been lost in the collapse of Roman civilization. So while Leonardo da Vinci wears the famed tag of "Renaissance Man" through his multiple interests and talents, a more accurate example of the rebirth of the classical spirit was Erasmus of Rotterdam (1467 – 1536). In his studies of the Greek New Testament and the early church fathers and in his vigorous defense of the pagan classics, Erasmus became a champion of Renaissance discovery.

From the Renaissance came the creation of what many have called "humanism." As the name implies, much of this was simply a celebration of the humanities and humanity itself. Giovanni Boccaccio's *The Decameron*, celebrating life and sensuality, marked a turning point in literature. In art, the medieval hesitance to capture the human image became a distant memory as portraits — both painted and carved — burst onto the scene. Typified by Michelangelo's towering, fourteen-foot sculpture of David, the human body had been "transfigured into heroic proportions and attitude, not seen since ancient times."

At first this humanism did not undermine the well-established Christian worldview. In many ways it invigorated it, for the learning was taking place within the Christian context that was still in effect from the Middle Ages. As a result, it merely served to expand the existing Christian vision. Social historian Fernand Braudel referred to the early humanism of the Renaissance as a robust and complementary "dialogue of Rome with Rome," meaning pagan Rome and Christian Rome, and between classical and Christian civilization. So during the sixteenth century, Raphael painted the pagan god Apollo on the walls of the papal apartments in Rome. This was not done as a sign of acceptance but of cultural appreciation. This reveals the confidence of the time that knowledge and art were pursued within the context and under the authority of the Christian faith.

So while the early humanism of the Renaissance was built around a return to things classical, it was done in light of the Creator. This was a Christian, or sacred, humanism. Despite some bumps along the road, the early humanism of the Renaissance was actually a call for a richer and more well-rounded Christian culture. The cry *ad fonts* — "back to the sources" — provided devout men and women with the impetus to reach back into the past, beyond any corruption that might have developed in and through the medieval church, to the golden age of the apostolic era. No group would take greater advantage of this than the Reformers. Though disagreement would erupt between the Reformers and the Renaissance humanists, it is often observed that Luther hatched the egg that Erasmus had laid.

Only when humanism was ripped from its Christian moorings and became a secular humanism did the interplay between Renaissance humanism and Christianity become adversarial. As Francis Schaeffer puts it in *Escape from Reason*, when humanism became autonomous — meaning divorced from the anchor of biblical revelation and a Christian worldview — it became destructive. Such a return to Athens, independent of Jerusalem, increasingly elevated Protagoras's contention that "Man is the measure of all things."

With "man," as opposed to God, as the measure of all things, many became ambivalent about this new humanism and the future it would bring. Yet others declared this new humanism the beginning of an age of "Enlightenment."

For reflection and discussion

- Have you ever enjoyed the discovery of something ancient as something new?
- In what ways do you think the gospel makes for a better humanism?
- In what ways can cultures die? How are cultures reborn? What is a "culture of life"?

Theodicy

theodicy: \ thē ŏd´‑ə sĭ \ vindication of the divine attributes, particularly holiness and justice, in respect to the existence of evil.

THE AMERICAN COLLEGE DICTIONARY

By Lee Strobel, bestselling author. Adapted from *The Case for Faith: A Journalist Investigates the Toughest Objections to Christianity*. A writer for the *Chicago Tribune*, Strobel turned his journalistic skills to address challenges to the Christian faith. In this reading, Why does God allow such suffering and evil? he interviews Boston University professor Peter Kreeft.

Peter Kreeft gestured toward the hallway. "On my door there is a cartoon of two turtles. One says, 'Sometimes I'd like to ask why he allows poverty, famine, and injustice when he could just do something about it.' The other turtle says, 'I'm afraid God might ask me the same question.' "

I responded, "That cartoon reminds me of the way God likes to turn questions around."

"Yes, he's constantly doing that. This happened to Job. Job was wondering who God was because it looked as if God was a cosmic sadist. At the end of the book of Job, God finally shows up with the answer — and the answer is a question.

"He says to Job, 'Who are you? Are you God? Did you write the script? Were you there when I laid the foundations of the earth?' And Job realizes the answer is no. Then he's satisfied. Why? *Because he sees God!* God doesn't write him a book. He could've written the best book on the problem of evil ever written. Instead, he shows himself to Job."

"And that satisfied him — "

"Yes! It has to — that's what's going to satisfy us forever in heaven. I think Job gets a foretaste of heaven at the end of the book, because he meets God. If it were only words that God gave him, that would mean that Job could dialogue and ask God another question and God would give him a good answer and Job would ask another question the next day and the next day, because Job was a very demanding philosopher. This would go on and on and never end. What could make it end? God's presence!

"God didn't let Job suffer because he lacked love but because he *did* love in order to bring Job to the point of encountering God face to face, which is humanity's supreme happiness. Job's suffering hollowed out a big space in him so that God and joy could fill it.

"As we look at human relationships, what we see is that lovers don't want explanations, but presence. And what God is, essentially, is presence — the doctrine of the Trinity says God is three persons who are present to each other in perfect knowledge and perfect love. That's why God is infinite joy. And insofar as we can participate in that presence, we too have infinite joy."

"The answer, then, to suffering," I said in trying to sum up where we'd come, "is not an answer at all."

"Correct," he emphasized. "It's the Answerer. It's Jesus himself. It's not a bunch of words, it's *the* Word. It's not a tightly woven philosophical argument, it's a person. *The* person. The answer to suffering cannot just be an abstract idea because this isn't an abstract issue, it's a personal issue. It requires a personal response. The answer must be someone, not just something, because the issue involves someone — *God, where are you?*

"Jesus is there, sitting beside us in the lowest places of our lives. Are we broken? He was broken, like bread for us. Are we despised? He was despised and rejected of men. Do we cry out that we can't take any more? He was a man of sorrows and acquainted with grief. Do people betray us? He was sold out himself. Are our tenderest relationships broken? He too loved and was rejected.

"Does he descend into all of our hells? *Yes,* he does. From the depths of a Nazi death camp, Corrie ten Boom wrote: 'No matter how deep our darkness, he is deeper still.'

"In the end, God has given us only partial explanations," he said slowly, a shrug in his voice. "Maybe that's because he saw that a better explanation wouldn't have been good for us. I don't know why. As a philosopher, I'm obviously curious. Humanly, I wish he had given us more information."

With that, he looked fully into my face.

"But he knew Jesus was more than an explanation," he said firmly. "He's what we really need. If your friend is sick and dying, the most important thing he wants is not an explanation; he wants you to sit with him. He is terrified of being alone more than anything else. So God has not left us alone.

"And for that," he said, *"I love him."*

> The LORD is close to the brokenhearted
> and saves those who are crushed in spirit.
> PSALM 34:18

For reflection and discussion

If Jesus would walk through the door, we would thrill to his presence. And yet he is with us always, even to the end of the earth, shimmering through the dark glass. We are the ones learning to see him, trace his hand. We are learning to value his presence so that, like Job, we find he is enough.

- What circumstances in your own life, or the lives of others, have made you ask, Where is God? What have you learned in these circumstances?
- How have you offered your presence to someone who is hurting?
- Think of a difficult time when God has given you the gift of his presence, perhaps even when you did not feel anything but darkness and anguish.
- How can you seek and savor his presence today?

Malaria

By **Michael J. Behe**, PhD, professor of biochemistry, Lehigh University. Behe's books *Darwin's Black Box* and *The Edge of Evolution* have ignited a spirited conversation about intelligent design in academia.

Even today, in some regions of the globe, half of all children die before the age of five. Humanity's ancient nemesis, malaria, kills a million of those children each year.

Throughout recorded history, malaria, with its periodic deadly fevers, was little understood. Only around 1900 did British physician Ronald Ross discover that the disease is caused by a microscopic parasitic amoeba-like creature, which is transmitted from person to person by the bite of a mosquito.

Now we know much more about the disease. Once inside a human, the malarial parasite first travels to the liver and undergoes preliminary growth and metamorphosis. Eventually thousands of malarial cells enter the bloodstream. Using sophisticated molecular machinery, the parasite grabs onto a red blood cell, enters it, and begins to eat the cell's protein, hemoglobin. The food allows it to make copies of itself. The twenty copies then burst out of the destroyed human cell and seek out other blood cells to invade. Multiplying exponentially, in a few days a trillion malaria cells can consume half of a person's blood.

As horrible as malaria is, its genetic history affords our best insight into Darwin's claims of chance evolution. Over thousands of years, humans have acquired DNA mutations that afford some resistance to the disease. These have been touted as our clearest examples of evolution in action. Only in recent years, however, has science tracked down the exact nature of those random changes: They are all damaging.

The haphazard mutations all break, diminish, or warp working genes. One mutation yields the well-known sickle cell gene. One helps a person resist malaria. But if two copies are inherited (one each from a child's mother and father), a child develops sickle cell anemia. Another mutation throws out a whole gene that usually helps make hemoglobin, leading to a medical condition called thalassemia. Other mutations destroy genes that ordinarily help protect a red blood cell from damage by oxygen, making the cell more fragile.

Since malaria has been studied for over a hundred years and since the microbe reproduces so rapidly, scientists have tracked the evolution of malaria for what would be the equivalent of millions of years of human evolutionary history. But if we look for the kinds of constructive mutations Darwinists claim could build the sophisticated machinery found in all cells, we come up empty. At the terrible cost of much human illness and death, science's best evidence shows random changes do not explain the well-planned machines of life. Like a bull in a china shop, random mutations break delicate objects, which sometimes, fortuitously, can do a child a bit of good but at the sacrifice of degrading the human genome.

To make the sophisticated systems of the human body, a powerful directing intelligence was needed. Our physical bodies have been planned with a stunning depth of detail that no earlier generations could have known. The advance of science gives us fresh reasons to rejoice that we are fearfully, wonderfully, purposely made.

Yet, perhaps shockingly, we see that malaria itself is also fearfully and wonderfully and purposely made. Like us, it also has sophisticated molecular machinery to allow it to live. Pondering the mystery of malaria, I think of Job. When he questioned God about his suffering, God wasn't defensive; he reminded Job of his transcendence. He uses whatever he chooses for his purposes: armies, natural catastrophes, and even deadly microbes. We live in a world beset by suffering and cannot know all God's plans and purposes. But we know they are good. Our faith assures us that nothing penetrates God's protective hedge around our lives without his permission and that, finally, every tear will be wiped away.

For reflection and discussion

- How does this view agree or disagree with your views of creation and Darwin's theory of evolution? Does it raise any questions?
- Think about your closest encounter with a painful or ravaging disease. Was it more difficult to think about it as a random accident or as something under the control of God's providence? How might you respond to one who suffers from such a disease (2 Corinthians 4:16 – 18)?
- In the light of this reading, how do you respond to a God who has "fearfully and wonderfully made [us]" (Psalm 139:14) and holds together "*all* things" (Colossians 1:16 – 17)?

Gerard Manley Hopkins:
The Sacrament of Struggle

By Sue Stewart, MA, essayist, writing coach, and founder of Brain Builders Gymnasium, has taught college English.

Whether we like it or not, all of us occasionally step into the ring with God.

No one escapes a turn battling the rage and injustice of a broken heart, the grief of loss, the despair of meaninglessness, or the psychic and physical brokenness of disease. This God who purportedly made us and loves us seems especially good at the one-two punch: you lose your job, then your car breaks down; your mom gets cancer, then your dog dies. Sometimes we're down for the count, feeling the sick effects of childhood sexual abuse all our lives. Or the knockout punch of an unbeatable addiction. We're routinely outboxed — purpled, swollen, and ignominiously vanquished by the implacable One who seems to so unjustly inflict or spare as he sees fit.

In London 120 years ago, there was an earnest Jesuit priest named Gerard Manley Hopkins in just such a life-fight with God. As he was given to writing dense, ahead-of-its-time poetry, a "Terrible Sonnet" emerged from his soul's dark night — one that complained, explained, and finally vaulted him out of the pit in fourteen sprung-rhythm lines.

Looking back at his time of "now done darkness," Hopkins wonders what affected the exodus. Hear what he says to Despair in the first stanza:

> *Not, I'll not, carrion comfort, Despair, not feast on thee,*
> *Not untwist — slack they may be — these last strands of man*
> *In me, or most weary cry — **I can no more**. I can;*
> *Can something, hope, wish day come, not choose not to be.*[1]

Not, not, not, not, not, not. Six nots. In the swirling vortex of the despair pit, the power of *not* and the power of *can* mean the same thing: *"I can not kill myself."* Actually, even in the midst of the most intense despair, there's a little laundry list of things anyone could do: hope, wish the day would come, and choose life.

Father Hopkins, crouched and bleeding in the corner of the ring, accuses and interrogates his Opponent in the next stanza:

But ah, but O thou terrible, why wouldst thou rude on me
Thy wring-world right foot rock? Lay a lion limb against me? Scan
With darksome devouring eyes my bruised bones? And fan,
O in turns of tempest, me heaped there; me frantic to avoid thee and flee?[2]

"Why are you mauling me? he screams, *"when you're already clearly the winner? I must get away from you!"*

But escape isn't an option. Only examination. And that's the point, as he continues in the third stanza:

Why? That my chaff might fly, my grain lie, sheer and clear.
Nay, in all that toil, that coil, since (seems) I kissed the rod,
Hand rather, my heart lo! Lapped strength, stole joy, would laugh, cheer.
Cheer whom though? The Hero whose heaven-handling flung me, foot-trod
Me? or me that fought him? O which one? is it each one? That night, that year
Of now done darkness I wretch lay wrestling with (my God!) my God.[3]

He concludes that this sacramental struggle is for purification (our grain, sheer and clear) and that the very nature of the struggle *and the way through it* is a paradox. We must learn to love both the torturous rod of discipline *and* the hand that wields it. We must willingly examine the meaning of our suffering and humbly acknowledge the partnership between ourselves and God (which just *looks* like a prizefight!). God's rocky grace and benevolent sovereignty is transformative, but so, paradoxically, is our submission, our self-examination, our courageous wretchedness. Only in the heart of that paradoxical partnership can we lap strength and joy, laughing and cheering for the loving necessity of the fight.

For reflection and discussion

Try reading the poem without the commentary. What does it take to follow Hopkins' thoughts?

- Have you felt yourself in a similar standoff with God? How would you describe it?
- What helps you continue in faith?
- How is God showing you the "loving necessity of the fight"? How do you want to respond to him?

Johann Sebastian Bach

By Lael Arrington

For several generations, the Bach family had produced professional musicians. But they could never have anticipated the genius and worldwide acclaim that would come to Johann (1685 – 1750), the son who left the family's mark on history.

In his *Spiritual Lives of the Great Composers*, Patrick Kavanaugh describes one of the most famous examples of Bach's "word painting": "In his colossal Mass in B Minor, towards the end of the 'Crucifixus' movement, the voices and instruments quietly sink into their lowest registers as the body of Jesus is lowered into the tomb. This is immediately followed by an explosion of blazing glory in the 'Et Resurrexit,' an effect composers have copied for centuries."4

Beauty. Order. Comfort. Majesty. Despair. Joy! Longing beyond words. Like the poetic repetitions of the Psalms, the point and counterpoint phrases of Bach's music evoke an extraordinary bandwidth of human emotion and experience. Beethoven praised this musical genius, saying, "His name ought not to be Bach (German for 'brook') but 'ocean' because of his infinite and inexhaustible wealth of combinations and harmonies."5

Bach was a civil servant in Leipzig, Germany, overseeing the music in four churches, but nothing about his life was average. He was the father of twenty children. His published works fill sixty-five volumes of music, and perhaps that much again has been lost. He directed a musical service institute, and he wrote, rehearsed, and directed new oratorios (sometimes monthly and even weekly) for his churches.

Bach "was certainly the zenith of composers coming out of the Reformation," wrote Francis Schaeffer in *How Should We Then Live?*

> His music was a direct result of the Reformation culture and the biblical Christianity of the time, which was so much a part of Bach himself. There would have been no Bach had there been no Luther. Bach wrote on his score initials representing such phrases as: "With the help of Jesus" — "To God alone be the glory" — "In the name of Jesus." It was appropriate that the last thing Bach the Christian wrote was "Before Thy Throne I Now Appear."

Bach consciously related both the form and the words of his music to biblical truth. Out of the biblical context came a rich combination of music and words and a diversity with unity. This rested on the fact that the Bible gives unity to the universal and the particulars, and therefore the particulars [all individual things, even notes on a page] have meaning. Expressed musically, there can be endless variety and diversity without chaos. There is variety yet resolution.[6]

The pathos and transcendence of Bach's music emanated from a heart that sought God through great adversity. At the age of nine, Bach lost both parents. He was passed over for appointments and promotions for political reasons and once worked for slave wages to play the violin in a duke's private chapel. He and his first wife lost twins and two other infants. He then lost his wife. Of the twelve children his second wife bore, eight died before the age of five.

Bach lost another son to a lifestyle that incurred so much debt that twice his son had to flee to other towns to escape his creditors. "What can I do or say more?" his father wrote, entreating him to turn his life around. "My warnings having failed and my loving care and help having proved unavailing? I can only bear my cross in patience and commend my undutiful boy to God's mercy, never doubting that he will hear my sorrow-stricken prayer and in his good time bring my son to understand that the path of conversion leads to him."[7] His son died suddenly at the age of twenty-four.

Enduring a lifetime of sorrows, yet ever ambitious, hardworking, and hospitable, Bach always opened his home to visitors and his genius was widely acclaimed. Throughout his life, he continued to write magnificent music, completing his famous Mass in B Minor the year before he suffered a stroke and died.

For reflection and discussion

- What connection have you experienced with Bach's music? (Listen to "Air on a G" on YouTube or download from iTunes.)
- How do you think adversity and great music (great work) might be related? Do you think great music can proceed from a life of comfort and ease?
- How do you experience both unresolved tension and resolution in your life with God? How do you want to respond to God in prayer about this reading?

U2

By **Mark Joseph**, multimedia producer and columnist. Adapted from his book *Faith, God & Rock 'n' Roll*. Joseph is editor of *Pop Goes Religion* and producer of *The Passion of the Christ* rock CD; *www.markjoseph.com*.

In many ways U2 pioneered the idea that rock music that glorified God could be done for a mainstream audience. But if Bono, The Edge, and Larry Mullen were undercover agents in God's army, critics would argue that they were so successful that few fans really knew where they stood when it came to their faith. The CD title *The Joshua Tree*, for instance, could reference Christ's cross, Joshua being another rendering of Jesus and the tree another name for the cross.

Critics aside, U2 managed to stand in the center of pop culture and continue to turn out music inspired by its members' faith and reference the members' deeply held Christian beliefs, however vaguely.

By now the band's story is familiar: originating in Dublin, the group consisted of teenagers who married their own brand of rock with spiritual devotion. When tensions within their church, the Shalom Fellowship, escalated, the band seemed to divorce themselves from active Christian fellowship and determined not to use their music to overtly proselytize.

"I do not want to talk about it in terms of music," Bono remarked about his faith early on in his career. "Anything that has to be said on that personal level is in the music or on stage, and I don't want to go through the media."

U2's expression of faith seemed to go in waves and be linked directly to Bono's individual spiritual journey. Some fellow believers saw U2's faith ebb and flow at various points — ebb around the time of the *Pop* album and flow around the time of the release of *All That You Can't Leave Behind*, seen as a strong reaffirmation of faith.

On *Pop*, Bono offered a startlingly frank declaration questioning God: "Jesus, I'm waiting here, boss, I know you're looking out for me, but maybe your hands aren't free."

But by the time of the release of *All That You Can't Leave Behind*, he seemed to have undergone a spiritual epiphany. The band, likely at Bono's direction, decided to insert a secret message of sorts into the album's cover art: U2 was photographed in a train station and airbrushed over the *departure* sign was this message: J333 — rumored to be Jeremiah 33:3: "Call to me and I will answer you and tell you great and unsearchable things you do not know."

"It was done like a piece of graffiti," confirmed Bono. "It's known as God's telephone number."

Still more evidence of U2's increasingly ardent behavior came with the group's live shows, which found Bono quoting from Psalms as he openly worshiped God from the stage. For many fans, Christian and non-Christian alike, it was an unforgettable experience.

Bono has framed his increasing pursuit of social justice issues in starkly religious terms: "You cannot, as a Christian, walk away from Africa. America will be judged by God if, in its plenty, it crossed the road from 23 million people suffering from HIV. What's up on trial here is Christianity itself. Distance does not decide who is your brother and who is not." [He has rallied leaders and fans to engage the needs of the world at *www.one.org*.]

Bono believes that all music must ask the important questions without which rock simply couldn't live up to its promise:

"If there is a God, it's serious. And if there isn't a God, it's even more serious. Or is it the other way around?" he once joked. "I don't know, but these are the things that, as an artist, are going to cross your mind."

For reflection and discussion

- You can access U2's lyrics at *www.U2.com* or download from iTunes. Is there a particular U2 song that resonates with your experience? How so?
- How has U2's charitable initiative affected believers and unbelievers? How do you respond to Jesus' call to social justice (Matthew 25:31 – 46)?
- How do you see God at work in an arena full of rock fans listening to the Psalms?

God's Middle Knowledge

By **William Lane Craig**, PhD, ThD, professor of philosophy at Talbot School of Theology. Author of *Reasonable Faith*, Craig is an acclaimed expert on the existence of God and a debater who draws standing-room-only crowds in Europe, the US, and Canada; *www.reasonablefaith.org.*

Note: *Craig invites the reader to consider the much-debated question of how we understand God's knowledge, his providence, and human responsibility.*

Saul took his own sword and fell on it.... Saul died because he was unfaithful to the LORD.... So the LORD put him to death and turned the kingdom over to David son of Jesse.

1 CHRONICLES 10:4, 13 – 14

In these few verses we see in microcosm the mystery of divine sovereignty and human freedom. On the one hand, Saul took his own life; on the other, God killed Saul. How are we to make sense of this paradox?

Consider the proposal of the seventeenth-century Jesuit theologian Luis Molina. Molina's theory of providence is based on his ingenious doctrine of divine middle knowledge. According to that doctrine, God knows, logically, prior to his decree to create a world, what every free creature he could possibly create would freely do in any possible set of circumstances.

God's will is that every creature do the right thing in any set of circumstances. But, alas, God knows that creatures would often freely sin in certain circumstances. For example, God knew that if Saul were about to be taken by the Philistines, he would freely commit suicide. Since that action is freely done, there's nothing God can do about that conditional fact. He could, in light of his middle knowledge, decide not to bring about those circumstances or to place Saul in them. But he cannot do anything about the *conditional fact* that if Saul were in those circumstances (which involve no supernatural intervention), he would freely fall on his sword.

Now, in planning a world of free creatures, God takes into account what various persons would freely do in various circumstances and how those circumstances and decisions would in turn affect others. Being omniscient, God plans the world down to its minutest detail. Everything that comes to pass

WEEK 9

therefore does so either by God's directly willing it or permitting it. All the righteous actions are directly willed by God, but the sinful actions he merely permits, knowing that in the end his ultimate purposes will be achieved.

So, to return to Saul, God knew what Saul would freely do in those circumstances, and though he did not desire Saul to commit suicide, he permitted him to do so freely, knowing that by this means David would take the throne, which is what God wanted. (This is obviously grossly simplified; Saul's suicide has an ever-widening ripple effect down through subsequent history, which God also takes into account.) Thus, Saul freely took his own life, but the chronicler, looking at it from the perspective of God's plan, says the Lord slew Saul.

In reflecting on Molina's theory, we must not lose sight of the fact that the circumstances do not determine how people will act, for these are freedom-permitting circumstances. When the FBI conducts a sting operation, calculating that the drug dealer or child pornographer would take the cash if offered to him, the criminal always tries to use the excuse of entrapment. But if the FBI has done its job right, the courts consistently rule that, under the circumstances, the criminal behaved freely and it is, therefore, he, not the FBI, who is liable. So it is with God's sovereign direction of a world of free creatures.

Middle knowledge in the hands of a tyrant would be terrifying. Therefore, it's vital to keep in mind that we're talking about a loving heavenly Father who wills the good of his creatures. As Joseph said to his brothers, "You intended to harm me, but God intended it for good to accomplish what is now being done, the saving of many lives" (Genesis 50:20).

For reflection and discussion

- Think of a time when it seemed God had not come through for you. Have you ever glimpsed his purposes later?
- How do you respond to God when you can't understand how he works?

As the heavens are higher than us, as the design of the eagle nebulae and DNA is beyond us, so are God's thoughts higher than our thoughts. In the light of such complexities, we bring our questions with a heart of humility to our Maker.

- What questions or thoughts might you want to bring to him in the light of this reading?

New England: A City Upon a Hill

By Lael Arrington. Among sources used was *Errand into the Wilderness* by Perry Miller.

"For wee must Consider that wee shall be as a City upon a Hill,
the eies of all people are upon us."

GOV. JOHN WINTHROP, MASSACHUSETTS BAY COMPANY

The same King James I who was suspicious of Puritans and their Geneva Bible (and so authorized the 1611 translation that bears his name) made life impossible for Separatists from the Church of England. The Pilgrims fled first to Holland and then, in 1620, to Plymouth, Massachusetts. In the Mayflower Compact they solemnized their purpose: "Having undertaken, for the glory of God and advancement of the Christian faith and Honour of our King and Country, a Voyage to plant the first colony in the Northern parts of Virginia ..."

Ten years later an even more visionary group of Puritans formed the Massachusetts Bay Company and set sail for New England. In his lay sermon aboard the flagship *Arabella*, John Winthrop laid out the group's explicit covenant. They had drawn up "indentures with the Almighty." If they succeeded and did not get diverted into making money, God would reward them. But if they failed, if they were to "embrace this present world and prosecute our carnall intencions, seekeing great things for our selves and our posterity, the Lord will surely breake out in wrathe against us ... and make us knowe the price of the breache of such a Covenant."[1]

As Puritan pastor and historian Cotton Mather described it, New England was settled "to express and pursue the Protestant Reformation."[2] In a virgin wilderness, free of oppressive government and religious authorities, these settlers aspired to create ideal Christian communities ruled only by the Word of God, with the consent of the governed.

The Reformation sought to transform not just communities but families. In our time, the word *Puritan* has become synonymous with sexual repression. But in fact the Puritans glorified wedded romantic love and companionship and rescued pure marital sex from the legacy of exceedingly ascetic church fathers like Ambrose, who wrote that "married people ought to blush

WEEK 9

at the state in which they are living." The Puritans celebrated the "concert" of the marriage bed where husband and wife may "joyfully give due benevolence one to the other as two musical instruments rightly fitted do make a most pleasant and sweet harmony."[3]

Jonathan Edwards, one of the last leading Puritan voices, declared that we live entirely from our affections. And that "there is never any great achievement by the things of religion without a heart deeply affected by those things."[4] Later Puritans struggled to maintain their mission as religious affections declined and nonchurch members insisted on and were given the right to vote.

By 1679 a formal Boston synod prepared a response to explain why the new settlement was experiencing crop failures, Indian wars, epidemics, harsh weather, and disappointing sons and daughters. In addition to the rise of heretics, eleven more causes were diagnosed: a terrible decline in godliness, a corresponding increase in pride, quarrels and infighting in the churches, more swearing and sleeping through sermons, a failure to observe the Sabbath, the breakdown of parental authority, and a steady uptick in lawsuits. Drunkenness and immorality could be documented by counting heads at crowded taverns and bastards in need of charity. People were lying, cheating in business, and showing no inclination to repent. Within just sixty years of its founding, New England struggled to affirm a common civic spirit, much less a shared vision of a City on a Hill.

For reflection and discussion

Affection, especially affection for God, has always been notoriously difficult to pass along to children and neighbors. Even God's first children lost their first love.

- Do you think that our ultimate motivation for life in God's kingdom must flow from our affection for God? What role does duty play? Knowledge? In other words, in order to live well for Christ, what do we need most?
- Does your love for God flow more from duty or tender affection?
- How do you want to respond to God about this reading? About your reflection?

The Sociobiology of E. O. Wilson

By Drew Trotter, PhD, who writes on film and culture and is president of the Center for Christian Study in Charlottesville, Virginia. This entry is adapted from an article by Trotter in *Tabletalk* magazine.

Robert Wright, in his book *Three Scientists and Their Gods*, tells a story about recently deceased E. O. Wilson, the Pulitzer Prize – winning biologist and coiner of the term "sociobiology," the scientific study of the biological (esp. ecological and evolutionary) aspects of social behavior in animals and humans. Wright had already described Wilson as one who argues that "moral and ethical intuitions are shaped by the genes" and who satirizes those who hold "the alternative view — that morality is 'divinely given.'"[5]

Harvard was honoring Martin Luther King Sr. and King, as part of the festivities, was preaching at the Harvard Memorial Chapel. There was a large turnout. The reverend preached fervently and the congregation sang richly and one of the hymns hit home with Wilson — "one of the good, old-timey ones that I hadn't heard since I was a kid." Partway through it, E. O. Wilson — scientific materialist, detached empiricist, confirmed Darwinian — started crying.

As if in atonement, he has a perfectly rational explanation. "It was tribal," he says. "It was the feeling that I had been a long way away from the tribe."

Wilson was right: he felt that he had been a long way from the tribe because he, and anyone else who is a philosophical materialist, *is* in fact a long way from the tribe of created man. How so?

As a member of the tribe, he bears God's image, and that image reminded him of his own finitude and of God's infinite majesty. All of us bear that image, and, among other things, it reminds us of our connection to him as those who reflect his glory (Psalm 8). And perhaps it is in worship, when the praises of our lips ascend to him, that we feel most clearly the privilege of being his image-bearing creation. No wonder Wilson cried when singing God's praises. The tension created by knowing deep in his heart that he bore God's reflection, while denying with all his being that God even exists, seems to have been too much for his emotions to bear. Perhaps his sense of separation from the God who created him was overwhelming; at that moment he knew he was a long way from the tribe.

WEEK 9

Scripture declares our tribe to be without excuse for ignorance of God, and the very creation we investigate pleads with us to believe that God exists. Paul reminds us that the visible universe clearly demonstrates God's "eternal power and divine nature" (Romans 1:20). This barrage of evidence, pounding on our senses day in and day out, is bound to build up a powerful tension in the mind and heart of one who will not see such evidence, a tension released in worship and resulting in tears.

A burst of tears, followed by a cold reductionistic explanation of those tears, is just what the Bible indicates we should expect from those who, on the basis of their "science," elevate man above God. We must never let the examination of God's universe, with our science, push from his rightful throne the One who holds the universe together by the word of his power. If we do, we will also feel a long way from the tribe.

For reflection and discussion

- Why do you feel a person might cry, as Wilson did, during the hymn?
- Begin paying attention to what motivates your various actions and relationships. What would you ascribe to chemistry and survival? What else motivates you?
- What are you feeling as you help a friend? A stranger who will never help you in return?
- In what ways do you sense a moral law at work? Are you haunted by wrong choices? Assured by right choices?
- Do you feel that *beauty* means something? What?

The Periodic Table of Elements

By **Benjamin Wiker**, PhD. Adapted from the book *A Meaningful World: How the Arts and Sciences Reveal the Genius of Nature*, which he coauthored with Jonathan Witt. Wiker is a fellow of Discovery Institute, former professor at Marquette University, and now lives with his wife and seven children in Ohio; *www.ameaningfulworld.com*.

The suspicion of order is rooted in our very human love of patterns. Before they discovered the order of the Periodic Table of Elements, modern chemists suspected that the elements were ordered according to some grand, well-designed pattern. As is almost always the case, the underlying order was far more elegant than even the most conspiracy-minded chemists could imagine. They suspected a beautiful melody. They discovered a symphony.

By the early 1800s there were enough elements known *as* elements that scientists could begin to look for patterns in the "pile" of elements before them. One of the first to note patterns was Johann Döbereiner (1780 – 1849), who picked up on what he called "triads" — groups of three elements wherein the atomic weight of the middle element was (approximately) the mean between two other elements. For example, Dobereiner noted that the weight of strontium was a mean between the weights of calcium and barium.

About the mid-1800s, Jean Dumas noticed that elements that had the same chemical properties and increasing atomic weights could be related by simple mathematical patterns. Here were the atomic weights available to him:

$$
\begin{aligned}
\text{nitrogen} &= \text{atomic weight } 14 \\
\text{phosphorous} &= \text{atomic weight } 31 \; [14 + 17] \\
\text{arsenic} &= \text{atomic weight } 75 \; [14 + 17 + (44 \times 1)] \\
\text{antimony} &= \text{atomic weight } 119 \; [14 + 17 + (44 \times 2)]
\end{aligned}
$$

Unbeknownst to Dumas, he had listed the elements in the exact vertical order of Group V of the periodic table.

Working with Dumas's insights, John Newlands (1837 – 1898) discovered something even more amazing by doing something incredibly obvious. He simply lined the elements up, one after another, in order of increasing atomic weight, beginning with hydrogen. When he did, he noticed that every eighth element had similar properties. He called it the "law of octaves," named after the repeating pattern of notes on a musical scale. If we look at our periodic table, we note that the elements in each vertical row have notably similar chemical properties. There is, then, a kind of law of octaves, and this law defines the order of the periodic table.

One can imagine being the designer of the table and feeling a bit like a human father who has cleverly hidden an Easter egg and is watching his children searching diligently, uncovering first one clue and then another, getting closer and closer — all the while the surprise is hidden right under their noses.

It was left to the great Russian Dmitri Mendeleev to actually "seize the egg" and take the next bold step, for which he is credited with having finally cracked the code of the periodic table of elements. Whereas Newlands had used the octaves of music as his guide, Mendeleev shuffled through cards. On each card he put the chemical element and all its known properties, including the way it combined with hydrogen and oxygen. As is the case for pattern-loving creatures, he could not believe that nature would contain simply a pile of unordered elements like so many randomly strewn playing cards.

He worked and reworked the cards and noticed that, when they were arranged according to increasing atomic weight, a pattern began to emerge — the chemical properties recurred periodically, that is, regularly. That led him to place them in vertical columns, which he labeled Group I, Group II, and so on, up to Group VIII. Believing that nature loves patterns as well, Mendeleev refused to allow that the pattern of increasing weights in chemical properties would be disrupted. When there was no known element that had the requisite properties to fit into a particular group or when there was a suspicious leap in atomic weight, he boldly left a blank. Even more boldly he predicted that elements would be discovered to fill these blanks and, also, that they would have so and so properties and such and such atomic weights.

For example, he predicted the existence of an element between calcium and titanium, described its properties, and assigned it an atomic weight of 44. A few years later, in 1879, Lars Nilsen discovered it and named it "scandium."

Nature is not only ordered but ordered in a kind of tutorial fashion so that we, the knowers, can move downward, step by step, from what is knowable in our everyday visible experience, through the layers of previously unseen order to the deep order we grasp only intellectually. That movement describes the march of chemistry through history, and the tutorial ordering in nature that made it possible couldn't be the result of an indifferent and pointless cosmos. One level of accidental order could be the result of chance; multiple layers of integrated order, configured in a way that is strikingly amenable to discovery, implies a conspiracy.

If we find out through scientific discovery that the universe is intricately ordered in a way that invites discovery, then it's most reasonable to cease trying to imagine ourselves as the hapless creatures of a nihilist cosmos. As the history of chemistry reveals, when we reflect on ourselves as knowers, it is clear that we are pattern-seeking and pattern-finding creatures, creatures curiously made to be curious amid an order curiously designed to be discovered.

For reflection and discussion

- Is there a kind of pattern in the natural world that strikes you as meaningful? If so, how do you sense God speaking to you in that pattern?
- How do Wiker's insights connect with your views about creation and human nature?

When we consider Jesus as the Logos (the Word of John 1:1), we find that Logos conveys the idea of bringing meaning and order, logic and reason to that which is disordered and chaotic. Jesus is the very essence of order and reason clothed in a person full of stories, pathos, and grace.

- How might Jesus bring meaning and order into your life? How has he done so in the past?

Romantic Realism

By Lael Arrington

The best literature illumines both the recesses of our hearts and worlds beyond our own. In poetic imagery and unfolding drama, we come to grips with the *reality* of the often painful human condition and resonate with *romantic* longings for transcendence — the world as we know it should be. Historically the literary pendulum has swung between the two poles of romanticism and realism.

Romanticism arose in the late 1700s as a reaction to the age of Enlightenment. The exaltation of reason delivered humanity from a great deal of superstition and ignorance of the past, but the Deist "Clockmaker God" was remote and unknowable. Science, increasingly untethered from biblical faith, cast a vision of an orderly but impersonal world.

Weary of the deadening reduction of nature to grinding laws and machinery, romantic writers emphasized passion over reason, intuition over logic, and the majesty and mystery of nature over scientific analysis. William Blake invited his readers to "see a World in a Grain of Sand / And a Heaven in a Wild Flower."[6] Samuel Taylor Coleridge defended the importance of creative imagination with biblical analogies. Gerard Manley Hopkins joined the chorus of the Hudson River School painters: "The world is charged with the grandeur of God / It will flame out like shining from shook foil." Influenced by French philosopher Rousseau, romantics expressed new confidence in beauty and goodness, not only of nature but also of the human heart. William Wordsworth and Walt Whitman celebrated the self — the freedom and beauty of the common person and everyday life.

Romantic heroes challenged social conventions and social injustice, idealizing the "noble savage" who lived in harmony with nature (James Fenimore Cooper, *The Last of the Mohicans*). Other romantic writers (Sir Walter Scott, *Ivanhoe*) overlooked the misery of feudal serfdom and romanticized the past in medieval pageants of knights, maidens, and castle flags aflutter.

"Dark romantics" like Edgar Allen Poe used encounters with the supernatural to explore the more fearful and tortured range of human feelings.

Melancholy musings over a world so far from the ideal eventually sowed the seeds of realism.

Realists rebelled against the sentimentality and melodrama of romantic idealism. Where romantics celebrated glimpses of Eden, realists tightened their focus on the ashes of the fall. Committed to unflinching accuracy, realists depicted flawed heroes caught up in less adventurous, more psychological conflict set in everyday life.

Early realists like Jane Austen, George Eliot, Charles Dickens, and the great Russian writers Tolstoy and Dostoyevsky wove together grim portraits of human depravity with biblical optimism in God's redemptive work. Mark Twain's work showed increasing cynicism, and authors of the 1920s (Fitzgerald, Hemingway) dwelt on disillusionment and rootless careers.

Inspired by the rising popularity of Darwinism, naturalist fiction (Stephen Crane and Jack London) presented man's struggle to survive in an indifferent universe against the deterministic and overwhelming forces of nature. Realism has since become mainstream, but many strands of romanticism still flourish in romantic comedies, science fiction, and fantasy genres.

For reflection and discussion

In *World* magazine, editor Marvin Olasky describes the biblical worldview as "romantic realism." "Christianity," Olasky writes, "is both gruesomely accurate in its realistic depiction of abundant sin but also romantically hopeful — for the bridegroom, Christ, does not give up even when repeatedly spurned.

"The Bible is the romantic realist book that best shows both graves and grace. It doesn't pretend that life is either heavenly or hellish, but shows how we're all thigh-deep in muck yet able, through God's grace, to see the sun. Jesus not only turned water into wine but turned Simon, who dreamed of fish, into Peter, a fisher of men — and he can do that to each of us."[7]

Jesus invites us to join him in his redemptive work. Olasky cautions, "The biggest obstacle in many situations, as romantic realist Walker Percy shows so well in his novels, is that we become sunk into everydayness, comfortable with our routines and unwilling to uproot ourselves."[8] The world's realism leaches desire from our hearts and kingdom vision from our imaginations. But God is the great romantic realist. "Take the risk," he beckons. "If you are opposed or even crushed by the powers of this world, ultimately there is no risk because your name is written in the Book of Life" — the ultimate realistic romance.

- What aspects of your life point to a realist work? To a romantic work?
- How is God giving his grace to you as you endure the often difficult reality of your everyday life?
- How is God asking you to embrace his romantic promises of "hope and a future," shake off your everydayness and routines, uproot yourself, and follow him?

Norman Rockwell (1894–1978)

By Kelly Monroe Kullberg and David Kullberg

> I was showing the America I knew and observed
> to others who might not have noticed.
>
> NORMAN ROCKWELL

Born in New York City, Norman Rockwell enrolled in art school at age fourteen. While still in his teens, he was hired as art director of the Boy Scouts publication *Boys' Life*. In 1916, the twenty-two-year-old Rockwell painted his first cover for *The Saturday Evening Post*. Over the next forty-seven years, another 321 Rockwell paintings would appear on its covers.

In 1930 he married Mary Barstow, a schoolteacher, and the couple had three sons. The family moved to Arlington, Vermont, in 1939.

Little escaped Rockwell's notice. Through art he honored that which does not often make the evening news — quiet and common graces, innocence, wit, irony, puppy love, a grandmother's worn hands, a father awaiting the train that will take his son to college and likely to a life not on the family farm. He wrote in 1936, "The commonplaces of America are to me the richest subjects in art." And yet Rockwell did not avoid the serious questions of his times; rather, he did justice to them. In 1977, Rockwell received the nation's highest civilian honor, the Presidential Medal.

In his 1941 State of the Union address, President Franklin D. Roosevelt attempted to unite the American people to a common cause. Though the Japanese attack on Pearl Harbor was still almost a year away, the war was already raging in Europe and Asia. England was on the verge of collapse. President Roosevelt, faced with an isolationist-leaning America and the looming prospect of a second world war, set forth a vision that would inspire citizens to brave the sacrifices and perils he foresaw in a war against fascism. His vision consisted of four universal human rights: freedom of speech, freedom to worship, freedom from fear, and freedom from want. He saw these values as America's heritage, now threatened and needing to be defended.

The government launched an effort to communicate the "Four Freedoms." Artists, photographers, and writers were enlisted to the cause, but eighteen months later the American public had little knowledge of the freedoms, and no more than 2 percent could identify them correctly.[9]

During the summer of 1942, in the middle of the night, an idea came to Rockwell. He would create four posters, each painting expressing one of the freedoms. With sketches in hand, he went to Washington, D.C., where he was rebuffed by a man at the Office of War Information (OWI): " 'The last war you illustrators did the posters,' he said. 'This war we're going to use fine arts men, real artists.' "[10] When Ben Hibbs of *The Saturday Evening Post* heard this, he immediately asked Rockwell to create the freedoms for the *Post*.

When Rockwell's *Four Freedoms* were seen by the OWI, they were chosen despite pressure from liberal intellectuals to select the paintings of Nazi brutality by artist Ben Shahn.

The reception of Rockwell's paintings was overwhelming. His *Four Freedoms* were launched on a nationwide tour in April 1943. More than 1.2 million people viewed them and war bonds worth $132 million were sold. During the war four million posters were printed. The *New Yorker* reported in 1945 that the *Four Freedoms* were received by the public "with more enthusiasm, perhaps, that any other paintings in the history of American art." Rockwell's favorite was said to be *Freedom of Worship* even though it also had been the most difficult to paint.

In 1953, the Rockwell family moved to Stockbridge, in the Berkshire mountains of western Massachusetts. Norman Rockwell loved everything about Stockbridge, a small, culturally rich New England town. "Main street, barbershop, high-school prom, swimming hole and Sunday church services, Stockbridge seemed to exemplify the world that inspired Rockwell's works."[11] It is a fun fact of our Kullberg family history that my husband's New England cousins, aunt, and uncle — neighbors to the famous artist — modeled for many Rockwell paintings. You may recall a precocious redhead with his puppy and fishing pole in summer, dog and sled in winter.

During the 1960s, Rockwell began an association with *Look* magazine. His paintings illustrated some of his deepest concerns and interests, including civil rights, America's war on poverty, and the exploration of space.

Rockwell celebrated faith in not only the *Freedom of Worship* painting. Faith was also the topic in *The Golden Rule* and in his 1951 *Saying Grace*, a simple but profound painting that depicted an act of worship done unashamedly in public. Said to have "touched America's heart," *Saying Grace* was selected by *Post* readers as their all-time favorite.

America loved, and perhaps still loves, what *Smithsonian* magazine called "the comforting world of Norman Rockwell, the artist and illustrator famous for his observation and celebration of small-town America."[12] An elegant museum in Stockbridge now honors him and is home to 678 paintings and drawings, some of the legacy of an artist whose life was a celebration of the true, the good, and the beautiful.

For reflection and discussion

Do you know Rockwell's work? Whether you spend a day at his museum, with a library book, or browsing his paintings on the Internet (*www.nrm.org*):

- What does Rockwell evoke in your own life, your memory, your hopes?
- What scenes from your own life might Norman Rockwell have wanted to paint?
- When viewing some of Rockwell's paintings, what do you see to praise God for?

Burning Man

By Lael Arrington

A shark car zigzags through the shimmering heat waves of Nevada's Black Rock Desert. From the car's large papier-mâché mouth, wet-suited legs and flippered feet poke out in black humorous fun. A go-cart with a jet engine screams past, followed by a truck dragging a mattress, whipping up near-lethal billows of dust. Three mattress passengers in gas masks give their royals-in-their-carriage wave.

Welcome to the annual Labor Day Burning Man project where, for six days each year, a temporary city is home to 48,000-plus inhabitants (*www .burningman.com*). Scratched into the desert floor, concentric half-circular city "blocks" are subdivided by spoke-like arteries radiating from the hub. In the empty center, the participants erect a three-story avant-garde stick-figure man outlined in neon tube lights.

At Burning Man, you don't have to wear clothes, but you do have to pick up your trash. Except to insure safety, there are no rules to infringe upon the pursuit of life, liberty, and happiness translated as, "How can I push the envelope with something — my clothes-vehicles-art-behavior — *something* that someone isn't already selling on a T-shirt?" The style is "ironic juxtaposition." Take the old cards and shuffle them together in shocking new ways — a barbershop quartet sings the Beach Boys, a fire breather sports a Teddy Roosevelt monocle, safari hat, khaki shirt, and zebra leggings.

Nothing is for sale. Burners must provide everything they need, including food and shelter, toilets excepted. Some burners prefer to walk on stilts. Others chant and drum. Festooned with buttons that read "Fun Is a Spiritual Path," "Born Again Pagan," "Recovering Catholic," and "My Karma ran over your Dogma," they celebrate their commitment to radical self-expression and self-reliance to a degree not possible in day-to-day life. "We live on this fantasy plane of desire within a vicarious spectacle," says founder Larry Harvey, of America's entertainment culture. "But by preparing to actually survive in a place with 100-mile-an-hour winds — and I'm not kidding — you have to commune with your inner needs, you must face immediate outer realities. It will just shock you out of the seance, out of the spell."[13]

Every year the theme camps, art installations, and performance venues try to bring a different theme to life — Fertility, Time, Hell, Beyond Belief, and Hope and Fear, to name a few. People line up to experience the walk-in camera big enough to view the desert upside down, a bubble fountain complete with do-it-yourself bubble wands, the mass-naked photograph, and a drama about the "wound that never heals." At Viva Lost Vegas, an Elvis impersonator lip-synchs one of the king's rowdiest numbers, swiveling and sweating in the stage lights. Sleek young men in spike heels, sequined gowns, and lipstick back him up, their dance steps tightly choreographed. In the wee hours, a black-robed woman passes a chalice of red liquid around while her cohorts blow torch animal heads over fifty-five-gallon drums.

On Saturday night the community gathers for a techno-pagan surge of transcendence — the burning of the man. A pyrotechnic prelude explodes from his limbs and torso, and then the revelry pauses. The man's hands and feet are set ablaze. A few maintain their silence. Some sink to their knees. As the man slowly raises his burning hands, the drummers resume their frenzy and, for most of the celebrants, it's like touchdown at the Super Bowl.

Burners are asked, "What is this supposed to mean?" The most common answer is, "Nothing. It only means what it means to you." The Burning Man, like the desert playa, is intended to be a blank slate upon which you create or project your own meaning. When *Time* magazine asked Harvey, "Why do you do it?" the official response was, "Because, if we didn't burn it this year, we couldn't burn it again next year."[14]

Burning Man began as a Utopian experiment for radical individuals dedicated to the search for intense immediacy of experiences and relationships. "You could make a spectacle. Make a spectacle of yourself. Make a spectacle for others — and that is how you would escape the great American spectacle," says Harvey, bohemian critic of TV and the market's power to commodify everything, even our souls.[15]

Those who come merely to cruise and enjoy the seduction of the "new" and "creative" don't keep coming back. The ones who open themselves to community and transcendence do. "People go to Burning Man and they go home and say, 'Gosh, this connected me to myself, and this connected me to other people. It connected me to things even much larger than myself,'" writes Harvey.[16]

If you want to know where our culture is going, look at the Burning Man arts. In their flamboyant decoration, their tatooing, piercing, branding, drum-beating, and chanting, these desert fathers and mothers cry out in the wilderness — "We won't sell out! Make your own show!"

Consuming isolates and destroys. TV is killing us softly with sitcoms. Modernism has slain the life of the soul, and these postmodern pagans are bent on resurrection. Burning Man is a surge for the soul. A surge for meaning. A little more extreme than the skateboarder's half-pipe, surfing, or bungee jumping, but the same intense grab for something *real*. Something to make you feel *alive*. For them, ultimate reality is sensory, not in the modern, empirical sense, but sought through their own design of art, metaphor, story, communion, and liturgy. Where else, they wonder, could they find what they're looking for?

For reflection and discussion

- In what ways might you identify with the message of Burning Man? How do you respond to their prescription for escaping the numbing passivity of our entertainment culture?
- When it comes to a world thick with drama and meaning or a world that is thin, lacking both, which has been your experience in your life with Jesus Christ? Your Christian community? What step do you think you could take to move into more risk and meaning? Individually? In community?
- How do you want to respond to God about the richness or thinness of your own experience with him? With others?

Hearing God

By **Dallas Willard**, PhD, author, professor of philosophy, University of Southern California. Adapted from his book *Hearing God*; *www.dwillard.org*.

In the book *Hearing God*, I have tried to clarify what hearing God amounts to and to make a life in which one hears God's voice, in the way of Jesus, accessible to anyone who would enter it. But I am painfully aware of a *great barrier* to the spiritual life, what has been called, "the seeming overwhelming presence of the visible world."

The visible world daily bludgeons us with its things and events. They pinch and pull and hammer away at our bodies. Few people arise in the morning as hungry for God as they are for cornflakes or toast and eggs. But instead of shouting and shoving, the *spiritual* world whispers at us ever so gently.

We are hindered in our progress toward becoming spiritually competent people by how easily we can explain away the movements of God toward us. Of course his day will come, but for now he cooperates with the desires and inclinations that make up our character as we are gradually becoming the kind of people we will forever be. That should send a chill down our spine.

God wants to be wanted, to be wanted enough that we are ready, predisposed, to find him present with us. And if, by contrast, we are ready and set to find ways of explaining away his gentle overtures, he will rarely respond with fire from heaven. More likely he will simply leave us alone, and we shall have the satisfaction of thinking ourselves not to be gullible.

The test of character posed by the gentleness of God's approach to us is especially dangerous for those formed by the ideas that dominate our modern world. We live in a culture that has, for centuries now, cultivated the idea that the *skeptical* person is always smarter than one who believes. You can be almost as stupid as a cabbage, as long as you *doubt*. The fashion of the age has identified mental sharpness with a pose, not with genuine intellectual method and character. Only a very hardy individualist or social rebel — or one desperate for another life — stands any chance of discovering the substantiality of the spiritual life today.

Nearly all areas of life in which we could become spiritually competent (hearing God, praying, receiving guidance, leadership) confront us with the same type of challenge. They all require of us a *choice* to be a spiritual person, to live a spiritual life. We are required to "bet our life" that the visible world, while real, is not reality itself.

God is not insensitive to our problem of overcoming the power of the visible world. He invades the visible. Think of his many manifestations to Moses and the Israelites. He has spoken at times in an audible voice. But the tendency of life in Christ is progressively toward the inward word to the receptive heart. Jesus presses us toward a life with our "Father, who sees what is done in secret" (Matthew 6:6).

After his resurrection, Jesus appeared to his disciples in visible form over a period of forty days. He made himself visible to them just enough to give them confidence that it was he who was speaking in their hearts. Two of Jesus' heartbroken students were walking to the village of Emmaus. Jesus, unrecognized, heard their sad story about what had happened to Jesus of Nazareth and about how, it seemed, all hope was now lost. He responded by taking them through the Scriptures and showing them that what had happened was exactly what was to befall the Messiah that Israel hoped for. Then as they sat at supper with him, suddenly "their eyes were opened and they recognized him, and he disappeared from their sight" (Luke 24:31). But their recognition was more than a visual one, and that was the whole point. They asked one another, "Were not our hearts burning within us while he talked with us on the road and opened the Scriptures to us?" (24:32).

He would meet with them one final time as a visible presence. There in the beauty and silence of the Galilean mountains, he would explain to them that he had been given authority over everything in heaven and on the earth. Because of that, they were now to go to every kind of people on earth and make them his students, to surround them with the reality of the Father, Son, and Holy Spirit and to teach them how to do all the things he had commanded. His final words to them were simply, "Look, I am with you every minute, until the job is done" (Matthew 28:20 paraphrase). He is with us now, and he speaks with us and we with him. He speaks with us in our hearts, which burn from the impact of his word and his presence. This companionship with Jesus is the form that Christian spirituality, as practiced through the ages, takes.

Today, as God's trusting apprentices in the kingdom of the heavens, we live on the Emmaus road, so to speak. His word pours into our hearts, energizing and directing our lives in a way that cannot be accounted for in natural terms.

The presence of the physical world is, then, if I will have it so, no longer a barrier between me and God. My visible surroundings become, instead, God's gift to me, where I am privileged to see the rule of heaven realized through my friendship with Jesus.

For reflection and discussion

- Where do you notice the quiet initiatives of God in your life?
- What are the barriers that keep you from fully trusting them?
- What activities and practices help you move toward God?
- Where have you seen the invisible life with God making changes in your visible life?
- How might your friendship with Jesus infuse your world with possibility?

Ziegenbalg: India's First Missionary

By **Chris Gilbert**, journalist and filmmaker from the "land down under," who lives near Boston with his literary wife, Jo Kadlecek; *www.lamppostmedia.net.*

When King Friedrich IV of Denmark suffered the death of his favorite mistress in 1704, he granted a longstanding petition from both his wife and his mother. As reformist Lutheran Pietists, they wanted missionaries sent to his trading ports. So began the journey to India of the first ever Protestant missionary, Bartholomaeus Ziegenbalg, age twenty-three, from Halle in Germany.

Ziegenbalg suffered chronic stomach illness that interrupted his seminary training. But he shone in Berlin, mentored by a father of evangelicalism, Herman Francke, while teaching in schools that mixed the very poor with the very rich. Francke referred him to King Friedrich's chaplain as a missionary candidate.

In late 1705, Ziegenbalg sailed from Copenhagen with temporary mission partner Heinrich Plutschau. After eight months, they arrived at the Danish East India Company (DEIC) port of Tranquebar on India's east coast. Like evening arrivals in an Old Testament city, they landed without welcome from the Christian governor and European settlers. The missionary pair gladly accepted hospitality from a Tamil servant of the DEIC in the poorest part of the city.

So, Bartholomaeus Ziegenbalg began living with the Tamil people of the Coramandel Coast. The people were called by the Portuguese name "Malabarians," a name Danes used pejoratively to mean "beasts" because of the Tamils' dark skin, lowly estate, and strange language. Tamils returned the favor, labeling Europeans as "Paranghi's," or "beef-eaters," another derogatory label implying sexually immoral, unhygienic, and abandoners of bastard children. In this context, Ziegenbalg and Plutschau began to preach Christ. The Tamil hosts realized their missionary guests were different because they too suffered persecution from "Christian Europeans."

Within six months Ziegenbalg began to teach and preach in the Tamil of the ordinary people. Guided by Tamil mentors, he created a dictionary and a grammar text for Europeans. Because Tamils were forbidden by their Brahmin rulers from owning or reading the classical texts, spoken Tamil had no written form. London's Society for the Propagation of Christian Knowledge sent India's first mechanical printing press to Ziegenbalg. In the script he developed, as he translated for them, Tamils began to read their literature and the Bible for the first time. This was like introducing the Internet.

Literacy spread through the casteless schools he established, where for the first time in India girls received an education that didn't require them to become temple prostitutes. Modern Tamil Nadu's education system is based upon Ziegenbalg's written language and schools.

In each village, priests interpreted ancient Indian texts to the illiterate. Interpretations varied with priestly personalities, but most enslaved the many to the elite. In order to understand Indian religion, Ziegenbalg collected libraries of books and debated with religious scholars. He found their scriptures essentially moral and intellectually equal to European philosophy, however poorly applied. He became India's foremost eighteenth-century religious scholar. With respectful understanding, he taught passionately how Christ fulfilled the many gaps in their texts about ultimate truth. And 250 Tamils embraced Christ and the opportunity to propagate a lifestyle free of caste, illiteracy, and its consequent Brahmin and European subjugation. These Tamils were trained in Christian discipleship from within their own culture, and millions can trace their Christian faith through the New Jerusalem Church in Tranquebar. This was Ziegenbalg's great legacy.

In 1719, renewed European persecution inflamed his chronic illness, and he died an early death at age thirty-six. In July 2006, the nation of India — Hindu, Muslim, and Christian — spent a week celebrating the three-hundredth anniversary of Ziegenbalg's Christian legacy to Indian culture. Thousands went to Tranquebar. The post office issued a special stamp.

But Ziegenbalg is forgotten in the West.

For reflection and discussion

India, now home to over a billion people, is one of the most unique cultures in the world, vastly different from the West.

- What experiences have you had with Indian people or culture?
- When Hindus and Muslims celebrate Ziegenbalg, what qualities of Christ might they be recognizing?

Ziegenbalg was a peer among intellectuals and a friend to lowly Tamils. In this way he was a follower of Jesus Christ, who could talk philosophy with Pilate and fishing with the country folk of Galilee.

- Ziegenbalg saw beauty in Tamils, where his peers saw beasts. In whom might we discover Christ where others see only demons?
- How great is your need to be celebrated and remembered? What would mean more to you: to be made much of or to be delivered from needing to be made much of?

The Modern University

By J. P. Moreland, PhD, professor of philosophy, Talbot School of Theology. Excerpted from *Kingdom Triangle: Recover the Christian Mind, Renovate the Soul, Restore the Spirit's Power.* Moreland has authored, edited, or contributed to over seventy books, spoken at over two hundred college campuses, and is director of Eidos Christian Center; *www.kingdomtriangle.com.*

Note: *The earliest colleges in America, as in Europe, exalted Christ at the center of learning and knowledge. Harvard's original motto was "For Christ's glory." Princeton's read, "I bring life to the dead." Explore further, in Kelly Kullberg's book* Finding God Beyond Harvard, *how the quest for truth began and has unfolded in American universities.*

In her authoritative work *The Making of the Modern University*, Harvard professor Julie Reuben describes the transition from the American liberal arts college to the modern research university from 1880 to 1930. Reuben divides this time of upheaval into three overlapping periods: the Religious Stage (1880 – 1910), the Scientific Stage (1900 – 1920), and the Humanities and Extracurricular Stage (1915 – 1930).

During the first period, colleges took themselves to have two mandates: the impartation of wisdom and knowledge and the tools needed to discover them, and the development of spiritually, morally, and politically virtuous graduates who could serve God, the state, and the church well.

Because the Christian God was a single, unified mind and the source of all truths, the curriculum was unified in that every discipline was expected to shed light on and harmonize with every other discipline. College faculty and administrators were confident that knowledge existed in all fields of study. In particular, spiritual, ethical, aesthetic, and political truth and knowledge were real and on a par with truth and knowledge in other disciplines, including science.

As time went on, a fact/value distinction arose according to which truth and facts, along with the knowledge thereof, was the sole domain of empirical science. The realm of religion and values became noncognitive (knowledge is not possible in these domains). The idea that there exists a stable body of knowable truths gave way to the notion that truth changes constantly, that progress, not wisdom, is what matters, and that university education should focus on method and "learning how to think" rather than trying to impart knowledge and wisdom to students, especially outside the empirical sciences. Academic freedom, "open" inquiry, a spirit of skepticism, and specialized research became the central values of American universities.

The abandonment of Christian monotheism from the cognitive domain meant that there was no longer a basis for a unified curriculum. Great hostility arose to natural and revealed theology and their claim to provide knowledge of God and related matters; instead, religion was tolerated as long as it did not claim to be cognitive or factual. The new goal of the university was not the discovery of truth but the facilitating of research.

Administrators looked to professors in literature, art, history, language, and philosophy to unify the lives of the students and teach values for university life in general, and the curriculum in particular, but the humanities professors could not find any basis for agreement about whose values, whose justice, whose religion should be taught. So they could not mount a robust, common vision of moral and religious truth and knowledge apt for filling this mandate. As a result, ethical and religious training was punted to extracurricular activities.

Universities sought to provide a unifying, distinct university experience through faculty advising, living in dorms as vehicles for creating a sense of community, the office of Dean of Students, and freshman orientation.

The university's second mandate to impart moral and spiritual knowledge to its students devolved into the vague aim of developing a rich student life as part of the college experience. Morality soon became morale or school spirit, and the goal of making a college education a distinct experience turned out to revolve around athletic teams and the school spirit associated with them. The moral and spiritual wisdom of Plato, Aristotle, Moses, Solomon, and Jesus was replaced with football and school spirit.

For reflection and discussion

Sociologist David Brooks writes in *On Paradise Drive*, "If you ask professors whether they seek to instill character, they often look at you blankly. They are on campus to instill calculus, or nineteenth-century history. 'We've taken the decision that these are adults and this is not our job,' one Princeton professor once told me in an interview. 'We're very conservative about how we steer. They steer themselves,' said that school's dean of undergraduate students."[1] Here we see the difficulty of finding universal meaning for individual things — be it character values or individual courses — when the unity of absolutes and ideals is abandoned. We also see the difficulty of steering college students to develop a shared vision of character or purpose for their education when they are offered athletic and social experiences, both visceral and often visual, rather than a larger story in which to live and thrive.

- How does Moreland's description of the modern university compare to your own experience of the university's purpose? How might you offer a different explanation of its vision and goals?
- Founders of many schools dedicated and financially endowed those schools for learning within a Christian framework. In that light, do you think the shift to secularism is fair and just? How might we honor their intentions despite cultural changes?
- In the reality of today's diversity of beliefs and values, how do you think the university might approach the idea of instilling shared character values and ethics?
- How does your life with God connect with your own education, work, and goals?

DNA: The Beauty and Intelligence of the Designer

By Ray Bohlin, PhD, president of Probe Ministries. With advanced degrees in population genetics and molecular and cell biology, Bohlin is featured in the four-week DVD curriculum *Redeeming Darwin*; *www.probe.org*.

"What really astounds me is the architecture of life.... The system is extremely complex. It's like it was designed.... There's a huge intelligence there. I don't see that as being unscientific. Others may, but not me."

Sometimes words just jump off the page. Such was my experience when I read this quote from Gene Meyers in an article in the *San Francisco Chronicle* in February 2001.

Gene Meyers was one of the scientists from Celera Genomics, which had completed the sequence of the human genome along with the multinational Human Genome Project.

DNA (**D**eoxyibo**N**ucleic **A**cid) is composed of a sequence of nucleotide bases. Nucleotides are complex biomolecules. There are four types of nucleotides in DNA usually abbreviated A (adenine), G (guanine), T (thymine), and C (cytosine).

DNA exists in what is called a double helix, where two paired strands of DNA, oriented in opposite directions, wind around each other. A always pairs with T, and G always pairs with C. These are called base pairs. The human genome is composed of over 3 billion base pairs distributed over twenty-three sets of chromosomes.

Beneath this amazing and beautiful physical structure is the Genetic Code. We know that the physical properties of the As, Gs, Cs, and Ts do not determine the order in which they appear in the sequence. Yet their sequence is critically important.

Simply put, nucleotides are grouped together in threes, or codons, such as ACT, or TGC, or GGG. Each codon codes for one of twenty amino acids. Amino acids are the building blocks of proteins. The sequence of amino acids largely determines the function of the protein. Proteins are the workhorse molecules of the trillions of cells in your body.

Thousands of different proteins are made in different cells at different times and in different amounts. If the right proteins aren't made with the right sequence at the right time, you're in trouble. This incredible system is monitored and controlled with numerous feedback loops and sensory systems in the cell. The focus of molecular biology is trying to figure out how all these assembly and control systems work.

Most biologists maintain that the genome is a patchwork assemblage of genes and leftover DNA sequences accumulated by trial and error over millions of years of evolution. This never made sense to me. If there's a code, there's language. Where there's language, there's intelligence.

I remember sitting in seminars as a beginning graduate student where researchers presented their experiments in one-hour lectures. I would struggle to comprehend how the experiments worked, follow the reasoning, and understand how they interpreted their results. And that was usually just one small molecular pathway.

Eventually it would dawn on me that God not only understood everything about this one little pathway that took years to unravel but he fully comprehended the thousands upon thousands of interrelated molecular pathways in the entire cell! And not only that, he designed the whole thing in the first place!

I would silently worship and give thanks to the incredible Mind we were only catching glimpses of. I still feel the welling of tears and goose bumps, recalling those revelations.

I believe that in the next ten to twenty years, the incredible design and intelligence of the information systems of the cell will scream louder and louder of the Designer. Many more will exclaim as did Gene Meyers, "There's a huge intelligence there."

For reflection and discussion

In Psalm 139:17 – 18 David says, "How precious to me are your thoughts, God! How vast is the sum of them! ... When I awake, I am still with you." We marvel at the intellectual brilliance of God. And yet this exalted One comes near. From the moment we wake up, he gives us the gift of his presence.

- How does awareness of DNA affect your sense of connection with God?
- What does the presence of God mean in your experience?
- As you consider God's design of DNA, how might his knowledge and ability supply what you need to deal with some problem or challenge you are facing?

Hamlet: Shakespeare's Ingenious Design

By **Jonathan Witt**, PhD, senior fellow of Discovery Institute. Text adapted from *A Meaningful World: How the Arts and Sciences Reveal the Genius of Nature*, coauthored by Witt and Benjamin Wiker. Witt is a script writer for documentaries that have aired on PBS (*The Privileged Planet, The Call of the Entrepreneur*); *www.ameaningfulworld.com.*

Oxford zoologist Richard Dawkins uses a line from Shakespeare's *Hamlet* to argue that Darwinian evolution can mimic not just intelligence but the keen intellect of the Bard himself.

Dawkins describes a computer experiment that begins with a string of random letters exactly as long as Hamlet's comment "Methinks it is like a weasel." The program then randomly substitutes new letters for old in the string of gibberish. If any new letters bring the string closer to the Shakespearean line, the program locks in the new letters. Then the program substitutes a new set of random letters for the remaining unfixed set of letters, and the process continues. By the forty-third generation, the computer spits out "Methinks it is like a weasel." This, Dawkins claims, illustrates the power of Darwinian evolution to create new genetic information and, with it, new works of natural art like weasels.

The problem is, Dawkins' computer program does not mimic Darwinian evolution. First, the Shakespearean sentence is in the program from the start, serving as the target. Darwinian evolution doesn't have a distance goal in mind. Second, the string that begins the evolutionary process is dysfunctional gibberish, as are the intermediate steps until late in the process. Darwin's mechanism of natural selection eliminates dysfunctional things. It only selects for immediate function. Dawkins' program doesn't model Darwinian evolution. It models intelligently guided evolution.

Indeed, even if the program were forced to randomly generate the entire Shakespearean line in one fell swoop, it wouldn't mirror the challenge for Darwinian evolution. "Methinks it is like a weasel" finds its function and meaning in the context of the larger play. Hamlet is the medieval prince of Denmark. His father, the king, was secretly murdered by the king's brother, Claudius, who then marries the old king's widow a mere two months after the funeral and seizes the throne while Prince Hamlet is away. In the first act,

Hamlet, unaware of his uncle's unnatural treachery, broods over his mother's too hasty marriage.

Hamlet then learns the true cause of his father's death from his father's ghost. The prince's subsequent quest to avenge his father's death shapes the rest of the play and is the occasion for profound reflections on the nature of sin; human and divine punishment; love and loyalty; the divide between appearance and reality; and the tangled web of Providence, happenstance, and free will.

The "weasel" line comes in a scene between Hamlet and Polonius. Polonius was King Hamlet's right-hand man but now serves King Claudius, never mind that Claudius's grab for the vacant throne was unseemly at best. Polonius is the archetypal yes-man, a court toady, and Hamlet manages to illustrate this fact while pretending to be insane:

> *Hamlet.* Do you see yonder cloud that's almost in the shape of a camel?
> *Polonius.* By th' mass. And 'tis like a camel indeed.
> *Hamlet. Methinks it is like a weasel.*
> *Polonius.* It is backed like a weasel.
> *Hamlet.* Or like a whale?
> *Polonius.* Very like a whale.

Hamlet is mocking Polonius, who, in deference to royalty, will agree to almost anything a royal figure says, no matter how absurd.

Thus, the weasel line's meaning emerges only in the larger context of the play. By itself it fails to function. In the same way, strands of genetic information lack function apart from their larger, unimaginably more complex biological context. Thus, the problem Darwinism faces is to generate not a single short genetic phrase but an entire biological "play" in which the genetic phrase can actually function.

Dawkins inadvertently underscores the importance of context by ignoring relevant context and thereby misreading the *Hamlet* passage. He suggests a parallel between people who imagine someone shapes clouds to look like animals and those who mistake the appearance of design in biology for actual design. But neither Hamlet nor Polonius think the cloud even looks like a weasel, much less that a heavenly artist tried to sculpt a weasel-shaped cloud. The passage is not about seeing design where it isn't. Polonius's problem is just the opposite. In an act of willed blindness, Polonius attributes King Hamlet's death to natural causes when the evidence points strongly to death by intelligent design. The parallel to Dawkins is fairly straightforward: he too overlooks the evidence for intelligent design.

According to Dawkins, every living thing is ultimately just a string of chemical letters, including Shakespeare. But that is a fundamental error. No sensible person would say the analogical equivalent about Shakespeare's *Hamlet*. The play isn't essentially a string of letters or even lines. Its meaning is manifested from both the whole and its milieu. And its source is not the blowing of the wind, is not some mindless material mechanism, but the mind of a most intelligent artist.

What is true of *Hamlet* is true of life.

For reflection and discussion

- How does this reading encourage or challenge your view of Darwinian evolution (by natural selection and random mutation) or intelligent design? How do you respond to Dawkins' claim that Darwinian evolution can mimic the genius of Shakespeare?

Witt goes on to say, "That Shakespeare's art cannot be reduced to material mechanisms should be obvious, but the obvious has been obscured by the dogma that matter is all there is. Materialism has created a kind of flatland that crushes the life out of life, despoiling its native richness, denying its true depth, muddying over its brilliant and variegated hues."

- How does your perspective on your own life change as you see it in the larger context of God's creative and redemptive work?
- What do you want to say to God in response to this reading?

Handel's *Messiah*

By **Patrick Kavanaugh**, artistic director of the MasterWorks Festival. Adapted from *The Spiritual Lives of the Great Composers* by Kavanaugh, Emi Christian Music Group. A conductor and performer, he is director of the Christian Performing Artists Fellowship; *www.ChristianPerformingArt.org.*

London audiences for German-born George Frideric Handel's compositions were unpredictable, and even the Church of England attacked him for what they considered his notorious practice of writing biblical dramas, like *Esther*, to be performed in secular theaters. His occasional commercial success soon met with financial disaster as he drove himself relentlessly to recover from one failure after another, and finally his health began to fail. By 1741 he was swimming in debt. Prison seemed imminent.

On April 8 of that year, he gave what he considered his farewell concert. Miserably discouraged, he felt forced to retire from public activities at the age of fifty-six. Then two unforeseen events converged to change his life. A wealthy friend, Charles Jennens, gave Handel a libretto based on the life of Christ, taken entirely from the Bible. Handel also received a commission to compose a work for a Dublin benefit performance.

He set to work composing on August 22 in his little house in London. Within six days, part one was complete. In nine days more Handel had finished part two, and in another six, part three. Morning, noon, and evening his servant delivered meals to the composer and returned later to find them largely untouched. Once, as the servant swung open the door, the startled composer, tears streaming down his face, turned to him and cried out, "I did think I did see all Heaven before me, and the great God Himself." Handel had just finished writing a movement that would take its place in history as the "Hallelujah" chorus.

Handel completed the orchestration in another two days. In all, 260 pages of manuscript were filled in the remarkably short time of twenty-four days.

Handel did not leave his house for those three weeks. A friend who visited found him sobbing with intense emotion. Later, as Handel groped for words to describe what he had experienced, he quoted St. Paul, saying, "Whether I was in the body or out of my body when I wrote it I know not."

Sir Newman Flower, one of Handel's many biographers, summed up the consensus of history: "Considering the immensity of the work, and the short time involved, it will remain, perhaps forever, the greatest feat in the whole history of music composition." Handel's title for the commissioned work was, simply, *Messiah*.

Messiah premiered on April 13, 1742, as a charitable benefit, raising 400 pounds and freeing 142 men from debtor's prison. A year later, Handel staged it in London. Controversy emanating from the Church of England continued to plague Handel. Yet the king of England attended the performance. As the first notes of the triumphant "Hallelujah" chorus rang out, the king rose. Following royal protocol, the entire audience stood too, initiating a tradition that has lasted for more than two centuries.

Handel donated freely to charities, even when he faced financial ruin. The thousands of pounds that his performances of *Messiah* raised for charity led one biographer to note: "*Messiah* has fed the hungry, clothed the naked, fostered the orphan ... more than any other single musical production in this or any other country." Others wrote, "Perhaps the works of no other composer have so largely contributed to the relief of human suffering."

One writer stated that the music and message of *Messiah* have probably done more than all the theological works ever written "to convince thousands of mankind that there is a God about us."

For reflection and discussion

- You can listen to Handel's *Messiah* on YouTube or download it from iTunes. What can you say about its effect on the listener? Have other works of art reached you in this powerful way?
- How would you express your own worship to God if you could freely choose? In music, painting, design?

Our relationship to God is defined by sheer grace. Yet, there is about God what William Blake has called a "fearful symmetry." We often see it in his orchestration of a fitting balance between our choices and God's gracious movement in our lives.

- How do you see God at work in Handel's life?
- How does Handel's music (and his life) make you want to respond to God?

AIDS

By **Stephanie Powers**, who served in a Harvard AIDS project in Tanzania and remained in Africa as a missionary in Uganda. She now studies and works as a nurse at the University of Tennessee.

One of the few times their eyes are expressionless is when asked, "How did he die?" Especially if it was from AIDS. I worked in Tanzania with an HIV/AIDS nutrition research collaborative between the Harvard School of Public Health and a university in Dar es Salaam and later with a mission in Uganda. The challenges of cultural differences and heat, a bout of malaria, inconsistent electricity, and, at times, desperation from what I saw kept me on my toes (and on my knees). I was sustained by faith and the knowledge that God redeems and by a colorful and incredibly resilient people of faith, who always had a song in their hearts, music on their tongues, and tea to offer. Yet the destruction of malaria and AIDS was ever present and not a respecter of persons.

AIDS is the silent killer that few want to talk about, even though it has touched most families. I was constantly alarmed by deaths among the families of my staff, coworkers, and friends. The office assistant who served me daily tea died a few years after I left Tanzania. Gone. Leaving young children behind. I wish I could have been there to hold her hand — I hope someone else was.

The number of people that died of AIDS in 2006 (2.9 million) is equal to almost one thousand 9/11s. The loss of human life is staggering. They each came out of their mother's wombs, so precious, the apple of someone's eye. Many were themselves caregivers. Some had no idea they had AIDS, too scared to test. Some knew, and out of anger or denial and irresponsibility gave it to others. Some were purely victims of someone else's choices. Some were well-educated, but lived in denial. Some were so doped up and addicted that they ignored what they were doing with dirty needles. Some were HIV-positive at birth and struggled each day to survive. Some were the children of desperately poor parents who sold them into the sex trade.

More than 70 percent of AIDS deaths in 2006 were in sub-Saharan Africa — 2.1 million people. The ramifications are huge. By the year 2010, the number of orphans in Africa may rise to above 40 million. In the worst regions of southern Africa, such as Swaziland, as many as *one in three* people are living with HIV. In the past two years, the number of people living with HIV increased in *every region* of the world, with striking increases in East Asia, Eastern Europe, and Central Asia. In North America, at least 1.5 million people live with HIV/AIDS. New infection rates in the US are highest among men who have sex with men and injection drug users, and the heaviest impact is found in minority groups. In the US, 25 percent of HIV-positive people and as many as 77 percent of HIV-positive gay males living in large cities do not know they have the infection. This, along with irresponsible sexual behavior, further complicates an already heavy public health burden.

The gut-wrenching realities of AIDS are complicated and overwhelming. God so loves and longs to heal this broken and hurting world. I have seen his expert hand turn evil into good with amazing grace, crafting magnificent redemption through those who put their trust in him and *act on behalf of those in need*. Walking with Jesus in the midst of those realities means opening our hearts and embracing risk, pain, and cost while leaning fully on Christ, who conquered death because of his love for us. The joy of his love, and that leaning, will sustain us in the giving.

For reflection and discussion

First John 4:19 says, "We love because he first loved us."

- How is your life different when you believe you are *already loved* by God and can draw on that love as you give to others?
- What would it be like if you waited for others to love you before you loved?
- What have been your personal experiences with people with AIDS or HIV?
- What are your greatest concerns or fears about the disease? How do you relate this disease to your understanding of God's purposes and character?
- Are you connected to any groups that offer assistance, either to help prevent HIV or with caretaking help?
- Rejoice today in the reality that God has "first loved us" and wants us to give it away to others.

Interpreting the Bible

By Jack Arrington, ThM, pastor and former president, College of Biblical Studies, Houston.

In *Through the Looking Glass*, Lewis Carroll playfully addresses questions of meaning and interpretation that have sent heretics to the stake. Seeking to persuade Alice that un-birthday presents are better than birthday presents because there are 364 days a year for un-birthday presents, Humpty Dumpty observes,

> "And only *one* for birthday presents, you know. There's glory for you!"
> "I don't know what you mean by 'glory,'" Alice said.
> Humpty Dumpty smiled contemptuously. "Of course you don't — till I tell you. I meant 'there's a nice knock-down argument for you!'"
> "But 'glory' doesn't mean 'a nice knock-down argument,'" Alice objected.
> "When *I* use a word," Humpty Dumpty said, in rather a scornful tone, "it means just what I choose it to mean — neither more nor less."

Are words that flexible? Can they mean whatever we choose them to mean? Can historical documents such as the Bible be read for their original historical meanings? Do we have the ability or the objectivity to reconstruct the original author's intent? Perhaps all that is really important is one's personal experience and use of the text. Maybe all texts become living documents with floating meanings totally dependent upon the reader. Maybe.

Suppose I wrote the following to you: "My grandmother likes climbing vines."

Can those words mean anything you choose them to mean, à la Mr. Dumpty? Shouldn't you try to grasp my intention? She is *my grandmother*. Wouldn't it be something akin to robbery to commandeer my description of my own grandmother? Should any author be treated in that manner?

I'm being playful too, but surely we can see that it is neither ethical nor beneficial to ignore the intent of the original author. Do we not go to good books, to the Bible, to interact with the thoughts of the authors and Author? So, it is most desirable to pursue the author's original intent. Only then do we encounter the thoughts and truly come to know another person.

If words (written or verbal) cannot convey the intended meaning of another person, then neither communication nor intimacy is possible. Yet we know communication is possible from everyday experience. We can read an email and get the joke. We can read a cake recipe and bake a tasty treat. And I assume you've understood what I've written up to this point. You have encountered my thoughts through the established norm of written communication.

Is it possible to *mis*understand? Certainly. Any married couple will confirm that reality. Is it possible to use a text in a biased, nonobjective manner? Of course. But neither potential for miscommunication negates the possibility of accurate understanding, as experience proves.

So how do we find the author's intended meaning? Consider my grandmother. Most words have several possible meanings. They can mean some things but not others. "Grandmother" cannot be my uncle or my mother. If you were observant, you would have noticed that it could be the *vines* that climb or my *grandmother* who climbs. Possible word meanings, grammar, and syntax have given two probable interpretations.

How do we pick the correct meaning? Is it simply a matter of choosing the meaning we like most? No. Literary and historical context provide the keys which usually enable us to unlock the most appropriate meaning, whether a text is inspired or not. So if either context informed you my grandmother loved gardening, you'd have a different understanding than if you discovered her name was Jane and she lived with Tarzan.

We discover the thoughts of God expressed in the words of the Bible in the same manner. Words can mean some things, but they can't mean anything we choose them to mean. With grammar, syntax, and context, we discover the author's meaning. Only in this manner can we teach others what Jesus has taught us.

Your word, LORD, is eternal; it stands firm in the heavens.

PSALM 119:89

For reflection and discussion

- Can you think of a time when something you wrote or said was badly misinterpreted? How has that shaped your ideas about the value of the author's intended meaning?

- How does this understanding of language challenge or encourage your understanding of what words mean? What questions does it raise?
- How do you think the Holy Spirit guides believers into truth (John 16:12 – 13)?
- Perhaps you would like to pray some of Psalm 119 to God, both in thanks for his Word and in petition that he would help you understand his meaning.

The Enlightenment

By **James Emery White**, PhD, professor of theology and culture at Gordon-Conwell Theological Seminary. He is founding pastor of Mecklenburg Community Church in Charlotte, N.C., and the author of more than a dozen books. Adapted from his book *Serious Times: Making Your Life Matter in an Urgent Day*; *www.serioustimes.com*.

Those who lived in the eighteenth century had little doubt that they were living in an enlightened age, one that emerged from twilight. Between 1650 and 1750 lived such luminaries as Sir Isaac Newton, Gottfried Leibniz, John Locke, and Voltaire. Within this span of time the last remaining vestiges of the Middle Ages ended. But more ended than an era.

Historian Mark Noll writes, "An increasing number of European intellectuals used new ideas about the natural world, society and the nature of things to attack the established churches, to question traditional views of divine revelation, and even to doubt the existence of God." The divine was reduced to a philosophical category, a "first mover" in the grand scheme of things, but no longer a loving Father. With the Enlightenment came the "rise of modern paganism."

To properly understand the Enlightenment, it must be seen as more than an age — it was a spirit or mood. While the Enlightenment period produced the hymns of Isaac Watts, the music of J. S. Bach and Handel, German Pietism, the ministries of John Wesley and George Whitefield, and the First Great Awakening, the dominant spirit of the age was anything but Christian. The spirit of the Enlightenment held two propositions: the present age is more enlightened than the past, and we understand nature and humanity best through the use of our natural faculties. The motto of Immanuel Kant, a prominent thinker of the time, was, "Dare to use your own reason," or simply, "Dare to know."

There could be no authority over the exercise or conclusion of reason. This idea of authority is critical, for the Enlightenment was a rebellion against one source of authority and the enthronement of another — human reason. For someone like Voltaire, the Enlightenment offered emancipation from "prone submission to the heavenly will."

Most Enlightenment thinkers, such as Scottish philosopher David Hume, elevated sense experience above all other sources for gaining knowledge. Whatever could not be observed or repeated was met with skepticism. The fundamental idea was that we could begin with ourselves to gain the means by which to judge all things.

Theology had reigned over science and philosophy for centuries. It was not that science and philosophy were ignored — only that they were to be submitted to revelation for final interpretation or meaning. Even René Descartes, in concluding his *Principes de la philosophie*, wrote, "Above all, we will observe as an infallible rule that what God has revealed is incomparably more certain that all the rest." Yet by the end of the eighteenth century, with discoveries that seemed to contradict the church's teaching (though not the Bible's teaching), the church had been marginalized, theology dethroned as the queen of the sciences, and the Christian worldview reduced among the intelligentsia to a fading memory. For the first time since the fourth century, the church would face persecution.

A foundational shift had taken place: from "faith seeking understanding" to "faith requiring justification."

The most visible manifestation of the seismic shift toward secular humanism was the French Revolution, where a religion of "man" was established. A process of de-Christianization began, so much so that Alexis de Tocqueville would later write, "In France ... Christianity was attacked with almost frenzied violence." One of the more symbolic events took place on November 10, 1793, when Notre-Dame de Paris, the church of France — most famous of the Gothic cathedrals — was formally declared and transformed into the Temple of Reason, with busts of Rousseau and Voltaire taking the place of the saints.

Humans were left to be their own masters. Suddenly man lived in a disenchanted world, forced to submit everything to criticism and skepticism. And it gave us the world in which we now live.

For reflection and discussion

- Do you see ways in which the Enlightenment was positive for the world?
- Do you see ways in which the light of Enlightenment led to darkness?
- What might White mean by a "disenchanted world"?
- How does belief in God affect your daily life experiences?

The Ultimate Premise

By Phillip Johnson, JD, professor emeritus of law at the University of California, Berkeley, author of *Reason in the Balance* and *The Right Questions: Truth and Meaning in Public Debate*, the source of this reading.

Note: *While Enlightenment thinkers expressed terrific confidence in reason, Johnson invites the reader to consider the limits of logic and reason.*

In the beginning were the particles.
In the beginning was the Word.

Our logic cannot supply its own beginning. Logic is merely a way of reasoning correctly from premises to conclusions. The premises must come from elsewhere.

Rationalism is inherently self-defeating because the rationalist must pretend to derive his first premises by logical reasoning, which always rests on other premises. Empiricism faces the same dilemma when it becomes a total system because the empiricist always needs to know more than he can observe.

We cannot resolve conflicting ultimate premises by argument. These are essentially faith commitments from which life and logic should proceed; they are not doctrines that require proof. "God creates" and "God cares" are ultimate premises that underlie the Bible's teaching. Totally opposite from these you find "In the beginning were only particles and the laws of Nature, and all else comes from these."

Ultimate premises do not yield to arguments or evidence, but a premise that appears to be ultimate may turn out not to be ultimate after all. It is important to determine whether you are talking about a fact or an ultimate premise. Trying to prove an ultimate premise is an absurdity. Such an attempt at proof would have to proceed from something else that is both more fundamental and more certainly true. You cannot prove that "in the beginning was the Word"; it is something you accept or not.

If you are a rationalist, you will probably recoil at the thought of an acknowledged premise, a fundamental proposition that comes at the beginning rather than at the end of a chain of logical reasoning.

But the rationalist also has a first premise: the reliability of the autonomous mind and its powers of reasoning, powers that, according to scientific materialism, amount to nothing more than so many neurons firing in the physical brain. I wonder if anyone has ever held on to such faith in the aftermath of a stroke.

If anything I may say could move the rationalist/materialist to choose a better ultimate premise, it would probably not be my arguments, but the story of what happened to me in a hospital room after my stroke. It is only one of many stories that could be told by people who have undergone a serious ordeal.

In the early days of my stroke recovery, when my worst fear seemed a present reality, we prayed in my hospital room. Our friend Kate sang a simple hymn: "On Christ the solid rock I stand; all other ground is sinking sand."

I could think of nothing but the man described in the Sermon on the Mount. I built a house, and in some respects it was a very good house, but it was not thoroughly anchored in the rock. I knew the importance of asking the right questions, such as, "How solid is my foundation?" Too often, however, I had been distracted by the wrong questions, such as, "How can I make the house look impressive so the neighbors will admire it?"

The storm came and shook the foundation.

I had always prided myself on being self-reliant, and my brain was what I had relied on. Now the self with its brain was exposed as the shaky instrument it had always been. I was a Christian, but now all the smoke was blown away and I knew myself to be not so much a believer in Christ as a skeptic about everything else, a recovering rationalist who had lost his faith in the world's definition of reason, but who knew only the world's Jesus.

I had to decide then and for eternity where my hope was based, or whether I had any. As Kate finished her song, I knew that I had found solid rock and that I was already standing on it. I recalled the familiar words of the twenty-third Psalm: "Yea, though I walk through the valley of the shadow of death, I will fear no evil: for Thou art with me." I told my wife, "To me that has always been just a beautiful poem, but now I know what it means." I had walked through the valley of the shadow of death, and that psalm was now my own story.

Lord, I believe; please help my unbelief! That juxtaposition is not paradoxical to those who have been there. Despite the way my brain was affected by the stroke, I was clearer than ever that there is a source from which our reasoning powers derive, and it is far more trustworthy than the movements of molecules.

For reflection and discussion

- How would you describe the relationship between faith and reason in your life?
- How do you respond to the idea that the ultimate premises for everything you count as knowledge cannot be proven with logic or evidence, but proceed from faith or some metaphysical assumption?
- God could have made a world where he shows himself so plainly, so empirically, that no one could reasonably deny his existence or his will. Why do you think he has done otherwise?
- What is God showing you about his purpose or character when he calls you to live by faith?

Darwin's Surprising Voyage

By Kelly Monroe Kullberg and David Kullberg, adapted from Charles Darwin's *The Voyage of the Beagle*; available at Project Gutenberg, *www.gutenberg.org.*

At age twenty-two, Charles Darwin (1809 – 1882) left home for the adventure of a lifetime. In his introduction to Darwin's trip journal, *The Voyage of the Beagle*, George Parker wrote, "About 1831 the British Admiralty decided to fit out The Beagle. . . . It seemed important to all concerned that a naturalist should accompany this expedition. . . . [Professor] Henslow recommended Darwin not as a finished naturalist but as one amply qualified for collecting, observing, and noting anything worthy to be noted in natural history."

But Darwin didn't only observe and collect biological data. Toward the end of his journal we discover fascinating observations of the role of the gospel in the lives of human beings.

The *Beagle* sailed from England in 1831 and would not return until 1836. She crossed the Atlantic to the coast of Brazil, headed south to Tierra del Fuego, rounded Cape Horn, and turned northward to Chile, Peru, and the Galapagos Islands. Near the equator, the *Beagle* headed westward, crossing the Pacific to Tahiti and on to New Zealand.

A keen observer of humans as well as botany, Darwin recorded his observations of people and the interactions of New Zealand natives with Christian missionaries. Though his words reveal his assumptions about British and cultural superiority, they also show concern for native people and the missionaries who befriended them. We allow him to speak in his own words, from *The Voyage of the Beagle*:

New Zealand, December 22, 1835

I should think a more warlike race of inhabitants could not be found in any part of the world than the New Zealanders. Their conduct on first seeing a ship, as described by Captain Cook, [the English sea captain who discovered New Zealand in 1769] strongly illustrates this: the act of throwing volleys of stones at so great and novel an object, and their defiance of "Come on shore and we will kill and eat you all," shows uncommon boldness. This warlike spirit is evident in many of their customs, and even in their smallest actions. . . .

December 23

At length we reached Waimate. After having passed over so many miles of an uninhabited useless country, the sudden appearance of an English farm-house, and its well-dressed fields, placed there as if by an enchanter's wand, was exceedingly pleasant.... There were large gardens with every fruit and vegetable: asparagus, apples, pears, figs ... also many kinds of flowers.

All this is very surprising, when it is considered that five years ago nothing but the fern flourished here. Moreover, native workmanship, taught by the missionaries, has effected this change; the lesson of the missionary is the enchanter's wand. The house had been built, the windows framed, the fields ploughed, and even the trees grafted, by a New Zealander....

When I looked at this whole scene ... It was not merely that England was brought vividly before my mind; but rather the high hopes thus inspired for the future progress of this fine island.

Several young men, redeemed by the missionaries from slavery, were employed on the farm.... These young men and boys appeared very merry.... The young women.... [were] clean, tidy, and healthy in appearance ... a wonderful contrast with the women of the filthy hovels in Kororadika....

December 23

Late in the evening I went to Mr. Williams's house, where I passed the night. I found there a large party of children, collected together for Christmas Day, and all sitting round a table at tea. I never saw a nicer or more merry group; and to think that this was in the centre of the land of cannibalism, murder, and all atrocious crimes!...

December 24

In the morning, prayers were read in the native tongue to the whole family.... I took leave of the missionaries with thankfulness for their kind welcome, and with feelings of high respect for their gentlemanlike, useful, and upright characters.

December 25: Christmas Day

We attended divine service in the chapel of Pahia.... Whilst at New Zealand we did not hear of any recent acts of cannibalism.... It is probable that the moral state of the people will rapidly improve.... One of the young men [of the island] read the Bible with difficulty by the light of the fire, to the others. After this the party knelt and prayed: in their prayers they mentioned Mr. Bushby and his family....

December 30 — leaving New Zealand

In the afternoon we stood out of the Bay of Islands, on our course to Sydney. I believe we were all glad to leave New Zealand.... I look back but to one bright spot, and that is Waimate, with its Christian inhabitants.

From New Zealand the *Beagle* sailed for Australia, then traversed the Indian Ocean, rounded Africa's Cape of Good Hope, and headed home for England.

For reflection and discussion

It is debatable whether Darwin's attribution "To the Creator" in his *Origin of the Species* was heartfelt or political. Darwin often dismissed the idea of a loving Creator intimately involved in our lives, and, yet, he never forgot the missionaries and, some might say, the moral and cultural evolution of human beings influenced by Jesus Christ.

With the microscopes of Darwin's day, he could not have imagined the complexity inside one living cell. Some, like British atheist Anthony Flew, have come to faith by learning that one cell contains more information than the Oxford English Dictionary.

- How do you consider the relationship between evolutionary theory and the understanding of God as Creator — in Darwin's time and in our own?
- If we put ourselves in the place of the islanders, with no prior knowledge of God's love, let's thank God for Jesus Christ and those who've modeled Christ in our lives.

Note: *Charles Darwin was so impressed by the effects of the Christian gospel, and the missionaries, that he contributed financially to the South American Mission Society until his death in 1882.*

Moby-Dick: Not Mere Fiction

By James Scott Bell, JD, bestselling author. Bell's fiction titles include *The Whole Truth* and *Try Dying*; *www.jamesscottbell.com*.

Take heart, take heart, O Bulkington! Bear thee grimly, demigod!
Up from the spray of thy ocean-perishing — straight up, leaps thy apotheosis!
HERMAN MELVILLE, *MOBY-DICK*

Whenever I mention Herman Melville's singular tale among friends, I generally get one of three responses: Haven't read it, tried to read it but couldn't finish, and they made me read it in high school and I *hated* it. Indeed, the novel seems an anomaly in today's slimmed-down, fast-paced *Die Hard* world.

Moby-Dick is to current fiction as the Empire State Building is to Dunkin' Donuts. There's a ton of the latter, only one of the former. And *Moby-Dick* stands glorious in its inimitability.

The surface story, of course, concerns Captain Ahab's obsessive quest to kill the great white whale who took his leg. Narrated by one calling himself Ishmael, the novel details the rigors, both physical and psychological, of the nineteenth-century whaling industry. But the hunt soon becomes a metaphor for many themes — vengeance, monomania, alienation from God, and the multifaceted nature of evil. Ishmael is not just pursuing whales, he's searching for the root of his own soul.

And the writing! It is like the ocean itself. Undulating currents and crashing waves of narrative. Calms and storms and the occasional port. And long sections about whaling.

You don't find too many high schoolers these days who respond to that kind of writing. Not many adults, either. No patience for it. Most readers today prefer mere fiction.

Melville, forgotten and mostly out of print in his own life, perhaps could have made a good living writing penny dreadfuls. But he was after more than a living. He was pursuing that elusive dream of transcendent literature.

God love him.

Literature is many things. Sometimes it's a diversion, an entertainment. And there's nothing wrong with a little of that. But even in so-called com-

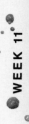

mercial fiction, those authors who strive to send their stories deeper than the gunshots and chase scenes are giving a nod to Herman Melville. For Melville taught us the glory of an artist stretching his hand beyond the grasping point.

Moby-Dick endures because it is everyone's story. Listen:

> Call me Ishmael. Some years ago — never mind how long precisely — having little or no money in my purse, and nothing particular to interest me on shore, I thought I would sail about a little and see the watery part of the world. It is a way I have of driving off the spleen, and regulating the circulation. Whenever I find myself growing grim about the mouth; whenever it is a damp, drizzly November in my soul; whenever I find myself involuntarily pausing before coffin warehouses, and bringing up the rear of every funeral I meet; and especially whenever my hypos get such an upper hand of me, that it requires a strong moral principle to prevent me from deliberately stepping into the street and methodically knocking people's hats off — then, I account it high time to get to sea as soon as I can. This is my substitute for pistol and ball.

Who among us has never endured a damp, drizzly November of the soul? Who doesn't sometimes think a few hats need to be knocked off a few complacent heads?

Who has never wondered where life's ship is headed?

Melville magnificently wondered for all of us in *Moby-Dick*.

For reflection and discussion

Perhaps you'd enjoy a quick overview of *Moby-Dick* at *www.sparknotes.com*, especially the plot summary and themes. Even read a chapter. Ishmael's story does not have a happy ending (chapter 135).

• Why do we want to do something difficult?

Like Ishmael hightailing it to sea, God beckons to us. "Come. Quest and question. Seek, search, pressing on, climbing, diving, higher up, deeper in. Board that sailing vessel, ascend that 655-page summit ... follow the mystery to my heart."

• How is God inviting you to live large in his kingdom story?
• What would you like to say to God about your own life quest?

The Impressionists

By Hans Rookmaaker, PhD, former professor of history of art, Free University, Amsterdam, and a director of L'Abri Fellowship. Adapted from *Modern Art and the Death of a Culture* [out of print but available at *www.piquant.net*]. Rookmaaker (1922 – 1977) came to a strengthened faith while in prison for challenging the Third Reich; (see Impressionist paintings at *www.artres.com*).

Monet, Renoir, and their friends set out to paint what they saw, what the eye recorded. In the early 1860s, Renoir painted an open-air dance with some of his friends sitting in the foreground [*Le Moulin de la Galette*]. Nothing special — though all would admit that the quality of the painting is very high, and his brushwork and use of color are superb. Nothing special? Look a bit closer. What are the light spots on the jacket of the man in the foreground? Perhaps he forgot to brush his jacket? Or has he leaned against a wall and got some whitewash on it? No, of course! They are simply "spots" of sunlight dappled by the leaves. And there are "spots" of light on the faces too and, most conspicuous, on the straw hat of the man behind the first group.

We must realize that it is the first time in history that things like this had been painted. Nobody had done it before. Of course, in ... Rembrandt ... and many others, spots of light had been included. But ... they never made the structure of the things depicted unclear. No one ever painted sunshine falling through leaves at random as Renoir did, or spots on a hat.... They would have thought that this falsified reality.

[We] look at a later Monet, of about 1880 [*Quai du Louvre*]. What do we see. Nothing special at first. It is not an important place. Monet just shows a "corner of nature."

A problem arises from a basic principle of the Enlightenment. Reality, the cosmos, is an unknown X and man can find out what it is like only by using his eyes and senses and then, with his brain, find a structure in the sensations coming from outside. [Already philosopher David Hume had raised the issue.] If I let a knife fall 999 times, how do I know that it will fall the next time?... Statistically we may take the chance that it will do so again the next time ... but we must admit that we can never be sure.... It was an epistemological problem, a question of the source of our knowledge of reality. Monet wrestles with it too....

So what do we see in the picture? Monet's brush strokes recording what he saw? In a way, no. Not *what* he saw. But he recorded what reached his eyes, the light beams that caused a sensation on his retina. The question is whether there is something behind them, a reality of things that caused the light beams. One may conjecture that there is a reality, in the same way as one is likely to take the chance that the knife will fall again, but one never knows for sure.

In the years before 1885 the Impressionists group became restless and nervous. Everybody who was in contact with this art realized there was something at stake. What is it? They were asking themselves. Where are we heading? Are we losing painting altogether? This world we are depicting, is it really reality?

Only Monet seemed to be sure of himself. He simply went on, and in 1885 dared to take the great step. The decisive step. The step over the threshold, the second step toward modern art. No, one never knows whether there is a reality behind the sensation we receive. There is no reality. Only the sensations are real.

If we look at his paintings after 1885 we see the difference [*Poplars at Giverny, Sunrise*]. He went on in the Impressionist line, more consistently than ever. He did various series of paintings depicting one spot — a row of trees by a river, Rouen Cathedral — but in different conditions: in rain and snow, in the morning, in the afternoon. It could not have been more naturalistic ... yet this is not the impression you get when you look at these pictures. They are more like dream pictures, pictures showing the world that is immaterial, ghost-like. The colors are beautiful, and one can sense that there was a world that induces sensations — the picture had some relationship to a real cathedral, for instance — but the reality does not seem so real.

In 1891 Kandinsky saw a painting of a haystack at a large exhibition of French painting in Moscow. He tells us how he looked at it, how magnificent he thought the painting was, the colors brilliant — but that he could not make out what kind of reality was represented. Was there a subject? He saw only color. Only after he consulted the catalog did he see what was meant. A strange picture, he thought. Beautiful, yes — but what about the reality depicted? It gave him, some twenty years later, the courage to paint an abstract picture.

For reflection and discussion

- If you appreciate Impressionist art, how would you express your attraction to the colors and images? How does your favorite Impressionist or realist painting or artist connect with you?
- If all we can be certain of is the particular sensation on our retinas, how would that impact our knowledge of reality? Would "Seeing [still be] believing"?
- What do you think the Bible means when it says we can perceive with the "eyes of your heart" (Ephesians 1:18)?
- How do you think visual perception gives you knowledge about God? How does perception of the eyes of your heart give you knowledge about God? Which do you find more reliable?
- How do you personally experience the reality that can be "seen" in Ephesians 1:18?

Tending the Garden Planet

By **Vera Shaw**, a chemist, and husband Jim were much-loved faculty advisers to the Harvard-Radcliffe Christian Fellowship for fifty years. Shaw is author of *Thorns in the Garden Planet: Meditations on the Creator's Care* and a contributor to *Finding God at Harvard*, both of which contributed to this adapted entry.

Much of Christ's teaching concerns the pollution of our inner spiritual environment and the glad news of the redemption and recycling that he offers. But is Jesus' message of the kingdom of God "within us" relevant to the global discussion of the moral and ethical problems of pollution and creation stewardship?

The messianic traditions of both Jews and Christians look forward to resolving the disharmony between God, humanity, and nature. The apostle Paul described the relationship between man and nature in his letter to the Romans (8:19), emphasizing that renewal of the earth is inextricably linked to man's renewal: "The creation waits in eager expectation for the children of God to be revealed." Paul goes on in the passage to say that as part of the creation, we ourselves "groan inwardly as we wait eagerly for our adoption, the redemption of our bodies." How accurate a description of our human condition even now, almost two thousand years later.

The heritage of Scripture includes a love for the whole creation. The psalms overflow with a sense of the beauty and grandeur of the creation and the Creator. God's delight in his creation in Genesis is carried forward in the garden theme throughout the Old and New Testaments and culminates in the book of Revelation, when access to the Tree of Life is restored.

The Creator's care for the creation is seen in the three gardens in the Bible: the garden of Eden, a garden of beginnings and calling as life-givers and preservers; the garden of Gethsemane, a garden of suffering and cleansing; and the garden of the Resurrection and new creation. Each garden tells its own story. In each garden, the Creator, who gives us life and responsibility, engages us in a dramatic dialogue which reveals our relationship to him, the earth, and our neighbor.

Environmental responsibility is part of the core of Christian life and faith. From Eden onward, the story of the Bible is the story of a God who seeks to fully redeem and re-create that which, and those whom, he made and loves. Indeed, the Christian message offers hope for the alarming pollution of the planet by first redeeming and recycling the human heart and spirit.

With the mind and spirit of Christ, we become gardeners, or stewards, of the earth in its fullness. Transformed lives are marked by maturity, wisdom, and self-control. We reject the driving, groping pace of consumerism and careerism. We name and constructively solve real problems. We develop the capacity to love and to share with those in poverty so that they are not forced to use the earth's resources in unsustainable ways. We seek to understand and live out an ecology of life that preserves both interior and exterior environments. We begin, like Christ, to see dumping grounds as gardens and then roll up our sleeves.

We can no longer afford to focus on the present at the expense of the future. When we look into the New Testament, we see that Jesus not only lived a profound ecological ethic but he created a redemptive community to live out creative solutions to any challenge the world could offer.

For reflection and discussion

In the words of Vera Shaw's friend biologist Calvin DeWitt, "A true grasp of faith leads us to a vision of harmony between human beings and nature, and the new life that has come to us through our relationship to Jesus Christ implies power to achieve that vision."[1]

A good starting place is to learn the environmental history of the area where we live, and what influences are protecting or destroying its natural beauty. Then try working together, as neighbors around the world, to preserve the beauty of life in the threatened garden planet.

- What gardens can you identify in your personal life? Your workplace? Your neighborhood? Your community?
- What practical steps have you taken to enhance these gardens? What steps do you want to take? How might our choices have a "ripple effect" among others?
- How can you offer help to others to make this garden planet better for them too?
- When you pray, how does God's care for the earth affect what you ask or ask for?

The Virtue of Holiness: A Vivid Thing

Note: *You'll notice that several entries this week share a call to holiness and reform, both for individuals and for the culture at large.*

By Betsy Childs, former associate writer for Ravi Zacharias International Ministries, whose work originally appeared in the organization's Internet daily feed "A Slice of Infinity."

WEEK 12

In a short essay called "Piece of Chalk," G. K. Chesterton describes one of his favorite childhood pastimes: drawing with chalk on brown paper. He prefers brown paper to white because the colors of the chalk stand out more vividly against its rough, dark background. The most essential piece of chalk in his collection is the white one. He writes, "One of the wise and awful truths which this brown-paper art reveals is this, that white is a color. It is not a mere absence of color; it is a shining and affirmative thing, as fierce as red, as definite as black."

I suspect most of us have been guilty of thinking of white as an absence of color; in fact, white light includes colors of every other wavelength. Chesterton draws a parallel between our mistaken thinking about the color white and our mixed-up perspective on virtue. He writes, "The chief assertion of religious morality is that white is a color. Virtue is not the absence of vices or the avoidance of moral dangers; virtue is a vivid and separate thing, like pain or a particular smell."

Have you fallen into thinking of virtue as the mere absence of vice? I have, on more than one occasion. I once led a Bible study on the subject of pride, and one of the participants asked if we were going to also study humility. "Oh, no," I responded. "If you can conquer pride, you've achieved humility." However, more study and a few more years of battling my own pride convinced me that I was dead wrong. It is only by pursuing the positive fruit of humility that we can ever hope to battle pride. Humility is not the mere absence of pride, any more than white is the absence of color. Humility is a "vivid and separate thing," a prize worth pursuing. It is only when we learn through humility to think on things greater than ourselves that we will be able to abandon our pride.

C. S. Lewis noted a similar misconception in his sermon "The Weight of Glory." Lewis writes, "If you asked twenty good men today what they thought the highest of the virtues, nineteen of them would reply, Unselfishness. But if you asked almost any of the great Christians of old he would have replied, Love. You see what has happened? A negative term has been substituted for a positive."[1]

We should be careful to avoid substituting negatives for positives. When God commanded his people to be holy, he did not base his command first and foremost on the detestability of sin. He grounded this command in his own character, saying, "You shall be holy because I am holy." Yes, God hates and abhors what is unholy, but this abhorrence springs from his delight in what is good and true, namely himself. Like him, we should not look at the joyful pursuit of holiness as the wearisome extermination of vice. We should not merely hate what is evil, we should also cling to what is good. In doing so, we move from the defensive to the offensive, a move that is a major turning point in the winning of any war.

For reflection and discussion

- Does anything surprise you in this entry? Explain.
- In the past, how have you thought of "holiness"? Does it seem optional? Or "religious"?
- What about Jesus Christ stands out to you as shining and affirmative and fierce?
- What virtues among your friends stand out as "shining" and "white"?
- Is there a particular area in which God is leading you into shining virtue?

The French Revolution:
Lessons in Spiritual Influence

By **Keith Bower**, PhD, pastor, speaker, and author of *Courageous Faith: Trusting God When Times Are Tough*. Bower has taught Western civilization and is adjunct professor in theological studies at Dallas Theological Seminary and a Disneyphile.

WEEK 12

They had become a familiar sight as they made their way through the streets of revolutionary Paris. Once a spectacle, soon commonplace, these small wooden carts, the tumbrels, carried the enemies of the Revolution from their prison cells at the Conciergerie near Notre-Dame to the Place de la Révolution and the guillotine. Look at the condemned as they pass: men and women, young and old, educated and ignorant, rich and poor, aristocrat and commoner ... and clergy.

Estimates are that 6 percent of the tens of thousands beheaded during the Terror were clergymen. Once privileged members of France's "First Estate," churchmen and indeed the church itself came to be considered enemies of the Revolution. How different from post-revolution America, where religion thrived at the very center of life and culture. What had happened in France to drive the church from the hearts of the people?

One might suppose that Christianity, with its emphasis on things spiritual, had simply collapsed under the weight of Enlightenment skepticism. After all, a growing number of intellectuals throughout Europe, including France, were adopting a worldview that would increasingly consider miracles implausible and the notion of an intervening God unnecessary. Perhaps Christianity was just too spiritual for the New France.

But no. In revolutionary Paris, forces more powerful, more primal were at work. The French clergy were condemned not before the tribunal of Enlightenment skepticism but before that of popular outrage. The church had indeed failed the test, but not the test of intellectual credibility. The church had failed the test of social justice. The people renounced the church because the church had abandoned the people. When the poor needed a voice, the church kept silent. When the multitudes needed food, churchmen hoarded the loaves and fishes for themselves.

Those who experience the extravagance of Versailles often feel it, even today: the injustice, the provocation, the sense of revolutionary inevitability. Certainly no one living on an island of such opulence in a sea of such desperation could have been caught off guard. Yet the nobility were not alone on this island. The clergy were there too. Though the parish priests were typically commoners, the higher clergy were aristocrats as devoted to power, position, and possessions as their noble brethren.

What happened to the church in France? It's not that the French church was too spiritual, but that it was too worldly. It's not that it was insufficiently influential, but that it was insufficiently godly. It did not do the things that Jesus did. And it failed to heed his warning: "You are the salt of the earth. But if the salt loses its saltiness, how can it be made salty again? It is no longer good for anything, except to be thrown out and trampled underfoot" (Matthew 5:13).

When the people of God adopt the priorities of the world, we are tempted to comfort ourselves that power, possessions, and prestige can be useful, giving us credibility and influence to do God's work. Yet Jesus reminds us that the real source of our spiritual influence lies elsewhere: "Let your light shine before others, that they may see your good deeds and glorify your Father in heaven" (Matthew 5:16). We worship the Son of God for his lowliness, his humility (Philippians 2:5 – 8), for his willingness to be poor in earthly things that we might become rich in heavenly things (2 Corinthians 8:9).

For reflection and discussion

- What comparisons come to mind between the church in France and the contemporary situation in America?
- How do you think we can avoid the pitfalls of the political seduction of the church?
- What gift of service might you offer today as a testimony to the reality and worth of the Lord Jesus?
- How do you want to pray about your political involvement? About your service to others?

Rousseau

By **Nancy Pearcey**, PhD, former Francis A. Schaeffer scholar at the World Journalism Institute and now scholar of worldview studies at Philadelphia Biblical University. Adapted from her book *Total Truth: Liberating Christianity from Its Cultural Captivity*. Pearcey is editor at large of *The Pearcey Report*; *www.pearceyreport.com*.

Most of the ideologies that bloodied the twentieth century were influenced by Rousseau. His writings inspired Robespierre in the French Revolution, as well as Marx, Lenin, Mussolini, Hitler, and Mao. So if you get a grip on Rousseau's thinking, you have a key to understanding much of the modern world.

What exactly was it that made his worldview so revolutionary? Rousseau said the way to grasp the essence of human nature was to hypothesize what we would be like if stripped of all social relationships, morals, laws, customs, and traditions. This original condition he called the "state of nature." In it, all that exists are disconnected, autonomous individuals, whose sole motivating force is the desire for self-preservation. Social relationships are not ultimately real; instead they are secondary, or derivative, created by individual choice.

What did that mean for Rousseau's view of society? If our true nature is to be autonomous individuals, then society is *contrary* to our nature — artificial, confining, oppressive. That's why Rousseau's most influential work, "The Social Contract," opens with the famous line, "Man is born free, and everywhere he is in chains." He did not mean chains of political oppression, as we Americans might think. For Rousseau, the really oppressive relationships were personal ones like marriage, family, church, and workplace.

This was a stark break from traditional Christian social theory, which takes the Trinity as the model of social life. The biblical picture of ultimate origins is not one of solitary individuals wandering under the trees in a state of nature. Instead the picture is one of a couple — male and female — related from the beginning in the institution of marriage, forming the foundation of social life.

The implication of the doctrine of the Trinity is that relationships are just as ultimate or real as individuals; they are not the creation of autonomous individuals, who can make or break them at will. Relationships are part of the created order and thus are ontologically real and good. The moral requirements they make on us are not impositions on our freedom but expressions of our true nature. By participating in the civilizing institutions of family, church, state, and society, we fulfill our social nature and develop the moral virtues that prepare us for our ultimate purpose — to become citizens of the heavenly city.

This explains why it was so revolutionary when Rousseau proposed that individuals are the sole ultimate reality. He denounced civilization, with its social conventions, as artificial and oppressive. And what would liberate us from this oppression?

The state. The state would destroy all social ties, releasing the individual from loyalty to anything except itself. Rousseau spelled out his vision with startling clarity: "Each citizen would then be completely independent of all his fellow man, and absolutely dependent on the state." No wonder his philosophy inspired so many totalitarian systems.

Ideas have consequences, both politically and personally. Rousseau and his mistress had five children — and, one by one, each was abandoned on the steps of a state-run orphanage. Records show that most children in the orphanage died or became beggars. Knowing that, Rousseau felt a need to defend his actions, and he did so by arguing that the state is more qualified than parents to raise children. Was this personal rationalization the source of his political philosophy? Does it explain why he portrayed family ties as oppressive — and the state as liberator? In his final book, Rousseau lamented that he had "lacked the simple courage to bring up a family."

For reflection and discussion

- How do you experience the goodness of personal freedom in choosing your relationships and associations? How do you experience the goodness of commitment and obligation to family, friends, and community? How do you think they prepare you to be a kingdom kind of person, suited for life in a new heaven and a new earth?
- At the heart of the universe we find relationship, community in the Trinity. What implications do you find for your life with God? With others?
- How do you want to respond to God about this reading?

The Strange Small World
of Quantum Mechanics

By Michael G. Strauss, PhD, an experimental high energy and particle physicist currently teaching at the University of Oklahoma. He was an academic guide at the Stanford Linear Accelerator Center.

During the first few decades of the twentieth century, physicists began to probe into the structure of the atom and unlock the secrets of the subatomic world. Their discoveries revealed that our everyday perception of how things "should be" didn't really operate at very small distances. The theory that emerged, quantum mechanics, perfectly describes the universe at distances about the size of an atom and smaller, yet it defies our common logic.

I first encountered this strange quantum mechanical world while studying physics as an undergraduate student and found the predictions of quantum mechanics hard to understand and harder to believe. Yet every one of these predictions has been verified in the laboratory and been shown to be true. If you or I were able to shrink to the size of an atom, we would encounter a very unfamiliar world. For one thing, we could be in two places at one time. I could be at home mowing the lawn at the same time I was lying on the beach in the Bahamas. Doesn't that sound great! Unfortunately, I can only be in two places at one time as long as no one sees me. As soon as a neighbor sees me mowing, then I cease to exist in the Bahamas and exist only in my yard. How disappointing!

In our subatomic world, objects often pop into existence out of nowhere, then quickly disappear. It's as if two pieces of cherry pie appear on your table, but before you can eat them, they disappear. Then two golf balls appear and disappear, and so forth. These things always appear and disappear in pairs because one of the objects is made of matter and the other object is made of anti-matter. So you really would get one piece of pie and one piece of anti-pie.

In the quantum mechanical world, it is impossible to simultaneously know the exact position and momentum of an object. This makes it very difficult to throw a baseball back and forth with someone. If I know where the baseball is, I don't know how fast it is moving, so I can't tell when it will get to my baseball glove. If I know how fast it is moving, then I can't know exactly where the ball will be or where I should place my glove. There are many more examples of how strange and mystifying our universe is when we shrink to the size of an atom, but I'm sure you get the picture.

Maybe the most remarkable aspect of quantum mechanics is that all of these bizarre properties are mandatory if we are to exist. Quantum mechanical features make the chemistry of life possible and fine-tune the fundamental constants of nature. Without quantum mechanics, there would be no life. I am truly amazed at this. The Creator of the universe is so imaginative that he designed a subatomic world totally different than anything we normally experience, yet if it were any different, we couldn't even exist.

The prophet Isaiah writes, " 'For my thoughts are not your thoughts, neither are your ways my ways,' declares the LORD. 'As the heavens are higher than the earth, so are my ways higher than your ways and my thoughts than your thoughts'" (Isaiah 55:8 – 9). When I can't figure out what God is doing in my life, or when the world around me just doesn't seem to make sense, I remember the lessons from quantum mechanics: The God of the universe often does things quite differently than I would ever imagine, but his ways are always perfect and masterfully designed to accomplish his divine plan.

For reflection and discussion

This seems odd, humorous, and mind-boggling, almost as if God could never be reduced to a predictable formula (even though quantum mechanics has some good formulas). Perhaps it's because he, the Creator, is in real time holding the universe together, and that without his present love and control it would all fall apart. "Mystery," wrote Flannery O'Connor, "is a great embarrassment to the modern mind." Things aren't always figurable.

- How do you read and make sense of quantum mechanics from this entry?
- Does it connect in some way to your own life?
- How might this give you peace in what at times seems to be a chaotic world?
- Let's thank God for holding the universe, and us, all together. (. . . and for humor, the Bahamas, golf balls, and cherry pie.)

Oscar Wilde's Portrait of a Soul

By Kelly Monroe Kullberg

Irish novelist Oscar Wilde (1854 – 1900) was a literary genius known for his sardonic wit. After two decades of that wit deployed against traditional morality, Wilde wrote *The Picture of Dorian Gray*. Readers were stunned by Wilde's piercing clarity about immorality's corruption of the soul and the pride that would objectify others for personal pleasure and power. Once common fare in schools, *Dorian Gray* is now often dismissed as a "morality play." And Wilde's deathbed conversion is rarely mentioned in literary circles. But the writing and story are brilliant. It is Wilde's magnum opus.

In the novel, the young Dorian Gray, strikingly pure and handsome, catches the eye of a fine portrait artist named Basil. As Dorian sits for his portrait, an older and capricious onlooker named Lord Henry begins to reorient and mentor Dorian in the wisdom of the world and the superior value of physical beauty, pleasure, vanity, luxury, and youth. Over time, Dorian begins to shed the people of humility and charity in his life in deference to other voices, new intrigues, and secret knowledge. No sensation, if pleasurable or taboo, is avoided. Lord Henry had a disciple.

The painting took on special importance. Like Narcissus, Dorian fell in love with his own image. And he wondered how he might preserve forever his appearance of youth, innocence, and beauty. He feared growing old, knowing his beauty would then be gone. Desperate to retain the youth of the portrait, he made a deal with the Devil — an exchange — and lost his soul.

Years passed and Dorian kept his youth and his beauty, as if he would forever look like that painting by Basil. Scandal entered his life. First there was the suicide of a woman he loved. Then he had other women and prostitutes, bouts with opium, and men whose reputations and lives were ruined by Dorian's seductions. For two decades, given the human tendency to confuse beauty with goodness, society allowed Dorian to roam free.

The portrait changed, showing the effects of Dorian's vanity, cruelty, and lust. It became increasingly hideous and mocking until Dorian finally locked it away in a closet.

One night while Dorian played the piano, Lord Henry, who had taught him the value of beauty and pleasure, said, "By the way, Dorian, what does it profit a man if he gains the whole world and loses — how does the quotation run? — his own soul?"

Then the artist accidentally discovered the painting and is shocked by what he sees. He finally understands how Dorian has been able to remain beautiful despite his sinful life. He tells Dorian to trust in Christ and repent. Tells him his "sins, though scarlet, will be white as snow."

Dorian refuses and becomes so enraged, he murders Basil to silence him. And, to remove every reminder of his deal with the Devil, Dorian Gray uses the knife on what has become the hideous portrait of his soul. (I'll leave the ending for you to read, at *www.gutenberg.org*, but I recommend the book.)

Oscar Wilde's insights are so vivid because he was writing about his own life. Like Dorian Gray, Wilde delved into aberrant sexuality and addictions, betrayed women (in Wilde's case, his wife), and injured various other women and men (and perhaps boys), who could not resist Wilde's fame and charm. Never at a loss for words, Wilde, in his thirties, would say, "When you are as old as I am, the only thing worth living for is sin." Another of his witticisms: "The only thing worse than being talked about is *not* being talked about."

In 1895, at the age of forty-one, Wilde was convicted of the crime of "gross indecency" and imprisoned for two years. In jail, he had the time and the inclination to read the Bible and the writing, *Pensées*, of a different kind of genius, the mathematician and author Blaise Pascal, who believed that life, art, and beauty soar when bounded by holiness.

Soon after his release from prison, at age forty-six, Wilde lay dying of syphilis, isolated and in poverty. Though Dorian Gray had refused mercy, Oscar Wilde seemed to want it very much. He seemed to realize that he'd misjudged where freedom, and pleasure, could be found. He asked for a priest to give him the last rites of the church he had spent his life fleeing. He was buried in Paris, in a church graveyard, near the tomb of Blaise Pascal.

For reflection and discussion

Note the kindness of God in Wilde's life, not condemning but rather appealing to Wilde in jail through Scripture, through *Pensées*, through believers. Paul said there is "a sorrow that leads to death" and "a sorrow that leads to repentance" and new life.

- How do you think a portrait of your soul would appear to you? To God?
- How can that image of a soul be renewed? Made pure again?
- How have you dealt with regret for mistakes in your life? And for mistakes against you?
- Can you trust God to forgive and forget so you can live moving forward?
- Are you called to reach out to someone with the message of grace?

Postmodern Architecture

Postmodern: *a challenge to (or rejection of) modern truth claims about language, culture, history, and identity, even truth itself; tolerance of contradictions; loss of faith in grand meta-narratives (stories) that try to explain origins, morality, meaning, or destiny.*

By Gene Edward Veith, PhD, provost and professor of literature, Patrick Henry College. Adapted from his book *Postmodern Times*. Veith is culture editor of *World* magazine; *www.geneveith.com*. View postmodern architecture at *www.greatbuildings.com/types/styles/post_modern.html*.

The modernist architectural aesthetic was based on the principle of "form follows function." Instead of designing a structure around some preexisting meaning or form, the function of the building should have priority. As those who worshiped in traditional [cross-shaped] churches were always reminded, worship is a matter of being gathered into his cross. The modernist approach to church design would first ascertain the practical functions the building needed to fulfill — accommodate a certain number of worshipers, classrooms for Sunday school, etc.

Those who built the Pruitt-Igoe housing project in St. Louis designed a form to follow the function of solving the housing problems of the urban poor. Designed according to every modernist principle, the project proved unlivable. In 1972 the city dynamited Pruitt-Igoe, marking the end of modernism in architecture.

Disillusioned with the modernist dogma that the present is always the best, architects and the public they serve rediscovered the value and beauty of the past. They started restoring old buildings. Whereas modern architecture is abstract, postmodern architecture is referential. Modern buildings look typically drab in their concrete and steel. Postmodern high-rises often flaunt bright colors and rich decorative detail. The ornamentation is flagrantly nonfunctional and often draws from past styles. A contemporary building may include Art Deco touches from the 1920s or updated classical columns or simplified Victorian bric-a-brac.

Postmodern architect Robert Venturi, author of *Learning from Las Vegas*, celebrates buildings that frankly cater to the whims and fancies of ordinary people (such as the gaudy luxury of Vegas hotels). He sees nothing wrong with buildings that are playful, funny, or in conventionally bad taste.

Much postmodernist architecture is like the New York City AT&T building (Philip Johnson, 1978). It pilfers various historical styles and works them into a pastiche (the characteristic postmodernist form), void of coherence or meaning. The combination of discordant styles (modernism, baroque, classicism) is a sort of joke. By lifting these incompatible styles out of history and tacking them together, the styles lose their significance. History is reduced to a smorgasbord of styles, to be sampled according to one's taste. The effect is to deconstruct style and relativize history.

Some postmodernist architects have set about overtly deconstructing their own designs, mocking both their forms and their functions. James Wine designed a series of Best stores that made people driving by do a double take. One of his stores in Milwaukee looked as if it were falling apart. The front wall was apparently peeled away in a pile of bricks, revealing shelves holding plastic replicas of lamps, toasters, and Barbie dolls. A customer would walk past this facade, past the plaster replicas, through the glass doors, and into the store with its shelves of real lamps, posters, and Barbies. With its fake rubble and gaping hole, the store was designed as a parody of itself, not so much a construction as a deconstruction.

Contemporary architecture has a curious feature, the confusion of interiors and exteriors. If you walk from the street into a new office building, the first thing you see inside may well be trees! Many buildings today include atriums complete with trees, nature paths, and bright sunlight.

Just as the atrium brings the outside inside, many postmodernist buildings bring the inside outside. Structural framework such as beams and ventilation ducts may appear on the surface. An extreme example is the Pompidou Center in Paris (1977). Support beams, tie-rods, and the plumbing appear to be on the outside of the building, painted in bright garish colors. An escalator snakes along the exterior of the building. It is as if the building were turned inside out. The effect is unsettling, like looking at a man but seeing only his insides — his lungs, blood vessels, and red guts.

What has been happening in architecture illustrates what has been happening throughout the arts and the culture since the collapse of modernism. The postmodern rejection of absolutes, it's triviality and relativism, and its penchant for self-gratification all undercut Christianity. The temptation is to capitulate to the new mind-set rather than work to redeem it. But the post-modern age also has room for Christianity in ways that modernism did not. The postmodern openness to the past, its rejection of narrow rationalism, its insistence that art refers to meanings and context beyond itself — these insights are all useful to the recovery of a Christian worldview.

For reflection and discussion

- What elements of postmodern style have been built in your area? How do you respond to their design, especially compared to the simple geometric shapes and the concrete, steel, and glass designs of modern structures?

Postmodernists take comfort in the demise of modernism's confidence that man, starting from his own reason, education, and technology, can solve our problems. They search to understand: How do we know what is true and good? Where have we come from? Where are we going? How do we find purpose and meaning? Yet they have little confidence that answers can be found. The journey is everything, and they find comfort in sharing it with a loving circle of people and place great value on relationships and authenticity.

- In what ways might this view resonate with you? What do you think post-modernism offers in a positive way?
- In what ways might you find a postmodern view lacking? Can the journey be better than the arrival at the destination?
- How do you think Jesus embodies or transcends these two viewpoints? What value does he place on truth and certainty? On relationships?
- How might God want to strengthen your confidence in his Truth? How might he want you to seek and speak truth in love, guarding relationships?

The Pursuit of Happiness

By **Catherine Hart Weber**, PhD, adjunct professor, Fuller Theological Seminary. Weber is a licensed marriage and family therapist and author of *Stressed or Depressed: A Practical and Inspirational Guide for Parents of Teens*; *www.hartinstitute.com*.

Two are better than one.... If they fall down, they can help each other up.

ECCLESIASTES 4:9 – 10

Despite ever-present cell phones and WiFi connectivity, the interpersonal infrastructure of America is weakening. Lifestyles are busy. We don't mean to, but it's getting harder and harder to keep relational connections, and we are suffering for it. "There is an epidemic of isolation and unhappiness in our society," says Dean Ornish, and it is associated with increased stress, depression, illness, and other health risks.

Robert Putnam in his book *Bowling Alone* draws on evidence including 500,000 interviews revealing how contemporary Western culture has become increasingly disconnected from family, friends, neighbors, and other social structures. He warns that if we do not reconnect with each other, we will continue suffering the impoverishing of our lives and our communities. Changes in work, family structure, suburban life, television, computers, women's roles, and other factors have contributed to this decline, and we need to reevaluate their impact on our well being.

God has wired us for connection. *Our health and our happiness depend on it to thrive.* Leading scholars in the new "Positive Psychology" movement are redirecting research away from what causes mental illness to discover what elevates life satisfaction and mental wellness. They pinpoint advertising and the consumer culture as culprits in creating a mindset that material things and status will bring instant happiness. Clearly they don't and money doesn't. How can we prioritize a balanced lifestyle, relationships, and health over work, money, and consumerism?

At the top of the list of greatest predictors of happiness are our intimate connections with people: family, friendships, and the groups we are part of. Data from the University of Chicago's National Opinion Research Center reveal that people with five or more close friends (excluding family) are 50 percent more likely to describe themselves as "very happy" than respondents with fewer. And overall, married people have been found to be happier than unattached individuals.

Community is at the heart of the Trinity, and it is not good even for God to be alone. Being created in the image of God, we've been designed for sociability, to be connected to God and interconnected together in unity, functioning as "the body" of Christ.

Other research findings show a connection between *close relationships* and *better coping skills* when confronted by stress, trauma, loss, and illness. Love and intimacy have healing qualities. There is value in friendship. Two really are "better than one." We do better together — sharing in bearing one another's burdens and rejoicing in celebrations. The support of others can ease devastation and disappointment and open up the possibility for healing and happier living.

This is remarkably illustrated in the true story of an unlikely friendship that came out of the December 2004 tsunami. Villagers in the small coastal town of Malindi rescued a frightened orphan baby hippo, who had been washed to sea. They took "Owen" to an animal sanctuary near Mombasa, where he was offered a home along with bushbucks, monkeys, and a giant 130-year-old Aldabra loner tortoise called Mzee. Owen was angry, weak, and exhausted from his stormy loss and capture and was not eating. Over the next few days, he began to follow the loner Mzee around, who slowly became friendlier. Then Owen started feeding right beside Mzee. Over the weeks, they became inseparable. They swam together, ate together, and slept next to each other. They rubbed noses and led each other around the enclosure.

Experts are still puzzled about how this unexpected friendship came to be. However, to the people who see their photos, read the reports, watch the films, and visit them at the park, what matters is that, although he suffered great loss and endured much, Owen isn't alone. It matters that Mzee's protective, calming presence saved a traumatized baby hippo's life.

Whether in animals or people, the connecting bond has the power to heal life-threatening loss and stress. As John Piper wrote, "For most people who are passing through the dark night of the soul, the turnaround will come because God brings unwavering lovers of Christ into their lives who do not give up on them."

Across nations and denominations, religious involvement is a positive predictor of happiness. Those active in organized religion — not self-fashioned spirituality — lead healthier, happier, and longer lives. In one study at the National Opinion Research Center, people who said they felt "close to God" were significantly more likely to consider themselves "very happy." C. S. Lewis goes even further, saying, "God cannot give us a happiness and peace apart from himself, because it is not there. There is no such thing."

The new scientific research confirms God's message to us: to pursue our own happiness is to pursue connection. On my own journey, I'm becoming more intentional about following the longings of my soul for "more" by taking the initiative to gather with others for meaningful interaction; serving, using my character strengths and spiritual gifts; being authentic and transparent in confessing and forgiving; and intentionally making room for intimacy with God in the rhythms of daily life. As we draw close to God, he draws close to us. And our lives are blessed with ensuing enrichment and happiness.

For reflection and discussion

- Where are you taking initiatives to build connection and intimacy with family members? Neighbors? Workplace associates? Fellow Christians? If you are an introvert, what unique challenges does that present? If you are an extrovert?
- As you look back over the readings this week, you'll find a frequently visited theme of radical autonomy vs. community. Which piece was the most meaningful to you in this regard? Why?
- What are you doing to develop your relationship with God?

The Fairness and Mercy of God

By R. C. Sproul, PhD, teacher, theologian, and pastor. Adapted from *Reason to Believe*. Sproul is founder of Ligonier Ministries, a TV/radio broadcaster, author of over sixty books, and producer of more than three hundred lecture series and eighty video series; *www.ligonier.org*.

Note: *We tend to think of God's fairness from the perspective of our life's experiences. This reading asks us to look at the issue from God's perspective.*

Let us suppose that there is a God who is altogether holy and righteous. Suppose that God freely creates mankind and gives the gift of life. Suppose he sets his creatures in an ideal setting and gives them the freedom to participate in all the glories of the created order. Suppose, however, that God imposes one small restriction upon them, warning that if they violate that restriction, they will die. Would such a God have the right to impose such a restriction with the penalty of forfeiture of the gift of life if his authority is violated?

Suppose that for no just cause his creatures disobeyed his restriction. Suppose when he discovered their violation, instead of killing them, he redeems them. Suppose the descendants of the first transgressors broadly increased their disobedience and hostility toward their Creator to the point that the whole world became rebellious to God and each person "did what was right in his own eyes."

Suppose God still determined to redeem these people and freely gave special gifts to one nation in order that, through them, the whole world would be blessed. Suppose God delivered this people from poverty and enslavement to a ruthless Egyptian pharaoh. Suppose this privileged nation, as soon as it was liberated, rose up in further rebellion against their God and their liberator. Suppose they took his law and violated it consistently.

Suppose that God, still intent upon redemption, sent specially endowed messengers to plead with his people to return to him. Suppose the people killed the messengers and mocked their message. Suppose the people then began to worship idols fashioned by their own hands. Suppose these people invented religions that were contrary to the truth of the real God and worshiped creatures rather than the Creator.

WEEK 13

Suppose in an ultimate act of redemption God himself became incarnate in the person of his Son. Suppose this Son came into the world not to condemn the world but to redeem the world. But suppose this Son of God was rejected, slandered, mocked, tortured, and murdered. Yet, suppose that God accepted the murder of his own Son as punishment for the sins of the very persons who murdered him. Suppose this God offered to his Son's murderers total amnesty, transcendent peace that comes with the cleansing of all guilt, victory over death, and eternal life.

Suppose God gave these people as a free gift the promise of a future life that would be without pain, without sickness, without death, and without tears. Suppose that God said to these people, "There is one thing that I demand. I demand that you honor my only begotten Son and that you worship and serve him alone."

Suppose God did all that. Would you be willing to say to him, "God, that's not fair, you haven't done enough"?

For reflection and discussion

- Considering the way God's mercy is described, what encourages you? Challenges you?
- What do you think of this article's fairness? Of God's fairness?
- If you might respond that what God has done is "not enough," what do you long for God to do? How might you offer those longings to God?

For over 1,500 years Christians have prayed the Jesus prayer as a way of being aware of God's presence throughout the day. Perhaps you would like to rest in the wide-open mercy of God as you pray throughout the day, "Lord Jesus Christ, have mercy on me."

The Great Awakenings and an Emerging America

By Kelly Monroe Kullberg and David Kullberg

Historians generally characterize the early 1700s in the American colonies as spiritually apathetic and morally corrupt. Into this void marched some of history's greatest revivalists, nationalists, and culture-makers.

In the late 1730s, a twenty-five-year-old Englishman named George Whitefield launched a new form of Protestantism in the American colonies. Whitefield had begun preaching outdoors in England because crowds gathering to hear him were too large to fit into the churches. In America he continued to draw record-breaking crowds, preaching in fields, as he traveled from Savannah in the south to Boston in the north. His sermon on the Boston Common in 1740 drew more people than the population of the city.

In the 1740s, revival and compassion began to spread throughout New England under the preaching of Whitefield, Jonathan Edwards, Gilbert Tennent, and others. The Great Awakening was all about spiritual rebirth and a personal knowledge of God's holiness. It drew more people than the civil rights movement and the campus and urban uprisings of the 1960s and '70s combined.

At first, world-renowned free-thinker and rationalist Benjamin Franklin (1706 – 1790) barely knew what to make of such revival. Franklin wrote in his autobiography, "It seemed as if all the world were growing religious, so that one could not walk through the town in an evening without hearing psalms sung in different families of every street." He wrote of the "extraordinary influence of [Whitefield's] oratory on his hearers."[1] At a Philadelphia gathering of thousands, Franklin recalls his own determination to hold on to the money in his pockets when Whitefield took up a collection for an orphanage. But alas, he succumbed. Franklin found himself emptying his pockets of all his silver and gold. The resulting Bethesda Home for Boys still operates today, with countless alumni who otherwise might have lived in poverty all of their lives.

In the cultural milieu of politics and nation-building in the decades to

WEEK 13

follow, George Washington, John Adams, Benjamin Franklin, and Thomas Jefferson would shape and lead America as a free nation. In his book *Serious Times*, historian James Emery White notes, "The American colony was embroiled in a contentious relationship with its mother country, Britain, which would erupt into a declaration of independence and eventually war. Instead of swift defeat at the hands of the British, the conflict birthed a new nation that in just over two centuries would be unrivaled in power and influence."[2]

John Adams (1735 – 1826) embodied the Puritan legacy of devotion to hard work and moral duty and the Enlightenment's devotion to reason and education. His life was immersed in the Continental Congress, the American Revolution, the writing of a constitution for Massachusetts, and the negotiation of the Treaty of Paris. He served as the first American vice president under George Washington and became the nation's second president. Thomas Jefferson (1743 – 1826), strongly influenced by the Enlightenment, drafted the Declaration of Independence and served as the country's first secretary of state, second vice president, and third president. He secured the Louisiana Purchase and founded the University of Virginia.

"My friend," John Adams wrote to Thomas Jefferson near the end of their lives, "you and I have lived in serious times." Indeed they had.

"Serious times met with serious lives," James White wrote. "This is the anvil on which history is forged."[3]

Cultures rise and fall and have the opportunity to rise again. The mid- and late-1800s saw a Second Great Awakening in America — a biblically based response to the Enlightenment's aloof deity. Expressions of faith in the Second Great Awakening were heartfelt and emotional. Many joined boisterous celebrations at camp meetings and demonstrated selfless social activism.

Two organizations begun in England came to America. William Booth, an itinerant preacher, founded the Salvation Army in 1865 to serve the desperate in East London. The "Army" came to America in 1880 and today helps over 33 million people each year with food, shelter, and disaster relief. The YMCA was founded in London in 1844 by George Williams to address unhealthy social conditions brought on by the Industrial Revolution. The YMCA came to Boston in 1851 and today approximately 18 million men, women, and children in the US are served every year. Other examples of faith-based cultural renewal include the Temperance Movement to curb the abuse of alcohol, the Sunday School Movement to spread literacy, and the Abolition Movement to end slavery.

For reflection and discussion

Are you tempted to think our times are irredeemable? So did many Christians in former generations who lived to see revival.

- In what way do you think spiritual and cultural revival can work together?
- How might the first Great Awakening have breathed new life into an emerging nation?
- How might we become a part of a twenty-first-century awakening?

Let's pray and live toward this end.

A Professor Reconstructed

By **Mary Poplin**, PhD, professor of education at Claremont Graduate University and author of *Finding Calcutta*. This article is adapted from her chapter in John Dunaway's *Gladly Learn, Gladly Teach*.

I was a fully tenured professor teaching radical theories as they applied to my own field of education. I had been through structuralism, multiculturalism, radical feminist theory, and was well into critical theory and deconstructivism. Deconstructivists took apart texts and situations in such a way to reveal unstated assumptions and/or contradictions, intentionally complicating the meanings to make the familiar look strange and the strange familiar. This was particularly applied to Western culture to emphasize oppressive characteristics — in a sense, to pull the rug out from previous cultural meanings. Deconstructivism appealed to my desire to be different, radical, nonconforming, and to construct my own definition of reality; it allowed that anything that was ever called truth could be reanalyzed as true only for you, or only in this situation, or not true. Truth, if there was to be any, was simply a social construction ultimately bound to cultured, gendered, social, economic, and political conditions. All "meta-narratives" (truth statements) were suddenly illegitimate, except, of course, this new one.

In actuality I was not really all that novel myself, just following along behind the radical left, bringing their spokespeople to campus and enjoying being part of the in crowd. In reality, the movement did help educators break out of old concepts of educational equality, which were also not true.

At that time if you had asked me about my calling, if I could have answered at all, I would have said it was to stay on the edge of new trends and apply them to education. So I went through one theory after another. Each time the search ultimately would end in boredom. I was constantly trying to escape boredom. One graduate tells me that I told my students they could use any sources in their course papers except the Bible. All the while, I thought of myself as wildly open-minded. I also thought of myself as "spiritual"; I thought I was a "good person" surfing the spiritual net in every arena, from Eastern religious practices to New Age. The only place I would not look was Christianity. I had given up that "meta-narrative" long before trying to give them all up.

I believed the professors and colleagues who told me that Christianity was oppressive and the academy was no place for God; I became one of those professors. It hadn't occurred to me to look around the world to see where people were the least oppressed or to think that if there were a God who created the world and all that is in it, it would matter in the study of everything. This God might have some intellectual, social, economic, scientific, artistic, psychological, even educational principles that might differ from our secular "constructions." The truth is that we do "construct" and "deconstruct" what we believe about reality because we would hate to know that someone, especially God, already knew the truth and that truth had some requirements. For centuries, even most Christian scholars have given up trying to apply Christian principles to our problems and our work in the various disciplines, so the very idea seems either bizarre or strangely medieval, especially to secular colleagues.

In my personal life, I was also escaping boredom. I was like Rahab and had the favor of university colleagues. But soon after my conversion, I was to become something of a leper at the country club. I was to come to understand that Christianity, like any religion — from secular humanism to Buddhism — forms a worldview that holds implications not just for one's personal life but profoundly for the way one approaches one's academic discipline. I was also soon to learn that the radical diversity and academic freedom proclaimed by the university primarily favors leftist and nonmonotheistic worldviews. As George Marsden pointed out, we restrict religious expression often in the name of multiculturalism. I find in the social sciences that certain religious expressions are encouraged by multiculturalism, particularly the more eccentric and Eastern ones, but not so for Christianity, which is proclaimed by radical multiculturalists as part of the oppressive meta-narrative.

But in January 1993, I knelt down during a communion service in the tiny Glen Alpine Methodist Church in which my mother had grown up and said to God, "If you are real, please come and get me." And he did.

After years of secular philosophies, like constructivism and radical feminism, and years of New Age ideas, I began to write the New Testament, Psalms, and Proverbs out by hand, word for word. As I did, I felt my mind begin to clear and heal. I suddenly felt clean. Like Psalm 107 proclaims, "He sent forth his word and healed them" (v. 20 NIV).

Then I truly became a radical and have never since been bored.

For reflection and discussion

Poplin isn't bored because she is in relationship with God, and with people, and because the gospel is relevant to life. She asks us, Who could plumb the depths of the philosophic, social, economic, scientific, political, artistic, educational, and psychological principles of God? Which of us could ever wholly fulfill Jesus' command: "If you hold to my teaching, you are really my disciples. Then you will know the truth, and the truth will set you free." Despite the number of university buildings that have the last part of this command engraved in stone, this is not some secular promise about knowing the truth if we just work at it long and hard enough. It is a command for those who want to know the truth: that knowing and following the Truth are inseparable.

- What seems to have been the turning point for Poplin?
- What was the turning point in your own experience of following Christ?
- What ideas of Jesus strike you as radical? Untried? Scary? Intriguing?

A Scientist's Sense of Wonder

By **Walter L. Bradley**, PhD, distinguished professor of mechanical engineering, Baylor University. During summers, Bradley assists impoverished villages in Indonesia develop practical water, food, and sanitation projects. He has spoken on science and faith at many universities and, in his own living room, while at Texas A&M or Baylor, explored ideas and questions with students.

The psalmist exclaims, "The heavens declare the glory of God; the skies proclaim the work of his hands." (See Psalm 19:1 – 6, 8.) God has left his unmistakable signature for everyone to see. God communicates with us in unique ways as we enjoy the panorama of a starry night or a walk in the woods. In nature we see God's majesty and his power ... and sense his presence. Some of my earliest encounters with God were experienced as a young boy walking home from church on starlit Sunday evenings and camping with my Boy Scout troop.

In Jesus Christ we see and experience God's love for us. While a beautiful painting may thrill and inspire us, meeting the painter and allowing him to share with us more about his life and the ideas he is expressing in the painting would be even more exciting. God's creation draws us to him like the tantalizing smell from a bakery draws us irresistibly.

In Psalm 104, God's providential care for his creatures is described through his works in (not of) creation. In our scientific age, we might tend to dismiss these illustrations as metaphors without meaning, but this would be a deistic rather than theistic view. In the theistic (and Christian) worldview, the laws of nature are seen as describing God's customary and patterned way of caring for his creatures. Miracles describe God caring for his creatures in an extraordinary way. If the sun had come up only once in history, we would still be talking with awe about it today. But because the sun rises daily, we may easily take it for granted, failing to thank God for his providential care in this customary way. We should be thankful for the sunshine, the rain, the produce of earth, and the many ways that God provides for us. And the fact that these provisions may be "described" scientifically by secondary causes does not eliminate God as the primary Causer (Colossians 1:17), a point made clearly by Isaac Newton in his classic *Principia*.

WEEK 13

Maybe the most exciting development of science in the past century has been the emergence of a view of the universe that is very sympathetic to a theistic worldview. The claim in Romans 1:18 – 20 that evidence for the existence of God is "clearly seen, being understood from what has been made," is now supported with a richly diverse set of observations from modern science. "Big bang" cosmology is essentially universally accepted in the scientific community today. A universe that *began* in a big bang rather than a universe that eternally existed clearly supports theism over atheism. Robert Jastrow, founder of the Goddard Space Center and a preeminent astronomer (and agnostic), put it humorously, "For the scientist who has lived by his faith in the power of reason, the story (of the big bang) ends like a bad dream. He has scaled the mountains of ignorance; he is about to conquer the highest peak; as he pulls himself over the final rock, he is greeted by a band of theologians who have been sitting there for centuries."

Galileo asserted, "The laws of nature are written by the hand of God in the language of mathematics." Newton, Galileo, Kepler, and Copernicus, who helped to "birth" modern science, viewed the universe as orderly and capable of mathematical description precisely because a rational God had fashioned it thus. Nobel laureate Eugene Wigner notes, "The miracle of the appropriateness of the language of mathematics for the formulation of the laws of physics is a wonderful gift which we neither understand nor deserve." Albert Einstein saw the comprehensibility of the universe as one of the great and surprising mysteries of nature. Only a brilliant creator could make a universe where physical reality is described by such simple and elegant mathematical equations, each describing a characteristic of God's creation that is crucial to make a habitat for complex, conscious human life.

Another remarkable scientific discovery of twentieth-century science has been the recognition that the universal constants (e.g., the speed of light, Planck's constant, Boltzmann's constant, gravity force constant, the masses of the subatomic particles) must be very finely tuned to provide a universe suitable for complex, conscious life. Nobel laureate Arno Penzias notes, "Astronomy leads us to a unique event, a universe which was created out of nothing, and delicately balanced to provide exactly the conditions required to support life. In the absence of an absurdly improbable accident, the observations of modern science seem to suggest an underlying, one might say supernatural, plan." Princeton physicist John Wheeler adds, "Slight variations in physical laws such as gravity or electro-magnetism would make life impossible.... The necessity to produce life lies at the center of the universe's whole machinery and design." God's purposes are fully realized through his careful design of the cosmos for our benefit.

In Genesis 1:31, we are told that "God saw all that he had made, and it was very good." Modern science has confirmed this in a most remarkable way. In view of the many discoveries of modern science, it takes a great deal more faith to be an atheist than a theist.

For reflection and discussion

- What questions arise as you consider this entry?
- Where do you notice signs of God as creator?
- As you journey through this day, ask God to give you eyes to see in creation his majesty and power as well as his loving, providential care.

Note: *More details on how modern science points to the existence of a Creator can be found at www.leaderu.com/offices/bradley/docs/scievidence.html.*

Screwtape on *The Da Vinci Code*

By Eric Metaxas, author of *Amazing Grace: William Wilberforce and the Heroic Campaign to End Slavery*. A Yale graduate with a rowdy sense of humor, Metaxas is a former staff writer for projects as diverse as Chuck Colson's *BreakPoint* and *VeggieTales*. His unabridged original essay, in the style of C. S. Lewis's *The Screwtape Letters*, is at *www.ericmetaxas.com*.

My dear Wormwood,

I trust this finds you as miserable and stupid as ever. I am pleased to take a respite from our usual tutorial and today croak a paean of praise to a particular work of middlebrow nonfiction, The Da Vinci Code.

It is well worth discussing, inasmuch as it contains such a precariously towering heap of our very best nonthinking that it is quite dizzying! It has the genuine potential to mislead, confuse, and vex millions!

Its principal delight for our side is that in the tacky plastic shell of some below-average "fiction," the book parades as "fact" a veritable phalanx of practical propaganda and disinformation that would make our dear Herr Goebbels (Circle Eight, third spiderhole on the right) jade green with envy.

But where to begin in describing to you its myriad delights? First, a brief synopsis of the plot: a museum curator is murdered by a fanatical albino Christian bigot (nice opening, no?); the curator's granddaughter and an American "symbologist" try to find the real killer and are launched on a wildly implausible and fantastically cryptical search for the proverbial Holy Grail, all the while chased by angry gendarmes and the aforementioned unhinged albino. In the process they (and the lucky reader) discover that: the Church is murderous and evil; the Bible is a hoax; Jesus is not divine, but merely a married mortal and an earnest proto-feminist (!); there is no such thing as Truth; and oh, yes ... orgasm is the truest kind of prayer. Can you stand it? It's as if the author's somehow squeezed all of hell into a walnut shell.

But that's just the irresistible plot, Wormwood. It's the author's technique in so many other areas that is particularly worth our attention. For example, the book seduces its reader by holding out the carrot of "inside knowledge." Make note, Wormwood; it worked wonders for us in Eden and works for us still. The author trots out the moth-eaten, bedraggled idea that all of history is a grand "conspiracy" conducted by some hidden elites! And for the mere price of purchasing this book, the lucky reader will learn the "real" story behind the "official" story that all the other saps have been buying for lo! these many centuries. Heady stuff, eh, Wormwood? This temptation has always been too great for the humans to bear. They ache to be part of that "inside" group that knows what's "really" going on and fall for it every time.

Another extremely admirable facet of this book is the author's intimate knowledge of his audience's skyscraping ignorance, which he exploits to devastating effect. One must ever endeavor to capitalize upon ignorance, Wormwood. This is one of the chiefest weapons in our arsenal. Our subjects' ignorance of history and theology both is of an absolutely unprecedented greatness. Never before have so many known so little about so much of great importance.

Ask your average fellow in the street the slightest detail of a daft sitcom of forty years ago and he will move heaven and earth to supply you with the answer. But ask him to tell you about the Nicean Council, and you will suddenly find yourself in the presence of a weather-beaten cigar store Injun! But then go ahead and ask him who played drums for The Monkees and you will think yourself in the presence of a Voltaire! Our television executives Down Under have been awfully successful!

As I say, this book exploits the ignorance of its readership with an exemplary élan. There's that double whopper with cheese, about how the Emperor Constantine "invented" Christianity in the fourth century! Never mind that people had been believing it for all those years before it was "invented." And in the same masterstroke the author undermines the authority of the Bible by declaring that what it contains arrived on a strictly "political" vote. All of those wonderful "Gospels" that didn't fit with the "patriarchal" version of things were cruelly — always "cruelly" — suppressed and rejected; the oppressive messages it now contains were slipped in to fit Constantine's political agenda! Who among this book's readers will know that for three centuries most of those same Gospels were already considered a part of the scriptural canon? Who among his readers even knows the meaning of the word canonical! My nostrils flare in admiration.

And at the creamy center of the story is the swaggeringly wild idea that Mary Magdalene married Our Chief Enemy! Oh, fatuosity! But it shrewdly plays into what the reader so wants to believe: that Jesus was not divine, and that all the demands that go along with his divinity may be conveniently ignored. And, perhaps most cunningly, it does not dismiss Jesus entirely, but patronizingly reduces him into a toothless "nice guy." And oh, yes, hold onto your horns, Wormwood: Mary Magdalene is the Holy Grail! You see, her womb ... oh, never mind! It's just too rich!

Well, Wormwood, if you can slither past the Early Reader prose and the overcaffeinated, goggle-eyed plot, I think you'll find that you've a veritable textbook on your hands as you stagger downward in mastering the grand and ignoble art of leading souls, one by one, toward a fathomlessly bleak eternity. Cheers.

Your affectionate Uncle,
Screwtape

For reflection and discussion

- If you've read *The Da Vinci Code* or seen the movie, do you share Metaxas's take on this story by Dan Brown? How do you account for its popularity?
- Do you think sarcasm can be successful as a means of persuasion? What are the potential drawbacks? If you've read *The Screwtape Letters* by C. S. Lewis, do you think it worked for Lewis? Why or why not?
- How do you think an understanding of church history can strengthen our faith?
- How might you engage an enthusiastic reader of Brown's book in a redemptive conversation?
- How might you want to pray about these concerns?

Composing for the Twenty-first Century

By Keith Getty. Irish composers and musicians Keith and Kristyn Getty are reinventing the hymn. Throughout Europe and in the US, their music is crossing genres and bridging generations. "In Christ Alone" has been recorded more than two hundred times — including arrangements by popular artists Natalie Grant and The Newsboys; *www.gettymusic.com.*

As we enter the twenty-first century, the Christian church is growing in more countries and languages than ever before. However the sad truth may be that biblical understanding is lower among Christians and church leaders than ever before. The need for depth, and for Christianity to "take root" on a global scale, has never been greater.

Music and lyrics help shape our faith. As "modern worship" is increasingly influential around the world, we must consider the implications of what we sing. To that end, six years ago I began focusing my energies toward the goal of re-creating contemporary "hymns" for today's church.

But don't hymns merely string together dry words that don't engage our interest, never mind our passion? I wondered if anyone would sing them. Would this not take the church back a hundred years, leaving us culturally irrelevant? What is a hymn anyway?

I set out to write hymns with two goals: to teach faith through song and to write in a "timeless" style that every generation could sing. I did not initially call them hymns, but others did, which made sense as these two goals seemed consistent with congregational song-writing through past generations.

In terms of teaching the faith through lyrical content, I wanted to write hymns that recalled the great stories of faith, taught core doctrines, and brought the gospel to the center of worship. Some songs introduce times of repentance or preparing to hear the Word. Many core facets of God's character we find in the Bible, and in particular in the Psalms, have gone without mention in our modern worship songs. Yet to have authentic worship, we need to present an authentic picture of God, as revealed in the Bible, in our music.

To write in a "timeless" and, I hope, enduring style, I lean toward beautiful melodies of my native Irish folk music, my classical sacred training, and even the influence of George Gershwin. A modern hymn style draws congregations together, from ages six to ninety-six, and it can work with an organ, choir, orchestra, or contemporary band.

We try to write songs that are easy to sing, helping congregants enter into worship rather than observing a performance. While the generational appeal has been hugely popular with older folks who feel disengaged with modern worship, the biggest support we've found is among student pastors who've been looking for a new vision for music in the twenty-first-century church.

Hymns also have the ability to endure. Meaningful lyrics are easily remembered. My grandfather would quote hymns, even when he was losing his memory. A pastoral friend challenged me with this thought: "What will new generations remember when they are older if they only sing songs for two years at a time?" He encouraged us to write music and words that are enduring, full of the unchanging riches of God and accessible to as many people as possible.

In the creative spirit of believing artists through the centuries, may God fill us in our day. May he give us mind-renewing worship that endures beyond us and inspires the world in this exciting new century, to the praise of Christ.

For reflection and discussion

Many younger people are surprised to discover the depth of theology and poetry in hymns that are a century or more old. Many older believers are surprised to discover the beauty of new hymns written each year.

- What popular music are you most drawn to? Can you identify what qualities attract you? Do these carry over into church music?
- What worship music has most influenced you? How does music enter into your personal times of worship and prayer? Do both the sound and the lyrics influence you?
- Is there music that you once loved but have lost? Are you open to new music? To "timeless" music?

The Graying of America: Aging, Dying, and Hope

By Kelly Monroe Kullberg and Lael Arrington

Life on a space-time continuum means, among other things, that we are aging. And the very large post-World War II "baby boomer" generation now enters their "sunset years." Implications are enormous for health care and economics and human resources of wisdom.

Experiencecorps.org reports that the number of Americans age fifty-five and older will almost double between now and 2030 — from 60 million today (21 percent of the total US population) to 107.6 million (31 percent of the population). Americans reaching age sixty-five today have an average life expectancy of an additional 17.9 years (19.2 years for females and 16.3 years for males).

The next generation of retirees can anticipate far more from their fourth quarter than previous generations. They will be the healthiest, longest lived, and best educated seniors in history. According to a 2002 survey conducted for Civic Ventures, 59 percent of older Americans see retirement as "a time to be active and involved, to start new activities, and to set new goals." Twenty-four percent see retirement as "a time to enjoy leisure activities and take a much deserved rest," like the couple reported in *Reader's Digest* who took early retirement at fifty-nine and fifty-one. "Now they live in Punta Gorda, Florida, where they cruise on their 30-foot trawler, play softball and collect shells."

Whether seeking pleasure or joy, many seniors anticipate time to create, to study and teach, to grow and share food, to tell and write stories, to paint and photograph, to mentor and grandparent children with needed wisdom, time, and attention — for the best art comes from love, and no one knows the value of love like those who've survived the losses of it ... our elders.

And yet, as we age we grieve the loss of our strength and beauty — the way we were when our muscles were taut and our neurons were firing. As quoted in *Time* magazine, Charles Baird, chairman of a private equity firm in Connecticut, says, "The average seventy-five-year-old will tell you they'd give up 95 percent of their net worth to feel forty-five again."[4]

WEEK 13

We live in a world that worships youth and longs to fly away forever young. If our dreams are all in this world, then time *is* a terrifying enemy and death is the end of our dreams.

But if our dream is to know God, to enjoy him as our greatest treasure, to delight in the Giver behind all the good gifts, to experience his presence in the long watches of hard pain, to dream of playing a crucial role in his eternal kingdom, then the ticktock of the clock brings us closer to the holiday at the sea.

We can say with Paul, "For to me, to live is Christ and to die is gain. If I am to go on living in the body, this will mean fruitful labor for me. Yet what shall I choose? I do not know! I am torn between the two: I desire to depart and be with Christ, which is better by far; but it is more necessary for you that I remain in the body" (Philippians 1:21 – 24 NIV). If we really see the wonder of Christ and his kingdom, we will feel torn. If we don't, we can't even imagine what Paul has seen.

But we are invited to imagine it.

In *Desire*, John Eldredge describes the "great party, the wedding feast of the Lamb. There will be dancing (Jeremiah 31:13). There is feasting (Isaiah 25:6). (Can you imagine what kind of cook God must be?) And there is drinking. At his Last Supper our Bridegroom said he will not drink of 'the fruit of the vine until the kingdom of God comes' (Luke 22:18). Then he'll pop a cork. And the next chapter of the great adventure will begin."[5]

And so we are wise, as Moses prayed, to number our days (Psalm 90). When we approach the Lord Jesus, we want to hold out far more than our collection of seashells. We want to offer him the kind of person that we will enjoy being and he will enjoy being with for all eternity — fruitful, able to offer his love to others in a way that is "necessary" for their wellness and joy. Able to live well because we are able to die well, knowing we are not getting older so much as we are getting closer.

For reflection and discussion

- Picture your eventual retirement. How do you envision it?
- How can you see aging and retirement enriching your relationships?
- Paul says, "I am crucified with Christ." How might our daily death ultimately make our physical death of little or no consequence?
- What are your primary concerns about aging and dying? How do you want to talk to God about them?

Heaven: Headed Home

By Randy Alcorn, founder of Eternal Perspective Ministries and author of more than twenty-five books of both nonfiction and fiction; *www.epm.org, www.randy alcorn.blogspot.com.*

God's people are aliens and strangers, looking for a country of their own. This world, as it is now, under the curse, isn't our home. But one day not only we but the earth itself will be remade. That earth, the new earth, will not only be a place made for us but the place we were made for.

Home as a term for heaven isn't simply a metaphor. It describes an actual physical place — a place of fond familiarity and comfort and refuge.

Scripture often speaks of banquets and feasts in heaven. We'll sit at tables with people we love, above all the Jesus we love. Revelation 21 and 22 tell us God will bring heaven down to this new earth by coming to dwell there with his people. There will be natural wonders, a great river, and the tree of life producing different fruit every month. We should anticipate great sights and sounds and smells and tastes and delightful conversation. On that new world "his servants will serve him" — that means things to do, places to go, people to see.

As resurrected people, we'll live on the new earth, not a non-earthly angelic realm for disembodied spirits. We'll live in our resurrected bodies on a resurrected earth, where the resurrected Jesus will rule on the throne of the new earth's capital city, a resurrected Jerusalem. And we will reign with him as righteous people ruling the earth to God's glory. That was exactly his design from the beginning. The Bible begins and ends with God and humanity in perfect fellowship on earth.

Because we've already lived on earth, I think it will seem from the first that we're coming home; the new earth will strike us as familiar because it will be the old earth raised, as our bodies will be our old bodies raised. The new earth will be the home we've always longed for.

The unbiblical stereotypes of heaven as a vague, incorporeal existence hurt us far more than we realize. They diminish our anticipation of heaven and keep us from believing it is truly our home. Graham Scroggie was right: "Future existence is not a purely spiritual existence; it demands a life in a

WEEK 14

body, and in a material universe."[1] Though many of us affirm a belief in the resurrection, we don't know what that really means. Our doctrine dresses up people in bodies, then gives them no place to go. Instead of the new earth as our eternal home, we offer an intangible and utterly unfamiliar heaven that's the *opposite* of home.

When we think of heaven as unearthly, our present lives seem unspiritual, like they don't matter. When we grasp the reality of the new earth, our present lives suddenly matter. Conversations with loved ones matter. Work, leisure, creativity, and intellectual stimulation matter. Laughter matters. Service matters. Why? *Because they are eternal.* Our present life on earth matters not because it's the only life we have but precisely because it isn't — it's the beginning of a life that will continue without end.

Jesus said, "I go to prepare a place for you." The carpenter from Nazareth knows how to build. He's built entire worlds, billions of them. He's also an expert at *repairing* what's been damaged — whether people or worlds. Romans 8 tells us this damaged universe groans, crying out to be repaired. Jesus is going to repair it, and we're going to live with him on resurrected ground. He's going to repair this earth because he's no more given up on it than he's given up on us.

For reflection and discussion

- What is your favorite literary, musical, or artistic picture of heaven? How might you be hindered by a failure of imagination about heaven?
- When you are finally home with Jesus, what (that is now broken) will you tell him you are most grateful that he repaired and made new?
- How do you want to respond to Jesus about your future and your hope?

Quiet Heroes:
The French Huguenots in World War II

By William Edgar, ThD, has lived in France and America, written books including *Truth in All Its Glory*, and plays jazz and blues piano. He is a prolific author, speaker, and professor of cultural apologetics at Westminster Theological Seminary near Philadelphia; *www.wts.edu*.

Nestled on a plateau in the middle of France are a few villages populated mostly by Huguenots (French Protestants). Life is hard for these farmers, although they manage to make ends meet. They are not particularly well-known, which is just the way they want it. Yet in the heavenly perspective, they are among the great heroes of the twentieth century. For during World War II they managed to harbor over five thousand refugees, most of them Jewish, and protect them from sure deportation to Nazi death camps. Some were even taken off Nazi trains at night. Why the risk? Simple. God, in Scripture, said to be hospitable to strangers and to protect the vulnerable. To do for others what we'd want others to do for us.

The largest of these villages is Le Chambon-sur-Lignon. During the war years their population doubled. They willingly took in these refugees and managed to include them in daily life. Many of them were children. Pierre Sauvage was born there and later went back to do a documentary film on this extraordinary episode. He returned to his birthplace to find a rather reluctant group. They simply did not think of themselves as heroes. As people of the book, they saw their duty to love God and to love their neighbor as the normal Christian life. Never mind that their lives were turned upside down and that they were constantly in danger of Nazi raids. Never mind that they had to make enormous sacrifices in order to feed, to house, and to respect the dignity of these thousands of escapees.

The award-winning documentary *Weapons of the Spirit* shows solid people, strong people, Christian people ready to die for their faith. The Huguenots of France know very well what persecution by a totalitarian power means. Throughout the eighteenth century, they were required to renounce their faith or die. Many of them fled to other countries, including America. Some stayed and resisted. So protecting the Jews was in a way something they had to do. But their low profile makes them so different from the standard celebrity hero of the media.

For reflection and discussion

One striking quality of the Hugenots interviewed in the film is the deep clarity of their faith as their way of life. Of course they would help. God brought Jews to their village. He said to rescue the oppressed. To be kind to strangers. End of discussion.

James 1:27: "Religion that God our Father accepts as pure and faultless is this: to look after orphans and widows in their distress and to keep oneself from being polluted by the world."

As followers of Christ, the "Chambonnais" were practicing what James calls "religion that God our Father accepts as pure and faultless." In the first century, orphans and widows were particularly vulnerable to injustice, and it was the joyful duty of the church to go and bring hope to them. Today the church has the privilege of carrying hope to slaves, war victims, and others who are hurting.

Second, James asks that we abstain from the pollution of the world. In any age, temptation to accommodate is rife. During World War II the temptation was strong to compromise with the forces of occupation. The Huguenots would have none of it. They did everything they could to subvert the occupation, short of violence. Today, the issues may have changed, but not the temptations.

- Who do you think of as a "nonheroic hero"?
- Why might the quiet heroes seem content to remain unnoticed?
- What do they tell us about the difference between "hero" and "celebrity"?
- Are there strangers in our midst we might surprise today with kindness?

The Sleep of Death

By Os Guinness, DPhil, was born in China and educated at Oriel College, Oxford. He is the author of many books, including *The Call* and *Long Journey Home*, and has spoken before countless thousands of students and leaders. Guinness, a writer and social critic, lives in northern Virginia. This excerpt is from *The Call*.

To come of age and come to faith in a tumultuous decade like the 1960s was a bracing privilege. No one could take anything for granted. For those who cared, everything had to be challenged, taken back to square one, thought through, and engaged with one's whole being and not just the mind.

When I was studying philosophy as an undergraduate, an aggressive humanism was the dominant faith on many campuses, and atheism was the reigning philosophy. Many religions were in vogue so long as they were not Christian, orthodox, or traditional.

In particular, hundreds of thousands of young people in the 1960s followed the Beatles, in mind if not body, when they flirted with Eastern religions. First introduced to the Beat movement by poet Gary Snyder and popularized in the newly emerging "counterculture" by one-time Anglican counselor Alan Watts, Eastern religions suddenly became the rage after the visits to the West by the Maharishi Mahesh Yogi and a bevy of Indian gurus and Zen masters. Meditation centers, communes, reincarnation, sitar music all became as familiar as blue jeans and rock music. The *Bhagavad Gita, The Tibetan Book of the Dead*, and Hermann Hesse's *Siddhartha* seemed as widely read as the Bible.

As a new follower of Christ, my desire to understand those on the physical or spiritual road to the East was so strong that I took to the road myself — physically, not spiritually. For more than six months I ranged "the hippie trail," exploring such crowded meccas as Kabul, Goa, Benares, Rishikesh, Katmandu, and Thailand.

Among a host of memories, two stand out because they were linked by the same phrase — "the sleep of death." The first time I heard it used was in Rishikesh, the famous center of the gurus in the foothills of the Himalayas. I was studying in an ashram not far from the Maharishi's, where the Beatles had gone. Most there were Indians, but my roommate was an Italian, a friend

WEEK 14

261

of film director Frederico Fellini, and there were at least twenty-five Europeans and Americans in various stages of initiation into Hinduism.

The guru, who spoke fluent English and was well versed in Western philosophy, would speak of the Westerners as "my refugees." When new people arrived, he would explain that they were refugees not just from the West but also from Western consciousness. They were "refugees from the sleep of death."

Sometimes the guru would expand on this phrase by referring to Plato's parable of the cave — like captive cave dwellers, he said, Westerners had no idea of the world of awareness outside their reason-and-science-bound cave. In Peter Berger's phrase describing the secular world, they were in "a world without windows." Or as Max Weber said famously, secularists are "unmusical" and "tone deaf" — sadly they cannot hear the music by which people of faith orchestrate their lives.

I later went to Katmandu where I again heard the phrase when I entered a cafe frequented by Westerners, accompanied by an English doctor who cared for those in the terminal stages of drug addiction. At least forty young Westerners were slumped with their heads down on the tables. As we entered, a shaft of sunlight broke into the smoky room, and a half dozen or so lifted their heads slowly and stared at us with glazed, unseeing eyes. They then settled down again to the zombie-like stupor in which they spent their days.

Watching to see my reaction to this sight he knew so well, the doctor said simply: "Poor things. They started out to escape a metaphorical sleep of death, and they've ended by succumbing to a real one."

For reflection and discussion

"The sleep of death" — what were the guru and the doctor referring to? These were allusions to romantic poet William Blake, who bemoaned the secular and mechanistic view of life. Mechanistic science, Blake believed, had petrified human life into a machinelike existence that was a form of captivity. Awareness of higher or different levels of reality, whether understood from a Christian, Hindu, or any supernatural viewpoint, was frozen out.

In the '60s, many sought escape from the lie that we are only animal, only machine, without transcendent spirits of some kind. Still today, something inside us rightly rebels from that same lie.

And yet flight from one lie can send us into another — the dangerous cave of sensory illusion and addiction.

Christ offers to fulfill both desires — the goodness of life in the body, in God's world, animated by his Holy Spirit. Followers of Christ flee neither spirit nor flesh and earth. God declares them both good. And he offers to live in and with us, all of our days.

- What is your most poignant memory or impression of the '60s?
- Have you embraced the beliefs and values of your youth? Or did you also decide that "everything had to be challenged, taken back to square one"? What were some of the turning points in your spiritual journey?

Human development scholar William Damon summarizes his research into young people's struggle to find their calling in *The Path to Purpose*: "Fewer than one in five young people in the twelve to twenty-two year age range expressed a clear vision of where they want to go and what they want to accomplish in life. About 55 percent had engaged in some potentially purposeful activities but had no realistic plans for pursuing their aspirations. The remaining portion of those interviewed — nearly a quarter — expressed *no aspiration at all* and little interest in acquiring any."[2]

- How do we experience the sleep of death today? In what ways do we flee into our caves?
- How do you want to pray about this reading? About shaking off the sleep of despair or escape?

Flying by Truth

By Robert Durfey, MPA, Harvard's Kennedy School of Government and US Coast Guard, chief of external affairs, District 1, is a former helicopter instructor pilot and commanding officer of two Coast Guard air stations. Durfey is a consultant in leadership development.

I fly helicopters and enjoy the responsibility and adventure of search-and-rescue missions.

Whether flying aircraft or navigating the trials of life, one's method for determining what is true, and what is false, is a matter of life or death. It's also a matter of abundant life. Flying by the truth, that is, knowing the exact nature of spatial, temporal, and physical realities, makes flight sustainable and missions successful. And, frankly, a lot of fun.

Beginning pilots fly by sight — what their own eyes and fluid in their inner ears tell them (spatial orientation). This is appropriate when the conditions of weather, visibility, and mechanics of the plane are all perfect.

As pilots advance in their training, they learn to "fly by the instruments," which means they submit their senses to the most accurate and sophisticated measures of reality. Advanced pilots are paying attention to their "attitude gyro" that tells them what is up (like the sky) and what is down (like the ocean). The altimeter tells us height above the ground (or not). And the compass tells us what direction we are heading.

Commercial pilots are flying "on instruments" the majority of the time, which is safer than flying solely by sight.

What is not safe, and often disastrous, is when pilots think they can fly visually. Whether low visibility is due to haze, darkness, or storm clouds, many flights have ended tragically short of their destination because the pilot believed something that was not true.

A tragic, public example was the death of John F. Kennedy Jr., with his wife and sister-in-law, off the coast of Massachusetts, en route to Martha's Vineyard. Although the visibility that night was five to eight miles, there was no visible horizon offshore, due to haze. The National Transportation Safety Board determined the probable cause of the accident was the pilot's failure to maintain control of the airplane during a descent over water at night, a result of spatial disorientation. Though the plane was operating normally, Kennedy's eyes and ears were telling his brain something that wasn't true. He wasn't instrument rated, but he believed he could fly visually.

Pilots must learn that disorientation comes easily, and that sight alone cannot be fully trusted. "Trust your instruments" is the mantra of the instructor pilot.

Life is similar. If we're to experience life fully, we must learn to "fly" (live) in stormy darkness, not just when the sky is bright and the sun is shining. Otherwise we're restricted to the hangar and never free to fly above the clouds and rescue those in distress and darkness.

We often have to fly (live) by faith in our instruments and not by our sight. For this reason I've come to see flying as a metaphor for my faith in God.

By trusting the One who is the ever-steady horizon, we can tell when we are turning or descending and we can focus on him. He never changes. When we learn to trust in what he says rather than what we simply want to believe, not only will we arrive safely at our destination but we'll be given many opportunities to help others who've lost their way.

Flying helicopters for the Coast Guard for twenty-three years, with over five thousand hours and four hundred search-and-rescue missions, I've come to appreciate that an "instrument-rated" life is a truly abundant life. While flying for the Coast Guard, I've seen over a hundred blue, gray, and humpback whales off the California coast; I've watched a comet through night-vision goggles over the Gulf of Mexico; I've taken off from the flight deck of a ship and danced along the tops of huge cumulus clouds near the Galapagos Islands; I've flown alongside eagles in the Cascade mountains and brightly colored parrots in the jungles of Central America. I've been blessed to be a member of rescue teams who've found lost children in the mountains, hurricane victims on Caribbean Islands, and desperate mariners at sea. Without my instruments, I would have missed all this because clouds or haze or darkness played a part in each flight.

I've flown over three thousand helicopter flights during the last three decades, but living each day as a follower and imitator of the Designer of flight and the Instructor of life is far more exciting. His "instruments" are trustworthy and life giving. Take the time to be proficient in using them.

For reflection and discussion

Durfey disciplined himself to fly by reality, not just his own judgment. As a result, he's had wonderful adventures and has lived to tell about them. He and his wife, Carolyn, have had some sleepless nights, but they've also had many joys, including rescuing people whom God loves. His rescue missions aren't virtual, they're actual. He lives in a great story, a real story.

Proverbs 3:5 – 6 reads, "Trust in the LORD with all your heart and lean not on your own understanding; in all ways submit to him, and he will make your paths straight."

- What practices or resources in the faith life work like "instruments" to guide you?
- When you do live according to the teachings of Scripture, of Jesus, what adventures, challenges, and greater purposes open up in your life?
- What do you observe about the results of discipline and guidance in the lives of others? In your life?
- Do you have any new goals as a result of thinking about flying by the instruments?
- Have you been called to any search-and-rescue missions? If so, what? Who?

Uncle Tom's Cabin

By Joy Jordan-Lake, PhD in English and American literature, author of *Whitewashing Uncle Tom's Cabin* and the recent novel *Blue Hole Back Home* dealing with racial tensions and redemption in the 1970s South.

She was a diminutive woman who wrote stories, mostly sentimental romances, to help pay family bills. As a woman living in the mid-nineteenth-century, she had no real political voice, and as the wife of a financially struggling professor, she wielded no economic leverage. A mother of six, she had nothing that even remotely resembled free time. Yet her faith led her to the convictions not only that slavery was a moral, ethical, and theological outrage, but also that she, politically powerless as she was, could help eradicate it from her country.

Harriet Beecher Stowe (1811 – 1896) had long been distressed by the existence of slavery in the United States. Having lived for eighteen years in Cincinnati, Ohio, just across the river from a slave state, she had witnessed bounty hunters pursuing fugitive slaves and had taught former slave children in the school the Beecher family ran. She had seen and heard firsthand slavery's atrocities. One Sunday while taking communion in her church, Stowe experienced a vision she believed came from God: a male slave was being beaten to death.

A letter from Stowe's sister-in-law suggested that such a gift for crafting stories as Harriet had demonstrated in domestic literature might be powerfully used for the cause of abolition. That letter marked a turning point. The daughter, sister, and wife of clergymen, Stowe determined to preach her own fiery sermons, only with a paper pulpit.

Personal tragedy, though, brought the issue beyond merely a topic of intellectual and political debate for her. During one of her husband Calvin's trips, the youngest of the Stowe children, baby Charley, fell ill with cholera and eventually died in his mother's arms. Stowe wrote her husband that she felt as if she could not endure the grief that threatened to swallow her whole. She could not go on bearing this sorrow, she confessed, unless she could believe that somehow God could bring some kind of good from her pain. She wept for her own loss, for the child that disease had wrenched from her. All the while,

WEEK 14

267

though, she pictured slave mothers on the auction block as they felt their own children wrenched from them by a perfectly legal system of commerce.

Together these three elements — a direct challenge on the part of a loved one who witnessed her gifts, a personal tragedy, and a spiritual vision — compelled her to begin writing a story that would highlight the horrors of human bondage, one that would change the course of history.

Uncle Tom's Cabin (1852), first released in serial form, became the first book by an American to sell more than a million copies. More to the point, it served as a catalyst in the American debate over slavery. Its images of slave parents and children being torn from each other's arms and of the self-sacrificing yet ultimately powerful Uncle Tom being whipped to death turned thousands of former political fence-sitters into active opponents of the South's "peculiar institution."

As an economically and politically powerless woman of the nineteenth century and a harried mother, Harriet Beecher Stowe had every right to insist she was too busy to be involved with social transformation. But Stowe believed the Christ of the crucifixion and resurrection asked more of her than listening to cultural dictates that insisted women should be publicly silent, the voices shrilling that her sole duty and commitment ought to be the running of her household. She listened to God, took seriously the potential for her own gifts to sway hearts and opinions — and transformed her world.

For reflection and discussion

- What particular kind of injustice most worries or concerns you?
- Despite your limitations and time constraints, can you see any way in which your skills or gifts could be used to confront the problem?
- Perhaps you see strong concerns and gifts in the life of a friend or a child. How could you be the one to encourage him or her to take action?

Bob Dylan: Slow Train Still Coming

By Terry Glaspey, a student of art, theology, and intellectual history with an MA in history. An essayist, Glaspey is the author of several books, including *Book Lover's Guide to Great Reading.*

Bob Dylan (1941 –) is an artist famously reticent to discuss the meanings of his complex and beautiful lyrics. He resists being co-opted by any political or religious philosophy or limited to any musical tradition. During his long and distinguished career, Dylan has worn a variety of hats: a protest folksinger in the Woody Guthrie tradition, a rock-and-roll surrealist poet, a country crooner, a dissector of his own inner demons, a fiery evangelist, and, always — a moralist in the tradition of the biblical prophets.

Dylan is a lyricist without parallel in the history of rock music. Just consider the scope and power of such remarkable songs as "Blowin' in the Wind," "Like a Rolling Stone," "Desolation Row," "Tangled Up in Blue," and "Every Grain of Sand." Each is marked by beautiful melodies and unforgettably poetic phrases, many of which have entered into our cultural lexicon. (View lyrics at *www.bobdylan.com*.)

Then there is that inimitable voice that, while not traditionally beautiful, is filled with an urgency arising from the depths of his own inner struggles. It's an honest everyman's voice, with a painterly sense of knowing how to shape a lyric in unexpected ways for maximum impact. Perhaps it might be helpful to think of Dylan as the Picasso of contemporary music. He ignored the normal standards of singing and writing, creating from his own inner muse a style uniquely his own.

Dylan's lyrics have always had a strong moral center, reflecting a Judeo-Christian worldview even before his later-in-life embrace of Christianity. His earliest songs of political concern are littered with biblical allusion and imagery, empowered by a passion for moral justice and social righteousness. He was always concerned with the personal element of morality, not just the desire for a more just society. In the late '60s and early '70s, a new spiritual tone entered his writing, presumably tied to a rediscovery of his Jewish roots. His album *John Wesley Harding* contained countless biblical allusions, and *New Morning* was even more explicit in the hymnlike "Father of Night."

In 1979 Dylan shocked the world of rock music by releasing *Slow Train Coming*, an overtly Christian album with a gospel sound and a hard-hitting, unambiguously evangelical message. At a time of personal and artistic confusion, he experienced a personal encounter with Jesus Christ that influenced his thinking and his performances. Audiences discovered a new side of Dylan, who now began to testify of his faith between songs and sing with a passion not seen since his earliest days. *Slow Train* and his next two albums, *Saved* and *Shot of Love*, were filled with evidence of the grace he had found in Christ and of his prediction of judgment for a world on the wrong course. These albums set aside much of the poetic ambiguity that had been Dylan's forte and expressed his new-found faith directly.

Then, in the albums that followed, Dylan returned to a more subtle approach to the issues of faith and doubt, although a biblical worldview clearly remained intact. Like many Christian artists, he passed through the "in your face" style of his early evangelistically minded work, exchanging it for a more nuanced and poetic expression.

Recent albums, such as *Time Out of Mind*, *Love and Theft*, and *Modern Times* have wed a prophetic concern for truth and justice with a world-weary realism about the nature of humanity. He writes of the battle between faith and doubt that is being fought out in every human heart. And few have written of it so memorably. To the one who listens closely, Dylan is still singing of a world teetering on the edge of apocalypse and a hope that is found in the God who holds the master plan.

For reflection and discussion

- As you recall a Dylan song you've heard, where does Dylan's poetry and music take you?
- What examples can you offer, from both a work of art and your own experience, of faith coexisting with doubt?
- As you think about Jesus' life, how do you see him responding to doubt (Mark 9:14 – 29)? To faith (Luke 7:3 – 10)?
- How do you see God responding to your own doubt? Your faith?

Today's Slavery

By **Jody Hassett Sanchez** has filmed in India, Pakistan, and Togo for her documentary *SOLD: Contemporary Abolitionists and the Global Slave Trade*; *www.soldthe film.com.*

LOME, TOGO — *Amazing Grace*, the film about William Wilberforce, concludes with what many consider to have been his greatest life work — the abolition of the transatlantic slave trade in 1807. But today, a walk through a dusty open-air market in Lome, Togo, makes it painfully clear that the slave trade is still flourishing, more than two hundred years later.

Tiny boys — they would be considered "preschoolers" in the West — strain to push overloaded wooden carts through the crowded market. Their workday begins before dawn and continues until late in the evening, when they are permitted to collapse beside their cart, in the dirt, for a few hours of rest.

Most of these young laborers can't remember what rural village they came from or who their families are. All they know is that they will be beaten and killed if they attempt to escape those who took them from their homes and force them to do this brutal work.

These child laborers are part of a global slave trade that is more complex and insidious than anything that William Wilberforce could have envisioned. Human bondage comes in many variations today: nine-year-old girls sold into brothels, preteen boys forced to kill for rebel armies, children shackled twenty hours a day to rug-weaving machines. An estimated 27 million people are currently enslaved around the world, operating in a shadow economy valued at approximately $12 billion.

How does one begin to think about taking on such overwhelming evil in the twenty-first century? Are there lessons to be gleaned from Wilberforce's example? It's tempting to regard him as one of history's great men, but the danger of such a view is that it lets the rest of us off the hook. Since most of us can't measure up to his extraordinary example, we convince ourselves that the best action is no action. We watch and wait for an obvious heir to the "Wilberforce legacy," someone we can support with our checkbook and prayers.

The reality is that Wilberforce did not act alone. His bold actions were bolstered by a curious coalition of individuals of differing theologies and political

WEEK 14

271

persuasions, who came together on the issue of slavery. With prayers, perseverance, and a savvy strategy, this coalition — which came to be known as the Clapham group — labored to change the way the British people perceived slavery. It took years, but they finally convinced the nation that slavery was not just an economic issue, it was also a moral issue that demanded redress.

Is a similar shift in the moral climate possible today in our globalized society? As a filmmaker who has spent the past two years documenting those on the front lines of today's abolitionist fight, I'm convinced it is indeed possible. Economic change and education are key components in this fight, but an understanding about human dignity, and the source of that dignity, is also essential. The concept that it is wrong for any individual to own and control another remains as powerful a catalyst for change today as it was in Wilberforce's time.

Piercing this darkness will require people of faith to put aside their theological and political differences — and their egos — to create a committed community. If we, like that curious coalition from Clapham, England, truly believe that every human is created in the image of a Creator, then we don't have a choice. We must take action.

For reflection and discussion

On October 28, 1787, William Wilberforce penned these words in his diary, "God Almighty has set before me two great objects in the suppression of the slave trade and the reformation of manners." It would take twenty years until Wilberforce would win the majority needed to stop the slave trade in 1807. The victory to abolish slavery in the British colonies was achieved just three days before his death in 1833. As we know in America, ending slavery took much longer and the attitudes that made slavery possible are among us still.

- Why is it so difficult to choose goodness and mercy over economic gain? How might you struggle with this problem in your own experience?
- How would you compare the joy of endurance to other joys?
- Do you have a few friends who might form a creative kinship with you to achieve a goal?

Certainly Wilberforce could identify with Romans 5:3 – 5: "We know that suffering produces perseverance; perseverance, character; and character, hope. And hope does not put us to shame, because God's love has been poured out into our hearts through the Holy Spirit, who has been given to us."

The Small and the Big Gospel

By **Scot McKnight**, ThD, professor of New Testament at North Park University and author of *The Jesus Creed* and *A Community Called Atonement* (*JesusCreed.org*). Adapted from the Christian Vision Project and *Christianity Today*.

Our problems are not small. The most cursory glance at a newspaper will remind us of global crises like AIDS, local catastrophes of senseless violence, family failures, ecological threats, and church skirmishes. These problems resist easy solutions. They are powerful, pervasive, and systemic.[1]

Do we have a gospel big enough for these problems? Do we have the confidence to declare that these robust problems, all of which begin with sin against God and then creep into the world like cancer, can be conquered by a robust gospel? When I read the Gospels, I see a Lion of Judah who roared with a kingdom gospel that challenged both Israel's and Rome's mighty men, gathered up the sick and dying, and made them whole. When I read the apostle Paul, I see a man who carried a gospel that he believed could save as well as unite Gentiles and barbarians with Abraham's sacred descendants.

I sometimes worry we have settled for a little gospel. But as close to us as the pages of a nearby Bible we can find the gospel that is much bigger than many of us have dared to believe. The gospel is the story of the work of the triune God (Father, Son, and Spirit) to completely restore broken image-bearers (Genesis 1:26 – 27), in the context of the community of faith (Israel, kingdom, and church) through the life, death, and resurrection of Jesus Christ and the gift of the Pentecostal Spirit, to union with God and communion with others for the good of the world.

The gospel may be bigger than this description, but it is certainly not smaller. The robust gospel is a story. Jesus' birth came in the midst of a story with a beginning, a problem, and a lengthy history. When Jesus stood up to announce the "gospel of the kingdom" (Matthew 4:23 KJV), the first thing his hearers would have focused on was not the word *gospel* but the word *kingdom* — the climax of Israel's story and its yearning for the eternal messianic reign — the kingdom of God.

The robust gospel deals with a robust problem. Genesis 1 – 3 teaches us that humans are made in God's image and likeness. These image-bearers

273

were in utter union with God, at home with themselves, in communion with one another, and in harmony with the world around them. When Eve, with her husband in tow, chose to eat of the wrong tree, the image was cracked in each of those four directions: God-alienation, self-shame, other-blame, and Eden-expulsion. The rest of the Bible, from Genesis 4 through Revelation 22, is about these cracked image-bearers being restored to personal union with God, freed from shame, placed in communion with others, and offered to the world. Any gospel that does not expand the "problem" of Genesis 3 to these cosmic dimensions is not robust enough.

A robust gospel has a grand vision. A little gospel promises me personal salvation and eternal life. But the robust gospel doesn't stop there. It also promises a new society and a new creation. When Jesus stood up to read Isaiah 61 in the synagogue at Nazareth, then sat down and declared that this prophetic vision was now coming to pass through him, there was more than personal redemption at work. God's kingdom, the society where God's will is established and lived, was now officially at work in his followers. That society was overturning the injustices and exclusions of the empire and establishing an inclusive and just alternative through its hospitality and generosity (Acts 2:42 – 47) in the Jerusalem churches. We find this in Jesus' opening words (Luke 4:18 – 19), in the Beatitudes (6:20 – 26), and throughout the Gospels.

A robust gospel includes the life of Jesus as well as his resurrection. Paul said he preached "Christ crucified," but the crucified Christ that Paul preached was an empty-cross Christ and an empty-grave Christ. This gospel incorporates us into the life of Jesus Christ, into his death with us, for us, and instead of us, into the resurrection that justifies and creates new life, and into the Pentecostal Spirit that empowers us to live together, as image-bearers of God, in such a way that we glow with his glory.

A robust gospel demands not only faith but everything. Inherent in the biblical view of the gospel is a view of faith that involves repentance, trust, surrender, commitment, and obedience.

A robust gospel emerges from and leads others to the church. A little gospel creates individuals who volunteer to attend church on the basis of their preferences in worship, friendships, sermons, and programs. The robust gospel knows that God's work, from the very beginning, has revolved around three words: Israel, kingdom, and church.

We cannot skip from the fall to the cross. Instead of sending his Son to redeem Adam and Eve in Genesis 4, God chose to wait. And what God did between the time of Adam and Eve and Jesus Christ was to work redemption in the form of community. The Old Testament is about Israel; the New Testament is about Jesus and the church. And the church is the focus of God's redemptive work on earth in the present age.

A little gospel gives the new believer a choice about the local church; the robust biblical gospel offers the new believer the church along with its Lord. Because ultimately, only a redeemed community is robust enough to do justice to the problems we confront — and the gospel we proclaim.

My physician tells me that the way I live during this decade will shape the way I live in the next decade. Likewise, the way we preach the gospel in this decade will shape the church of the next. A more robust gospel now will mean a more robust church for the next generation.

For reflection and discussion

- What big problems once existed in the world that have been overcome?
- Do you know about God's role in problems like the African slave trade, apartheid, the Cold War?
- What big problems in the world seem insurmountable right now?
- How might the gospel animate those problems with hope now and in the future?
- Let's pray to that end. And thank God for making a way where there was no way.

The Purpose of History

By Lael Arrington

In *The Year of Living Biblically*, A. J. Jacobs, general editor of *Esquire* magazine, writes, "Julie [his wife] always told me that things happen for a reason. To which I would reply, Sure, things happen for a reason. Certain chemical reactions take place in people's brains, and they cause those people to move their mouths and arms. That's the reason. But, I thought, there's no greater purpose."[2]

We all long to know where our lives in particular and history in general are going. When applied to history, Julie's view, that "things happen for a reason," is called "teleological": history reveals a larger *pattern* or *story* (meta-narrative), with some agency *directing* the course of human events.

AJ's view of purposelessness echoes that of today's neo-Darwinists: chance mutations and natural selection are the driving forces of history. With all species competing in the great race of life, all evolving like blind drunks with *no direction* or *purpose in mind*, history turned out to be the chance story of human progress — the "ascent of man." Had earth's climate favored gigantic rodents, history might have been written only in fossils, not books.

Darwin's theory of evolution blew fresh wind into the sails of the Enlightenment view of history. French thinkers had rejected the idea that God was directing the course of history, substituting instead their own teleology: *Directed by reason*, mankind would move toward a more perfect civilization. By blending Darwin's and the Enlightenment's visions of progress, modern thinkers offered a new purpose of history: Although there is no longer an author, there is still a grand story of progress enabled by science. Given enough money, technology, and especially education, mankind can create a utopia.

The brimming optimism of early twentieth-century thinkers hit the wall of reality in the trenches of World War I, the holocausts of World War II, and the atrocities of Stalin's and Mao's "more perfect civilizations." In our own postmodern times, people's confidence in reason and progress is flagging, but they are more honest: Perhaps, if there is no author, then there is no larger story. History may not be going anywhere. If chance, not progress, is the driving force, then life is a "tournament of narratives." A person can only create their own small story and make it as interesting as possible.

But the 9/11s of history and the brokenness of our own lives cry out for meaning. As Julie said, there has to be a reason. When chance displaces purpose, it also crushes hope. But believing in God's redemptive purpose in history is not just wishful thinking. A Christian worldview offers the most reasonable and coherent answers to the questions of origins, morality, meaning and destiny. God's master plan as set forth in the Bible is validated by compelling evidence in hard and social sciences, from physics to textual criticism, and sealed by the historical reality of Jesus' resurrection and the fulfillment of biblical prophesies.

The Bible declares that God, the living treasure, created mankind with a purpose: so that God could give himself as a gift to those who reach out and find him, though he is not far from each of us (Acts 17). He is directing a larger story in which we see him building his kingdom, redeeming lives, bringing light out of darkness. He promises ultimately to redeem all the tragedies of history. He will exchange the mourning of our personal lives with the gladness of his presence and a future beyond imagining.

Malcolm Muggeridge wrote in *The End of Christendom*,

We look back upon history and what do we see? Empires rising and falling, revolutions and counter-revolutions; wealth accumulated and wealth dispersed. I heard a crazed, cracked Austrian who announced to the world the establishment of a Reich that would last a thousand years. I've seen an Italian clown say he was going to stop and restart the calendar with his own ascension to power. I met a murderous judge and brigand in the Kremlin proclaimed by the intellectual elite of the world as wiser than Solomon, more humane than Marcus Aurelius, more enlightened than Buddha. All in one lifetime, all in one lifetime, gone — gone with the wind.

Hitler and Mussolini, dead and remembered only in infamy. Stalin, a forbidden name in the regime he helped found.... Behind the debris of these solemn supermen and these self-styled imperial diplomatists stands the gigantic figure of one person because of whom, by whom, in whom, and through whom alone mankind may still have hope. The person of Jesus Christ.[3]

For reflection and discussion

- What is your favorite picture of God at work in history?

- How do you see your own life story fitting into the larger story (Ephesians 1:4)?

If God is in control of history, then it means quite simply that he will keep his promises. Dallas Willard encourages us to see our daily struggles "in the larger world of a great and good God, who has all eternity, and resources beyond our wildest imagination, to ensure that the life of every individual who suffers, in whatever way, is ultimately one that even that individual will receive with boundless gratitude."[4]

- How is the God over all history inviting you to trust his promises today?

Blaise Pascal: Genius, Mind, and Heart

By **Kelly Monroe Kullberg**, with excerpts by Os Guinness from his book *The Call*.

Blaise Pascal (1623 – 1662) was born in France and raised in Paris. He was three when his mother died, but he was raised by a loving and capable father, Etienne Pascal, himself a student in mathematics, ancient languages, and poetry.

At the age of eleven, Blaise wrote a short treatise on the sounds of vibrating bodies, and at twelve he discovered geometric theorems without having yet studied geometry. He was then allowed to study Euclid and to sit in the monastery and listen to some of the greatest mathematicians and scientists in Europe.

Still a boy, Pascal developed a mechanical calculator to help his father calculate taxes. He advanced the study of fluids and the concepts of pressure and vacuum. At age sixteen he advanced research in projective geometry, and as an adult he developed probability theory which influenced the fields of social science and modern economics.

He wrote powerfully in defense of scientific method while at the same time opposing the nascent rationalism of René Descartes. Pascal humbly stated in *Pensees*, "Reason's last step is the recognition that there are an infinite number of things which are beyond it." Therefore, on the basis of reason, he was open to the supernatural or that which was revealed from beyond the realms of nature and logic alone. He burned with questions about God and eternity.

Describing Pascal, British sociologist Os Guinness wrote in *The Call*, "Mathematical genius, inventor, grandfather of the computer and modern risk theory, renaissance thinker well versed in physics, philosophy, and theology … among the most elegant prose stylists in the French language, Pascal is one of the supreme human thinkers of all time and author of a great masterpiece of Western literature — *Pensees*."[5]

But, according to Guinness, "Almost no one in Pascal's day and still too few in ours know of the experience that kept these achievements in perspective and lay at the core of his brief, intense, pain-filled, flame burst of a life. On the evening of Monday, November 23, 1654, he was thirty-one years old

WEEK 15

and had just experienced a close brush with death in a carriage driving accident. That night he had a profound encounter with God that changed the course of his life.

"Pascal's experience lasted from 10:30 p.m. until 12:30 a.m. It is often called his 'second conversion,' to distinguish it from his first, more formal conversion at Rouen when he was twenty-four. What he went through strained and finally shattered the capacities of his language: *fire*. But the experience was so precious and decisive to him that he sewed the parchment record of it into the lining of his doublet [coat] and wore it next to his heart.... It was only found by his sister, who felt the odd bump it formed, after his death in 1662 at the age of thirty-nine. The opening half of his 'Memorial' reads:

> **Fire**
> *God of Abraham, God of Isaac, God of Jacob,*
> *Not of philosophers and scholars.*
> *Certainty, certainty, heartfelt, joy, peace.*
> *God of Jesus Christ.*
> *God of Jesus Christ.*
> *My God and Your God.*
> *Your God shall be my God.*
> *The world forgotten, and everything except God.*
> *He can only be found by the ways taught in the Gospels.*
> *Greatness of the human soul.*
> *O righteous father, the world had not known thee,*
> *But I have known thee.*
> *Joy, Joy, Joy, tears of joy.*

Guinness continues, "Most of us cannot begin to understand Pascal's mathematical accomplishments, and we would not wish to experience the pain and suffering of his short life. But what lit and fanned into a blaze the deep potential of his character and gifts is something open to us all — the call of God."[6]

Pascal had entrusted his life to Christ even before his epiphany of fire, his "second conversion" yielding "certainty." Bill Tsamis of the C. S. Lewis Society wrote, "Transcending the idea of reason alone, the great philosopher recognized that God had purposed a degree of ambiguity in His creation in order that He might discover the faithfulness of the heart, rather than the certitude of the mind." Pascal wrote in his journal *Pensées*, "Acknowledge the truth of religion in its very obscurity ... for it is not true that everything reveals God, and it is not true that everything conceals God. But it is true at once that He hides from those who tempt Him and that He reveals Himself to those who seek Him."[7]

For reflection and discussion

- Do you agree with Pascal's statement "There is sufficient light for those who desire to see, and there is sufficient darkness for those of a contrary disposition"?
- What is it you desire to see?
- What experience or evidence gives you light to see by?
- What aspects of experience create darkness?
- How do you turn toward light?

God of the Galaxies

By **Jennifer Wiseman**, PhD, an author and astronomer who, at the Massachusetts Institute of Technology and Harvard, studied star-forming regions of our galaxy using radio, optical, and infrared telescopes. She discovered the comet Wiseman-Skiff; *http://hubblesite.org/newscenter/archive/releases/2006/07/image/a/*.

When I contemplate the heavens, I find several incredible qualities that permeate the universe. Among these are two I'll call simply *beauty* and *activity*. Beauty is easy to see but hard to explain. Why do we see beauty in a cluster of stars, shining like colored gemstones? Why do the majestic spiral arms of a galaxy bring us a calming humility?

The telescopes of the last century have revealed beauty to us from the heavens with detail never before imagined. Nothing can match the images from the orbiting Hubble Space Telescope (*http://hubblesite.org*) as it scans the heavens from a clear vantage above obscuring clouds. The Hubble has imaged thousands of galaxies, but my favorite grand spiral has the inspiring name NGC 1309 (astronomers aren't known for beauty when it comes to naming their discoveries). NGC 1309, a collection of stars, dust, and gas held together by gravity, has over time assumed a rotating spiral arrangement that looks like a giant symmetric pinwheel framing a bright central core. The light from across this spiral galaxy we see not as individual stars, which we cannot easily differentiate at this distance, but rather as the blended light of over a hundred billion stars shining forth in star clusters between clouds and swirls of interstellar gas. Even the background of this image is stunning. A careful look will reveal hundreds of other galaxies of various shapes and orientations. Some are even reddened in color due to their extreme distance and the resulting effects as their light transited billions of years to us through the stretching space of a universe we now know is expanding.

This brings us to the ubiquitous *activity* in the universe. It comes as a surprise to many to find out that stars and galaxies are not stagnant. Rather, galaxies that get too close to one another can distort each other with gravity and tidal forces, and sometimes even collide and merge. And galaxies like NGC 1309 and our own Milky Way are full of activity. Stars are actively forming by the hundreds of thousands within condensing pockets of gas and dust. Planets form in disks of material around young stars. Older stars that have used up all their inner hydrogen fuel become unstable, and the bigger ones explode in brilliant supernovae. Such explosions spew heavier elements into the interstellar gas, allowing the next generation of stars and their planetary systems to form with more elements like carbon and iron. Since NGC 1309 is relatively close to us, a "mere" 100 million light-years away, astronomers are using the measured brightness of supernova explosions in this galaxy to compare to those in more distant galaxies, to help calibrate the nearly unfathomable distance scale of the entire universe.

So what are we to think, knowing that galaxies like NGC 1309 and our own Milky Way each have over 100 billion stars and vigorous activity, and there are over 100 billion galaxies in the visible universe? We must first come to terms with the fact that our significance lies not in our particular place or lifespan in the universe. Our hope lies only in God's choice to give us significance and value. We can surely identify with the thoughts of the psalmist (Psalm 8:3 – 5, 9):

> When I consider your heavens, the work of your fingers, the moon and the stars, which you have set in place, what are mere mortals that you are mindful of them, human beings that you care for them?
> You have made them a little lower than the heavenly beings and crowned them with glory and honor. Lord, our Lord, how majestic is your name in all the earth!

But beyond thinking about ourselves, the beauty and activity in the universe give us some amazing spine-tingling hints about the very nature of God. What kind of God would create a universe with the ability to support hundreds of billions of active galaxies, teeming with stars and solar systems? And why is it that only now in the last few decades, after thousands of years of recorded human history, are we being enabled to discover so much of the vast size, makeup, beauty, and activity of the universe? I believe we cannot answer these questions, nor can we truly comprehend in our minds the magnitude of our astronomical discoveries. But let's look up from time to time to the heavens and remember that our God is truly an awesome God. And remember that when we say, "Jesus is Lord of all," that "all" is quite a lot more than we tend to think about in the world immediately in sight.

For reflection and discussion

Since Jesus says that the God who upholds the galaxies also cares for us — even to knowing the number of hairs on our heads:

- How should we be worshiping him?
- If someday intelligent life is discovered elsewhere in the universe, how would that affect your understanding of God and of salvation in Jesus Christ?

T. S. Eliot and Julian of Norwich

By Sandra Glahn, adjunct professor, Christian education and pastoral ministries, Dallas Theological Seminary. Excerpt from "Little Gidding" by T. S. Eliot. Glahn is editor of *Kindred Spirit* magazine and author of *Informed Consent* as well as the *Coffee Cup Bible Studies* series; *www.aspire2.com*.

> *And all shall be well and*
> *All manner of thing shall be well*
> *When the tongues of flame are in-folded*
> *Into the crowned knot of fire*
> *And the fire and the rose are one.*

Thus T. S. Eliot ends the final "Little Gidding" section of *Four Quartets* — the last poem in what is arguably the greatest literary achievement of the twentieth century's most influential poet. In the concluding sections of "Little Gidding," Eliot uses the phrase "all shall be well and all manner of thing shall be well" three times.[8] He borrowed it — and others — from English medieval anchoress Julian of Norwich.

According to Julian's own account, when she was thirty, she became ill. As she lay dying, she had a series of sixteen "shewings," or revelations, about God, the Trinity, and the crucified Jesus. Afterward the fourteenth-century mystic recovered completely and recorded her experiences.

Julian's *Sixteen Revelations of Divine Love*, known today as *Revelations of Divine Love*, was the first English book known to be written by a woman. While this accomplishment may seem significant today, in Julian's time English was merely a local dialect. She — like most women then — was unlearned and sought to live in relative obscurity. In fact, she may have had to learn her ABCs before she could even record her "shewings." After she did so, her work remained unpublished until 1670.

About six hundred years after Julian lived, T. S. Eliot chose to quote her. That she was from England and a woman influenced his choice as he drew on mystics from his adopted country's past. And hers was a credible voice, having gained the respect of even May Sinclair, the critic of modernist writing to whom we attribute the term "stream of consciousness." Sinclair disliked

Christian poetry, claiming it was neither written by poets nor supremely devotional.

For twenty years Eliot desired to prove Sinclair wrong, and in *Four Quartets* we see his deepest attempt. The statement that "all shall be well" is the summary of Julian's entire experience. Her optimism is not one of positive thinking but is based on an eschatological hope. Eliot shares her view that the One who can make even humans killing the God-Man into the still point of history can turn all lesser evils into good. Thus, "all manner of thing shall be well."

The words take on particular significance when viewed against the backdrop of Eliot's circumstances. A fire warden during World War I, he witnessed bombings and violence as everyday experiences. The evil around him demanded an explanation. And Julian's conclusion became Eliot's refrain. The basis of the wellness of which she speaks is her belief in Christ's power to renew all things to their original "making."

In reading Eliot's preconversion poems, such as *The Waste Land*, one wonders if he even believes in hope. But by the time he has penned the *Four Quartets*, well after his conversion, the poet has clearly come to affirm a hope of cosmic proportion — one that ultimately transcends time, sequence, geography, and history.

So the great modernist Nobel-winning wordsmith ends his masterpiece with the words of a humble, virtually illiterate medieval woman. Both witnessed overwhelming ugliness, brokenness, and suffering in the here and now. Her century saw plagues; his saw the wars. Though separated by six hundred years, their voices can and do affirm in unison the hope in Christ that all shall be well and, indeed, "all manner of thing shall be well."

For reflection and discussion

- Do you consider yourself a hopeful person? If not, where do you notice the absence of hope? What keeps you from being hopeful? If you are hopeful, what is the basis of your hope? How is your hope connected to faith? To Jesus?
- Julian was very sick when care was limited and plague was rampant. Yet her legacy is hope. What is the difference between optimism based on "eschatological hope" and optimism based on "positive thinking"? How do you respond to God's prophetic plans for the future?

Real Art: The Hope Beyond Ground Zero

By **Charles Colson**, JD, founder, Prison Fellowship, and author of *The Good Life*. From *BreakPoint*, Febrary 21, 2007; *www.breakpoint.org*.

In 2003 the White House announced that New York artist Makoto Fujimura was appointed by President George W. Bush to the National Council on the Arts for a six-year term. Perhaps it's the worldview behind his art that caught the president's attention. Working in his studio three blocks from Ground Zero, Fujimura was deeply impacted by the horrific events of September 11, 2001, and it caused him to challenge the artistic community to see the reality of our broken state of existence.

Fujimura says, "Art cannot be divorced from faith, for to do so is to literally close our eyes to that beauty of the dying sun setting all around us. Death spreads all over our lives, and therefore, faith must be given to see through the darkness, to see through the beauty of the valley of the shadow of death. Everyone has a Ground Zero to face."

Reflecting on his own conversion, he said, "I remember how I used to look at the landscape every day on my way to work, not believing what I saw was true or able to trust my own vision. I realized after my conversion that there was reality I could trust, and that I could also trust what was inside of me to express it. Reality is the foundation of creativity, and any artist who is honest has to make that assumption." Coming from Japan, with a Christian population of less than 1 percent, Fujimura's worldview shift in his art was radically countercultural and obvious to both his admirers and critics.

For Fujimura, art can be best understood in the context of the incarnation. In the Lord's Supper, ordinary substances become sacred. The immanent becomes transcendent. If God became man and humbled himself, this incarnational principle can be applied to every act of creativity, and, therefore, the results of artistic creation can become sacred. This is the theological understanding that flows through Fujimura's work.

Fujimura works in Nihonga — a medieval Japanese technique of painting using minerals. His works are painted in layers of mineral paints that become transparent over time, revealing the layers below.

When asked by art critic James Romaine how this technique relates to his faith, he said, "The underlying worldview of Japanese art is cyclical, and yet the technique lends itself to this notion that there is a beginning and an end." There is history and story in the painting, as this handmade paint is applied to handmade paper. "There is this rich fabric of story being woven as you work. That is something that is very significant to me, as I am someone who has come to understand that my worldview is a premise that allows for these stories to come alive. That understanding of the world or looking at yourself, as having a history, is very biblical. Because there is a beginning and an end, there is resolution; even in death itself, there is this purpose."

As a contemporary artist, creatively embracing and painting his way through the wreckage of September 11, Fujimura is an example of a Christian effectively using art as a vehicle to show us reality: its depravity and brokenness, but also the hope of restoration that the Great Artist himself, incarnate in Christ, brings to all things.

For reflection and discussion

Fujimura wrote that living and working near "ground zero" in Manhattan intensified his search for meaning. "The Twin Towers," he wrote, "were twin symbols of capitalism and materialism. Until September 11th, artists here worked both literally and figuratively in the shadows of these symbols. The devastation caused by the catastrophe created a hallowed sense of a presence greater than that of our so-called postmodern world."[9]

- Where were you on September 11, 2001? What do you feel when you see an image of the devastation?
- What works of art have offered you some connection to suffering? How have they helped you process loss or find healing?
- How might a devastation, a great loss, open up a space for a greater presence in your life?
- How might you express your thoughts to God about suffering and hope?

The Future and the Wonder of Being

By Charles Malik, PhD, served as president of the General Assembly of the United Nations and as Lebanese ambassador to the United States, coauthor of the original declaration of human rights (with Eleanor Roosevelt). After earning his PhD in philosophy from Harvard, he was awarded more than fifty honorary doctorates. His many books include *A Christian Critique of the University* and *The Wonder of Being*, from which this essay is adapted.

There goes on in the soul of each of us a most fateful struggle between two persons — the person of being and the person of not being. Which has the upper hand is the deepest question that can be asked about us at any given moment.

The person of being moves about in the world freely and joyously, wholly unentangled in himself, sometimes even wholly oblivious of his own existence — he is all the time out there, living and loving and laughing. The person of being trusts because there is essential integrity at the heart of existence to give him peace of mind. The person of not being cannot trust because he is at all times suspecting danger and disintegration and, therefore, you never find him enjoying rest and peace.

The person of being stands in awe before the wonderful plenitude of being, with its variety and wealth and content, its diversity of levels and orders. The person of being sometimes stops talking altogether because he is lost in contemplation and wonder. He rejects magic and chance and is always taken by the norm, the rule, that which for the most part is the case. The person of not being appears not to be interested in what is true as a rule, but always hunts the abnormal and the aberrant.

When you show a person of being Florence or Rome or the great cathedrals, when you take him to El Prado or the British Museum or to the Metropolitan Museum of Art, when you place in his hands Plato or Shakespeare or Tolstoy or the Psalms or the Gospels, he is profoundly grateful. Filled with awe, he is transported into another world full of stillness and meaning — a world of peace and creativity and life, a world of being, of God — a world of which these marvels, wonderful as they are, are nevertheless mere shadows and reflections and merest fragments, and he is profoundly grateful. Put a human person before a person of being, and the person of being comprehends him as a whole, amazed at his being.

What is it that calls forth the person of not being in us, and what is it that calls forth the person of being? Only Jesus Christ of Nazareth calls forth the person of being in us, whether or not we know it. I know why he does it — he does it because he loves us — but I do not know how.

No person of being will fail to be arrested by the phenomenon of Jesus Christ; he will therefore seek everything he can find about him — in the Bible, in the church, and in every historical-cultural manifestation. Here you have personal existence in history and time, confident, sure, unhesitating, full of matter and content, without the slightest attempt at coercion. Here you find yourself engaged at your deepest.

The person of being has no desire to explain Jesus Christ away. He is attracted by him as by nothing else. Jesus Christ powerfully convicts us of our sin and rebellion, yet no matter how much the person of being is thus shattered in the presence of Christ, he is not frightened or driven away by him.

In our heart of hearts we crave nothing more than to become authentic persons, to become intimately relational, to be repentant, to be forgiven, to enter life eternal. And yet modern existence diminishes and dissolves the person into his components, has no room whatever for repentance, never seeks forgiveness, and as for life eternal, this existence "lives" only for the moment or, at most, for the near future. This measures the magnitude of the anti-Christian revolution amidst which we are living and have been living for two thousand years.

The greatest event in history ... is his resurrection on the first Easter morning. This event utterly debunks the world and everything in it, proves its absolute lack of self-sufficiency, and provides the greatest real hope there is.

Do we find Jesus Christ everywhere — in nature, in history, in art, in our personal trials and sufferings, in our miseries and in our triumphs, in every human law and culture? Only the new creature, born from above, "born of the Spirit," can see everything in Jesus Christ and Jesus Christ in everything. And only this new birth and this mode of seeing in and through Jesus Christ is new in history. If you take him at his word, then nothing can be the same again for you in the world and in your life.

The Maker of heaven and earth is before you; the Creator of everything in the universe, visible and invisible, is before you; the Fullness of Being is before you. God himself, who took on human form to free us from not being, adopts us and grants us, through his resurrection, life everlasting with him and victory over the Devil and his works. He is before you. What can the thankful believer then do but fall on his knees and repeat from the Divine liturgy:

> *For unto thee are due all glory, honor, and worship,*
> *to the Father, and to the Son and to the Holy Spirit,*
> *now, and ever, and unto ages of ages.*

Excerpts from the following are used by permission with all rights reserved:

Week 1

Bible and Theology — A Christian Theory of Everything

Adapted from *One Thing: Developing a Passion for the Beauty of God* by Sam Storms. Copyright © 2004, Christian Focus Publications, Ross-shire, Scotland (*www .christianfocus.com*). Reprinted with permission.

Literature — Paradise Lost — Milton's Epic of Cosmic Betrayal

Adapted from *Reading Between the Lines: A Christian Guide to Literature* by Gene Edward Veith. Copyright © 1994. Used by permission of Crossway Books, a division of Good News Publishers, Wheaton, IL 60187; *www.crossway.com*.

Arts — Art — A Response to God's Beauty

Taken from *Scribbling in the Sand* by Michael Card. Copyright © 2002 by Michael Card. And from *Art and the Bible* by Francis Schaeffer. Copyright © 1973 by L'Abri Fellowship. Both used with permission of InterVarsity Press, PO Box 1400, Downers Grove, IL 60515; *www.ivpress.com*.

Contemporary Culture — A Conversation with Muslims

Reprinted by permission. *Soul Cravings* by Erwin McManus, copyright © 2006, Thomas Nelson Inc., Nashville, Tenn. All rights reserved.

Week 2

Bible and Theology — The Grand Affair: The Imago Dei and Intimacy

Reprinted by permission. *Desire: The Journey We Must Take to Find the Life God Offers* by John Eldredge, copyright © 2007, Thomas Nelson Inc., Nashville, Tenn. All rights reserved.

Week 4

Bible and Theology — God's Second Word: The Bible

Taken from *Finding God Beyond Harvard: The Quest for Veritas* by Kelly Monroe Kullberg. Copyright © 2006. Used with permission of InterVarsity Press, PO Box 1400, Downers Grove, IL 60515; *www.ivpress.com.*

History — The Genius of Jesus

Adapted from *The Divine Conspiracy: Rediscovering Our Hidden Life in God* by Dallas Willard. Copyright © 1998. Used by permission of HarperSanFrancisco, San Francisco, Calif. All rights reserved. And from *Finding God Beyond Harvard: The Quest for Veritas* by Kelly Monroe Kullberg. Copyright © 2006. Used with permission of InterVarsity Press, PO Box 1400, Downers Grove, IL 60515; *www.ivpress.com.*

Arts — Buddhist and Christian Ideals in Art

Reprinted from *Orthodoxy* by G. K. Chesterton. Copyright © 1994, 2001 by Harold Shaw Publishers. Used by permission of WaterBrook Press, Colorado Springs, CO. All rights reserved.

Week 5

Literature — Leo Tolstoy

Reprinted from *Soul Survivor: How Thirteen Unlikely Mentors Helped My Faith Survive the Church* by Philip Yancey. Copyright © 2001 by SCCT. Used by permission of WaterBrook Press, Colorado Springs, CO. All rights reserved.

Week 6

Philosophy — Seeing Through Cynicism

Adapted from *Seeing Through Cynicism: A Reconsideration of the Power of Suspicion* by Dick Keyes. Copyright © 2006. Used with permission of InterVarsity Press, PO Box 1400, Downers Grove, IL 60515; *www.ivpress.com.*

Week 7

Philosophy — The Fact/Value Divide

Adapted from *Total Truth: Liberating Christianity from Its Cultural Captivity* by Nancy Pearcey. Copyright © 2005. Used by permission of Crossway Books, a division of Good News Publishers, Wheaton, IL 60187; *www.crossway.com.*

Arts — Michelangelo: The Image of Renaissance Humanism

Excerpted from *How Should We Then Live? The Rise and Decline of Western Thought and Culture* by Francis A. Schaeffer. Copyright © 1976. Used by permission of Crossway Books, a division of Good News Publishers, Wheaton, IL 60187; *www.crossway.com*.

Week 8

Bible and Theology — Major and Minor Themes

Adapted from *Major & Minor Themes (Conversations: Volume 5)* by John Eldredge and the Ransomed Heart Men's Team. CD, copyright © 2006, Ransomed Heart Ministries. Used by permission. All rights reserved.

History — The Renaissance and Reformation

Adapted from *Serious Times: Making Your Life Matter in an Urgent Day* by James Emery White. Copyright © 2006 by Steven James. Used with permission of InterVarsity Press, PO Box 1400, Downers Grove, IL 60515; *www.ivpress.com*.

Philosophy — Theodicy

Taken from *The Case for Faith: A Journalist Investigates the Toughest Objections to Christianity* by Lee Strobel. Copyright © 2000 by Lee Strobel. Used by permission of Zondervan, Grand Rapids, Mich.

Contemporary Culture — U2

Adapted from *Faith, God & Rock 'n' Roll: From Bono to Jars of Clay: How People of Faith Are Transforming American Popular Music* by Mark Joseph. Copyright © 2003 by Sanctuary Publishing, London, UK. Used with permission of Omnibus Press.

Week 9

Philosophy — The Sociobiology of E. O. Wilson

Adapted from "A Long Way from the Tribe" by Drew Trotter in *Tabletalk* magazine, 14, no. 10:13 – 14. Used by permission.

Science — The Periodic Table of Elements

Adapted from *A Meaningful World: How the Arts and Sciences Reveal the Genius of Nature* by Benjamin Wiker and Jonathan Witt. Copyright © 2006 by Benjamin Wiker and Jonathan Witt. Used with permission of InterVarsity Press, PO Box 1400, Downers Grove, IL 60515; *www.ivpress.com*.

Week 10

Bible and Theology — Hearing God

Adapted from *Hearing God: Developing a Conversational Relationship with God* by Dallas Willard. Copyright © 1984, 1993, 1999 by Dallas Willard. Used with permission of InterVarsity Press, PO Box 1400, Downers Grove, IL 60515; *www.ivpress.com.*

Philosophy — The Modern University

Taken from *Kingdom Triangle: Recover the Christian Mind, Renovate the Soul, Restore the Spirit's Power* by J. P. Moreland. Copyright © 2007 by J. P. Moreland. Used by permission of Zondervan, Grand Rapids, Mich.

Literature — Hamlet: Shakespeare's Ingenious Design

Adapted from *A Meaningful World: How the Arts and Sciences Reveal the Genius of Nature* by Benjamin Wiker and Jonathan Witt. Copyright © 2006 by Benjamin Wiker and Jonathan Witt. Used with permission of InterVarsity Press, PO Box 1400, Downers Grove, IL 60515; *www.ivpress.com.*

Arts — Handel's Messiah

Taken from *The Spiritual Lives of the Great Composers* by Patrick Kavanaugh; EMI Christian Music Group. Copyright © 1992, 1996 by Patrick Kavanaugh. Used by permission of Zondervan, Grand Rapids, Mich.

Week 11

History — The Enlightenment

Adapted from *Serious Times: Making Your Life Matter in an Urgent Day* by James Emery White. Copyright © 2006 by Steven James. Used with permission of InterVarsity Press, PO Box 1400, Downers Grove, IL 60515; *www.ivpress.com.*

Philosophy — The Ultimate Premise

Taken from *The Right Questions: Truth and Meaning in Public Debate* by Phillip E. Johnson. Copyright © 2002 by Phillip E. Johnson. Used with permission of InterVarsity Press, PO Box 1400, Downers Grove, IL 60515; *www.ivpress.com.*

Arts — The Impressionists

Adapted from *Modern Art and the Death of a Culture* by Hans R. Rookmaaker. Copyright © 1970 by InterVarsity Press, Downers Grove, Ill. Permission granted by Marleen Hengelaar-Rookmaaker.

Contemporary Culture — Tending the Garden Planet

Adapted from *Thorns in the Garden Planet: Meditations on the Creator's Care* by Vera Shaw. Copyright © 1993, Thomas Nelson Inc., Nashville, Tenn. Used by permission. Also adapted from Shaw's contribution in *Finding God at Harvard: Spiritual Journeys of Thinking Christians*, Kelly Monroe, editor. Copyright © 1996 by Kelly K. Monroe. Used by permission of Zondervan, Grand Rapids, Mich.

Week 12

Philosophy — Rousseau

Adapted from *Total Truth: Liberating Christianity from Its Cultural Captivity* by Nancy Pearcey. Copyright © 2005. Used by permission of Crossway Books, a division of Good News Publishers, Wheaton, IL 60187; *www.crossway.com*.

Arts — Postmodern Architecture

Adapted from *Postmodern Times: A Christian Guide to Contemporary Thought and Culture* by Gene Edward Veith. Copyright © 1994. Used by permission of Crossway Books, a division of Good News Publishers, Wheaton, IL 60187; *www.crossway.com*.

Week 13

Bible and Theology — The Fairness and Mercy of God

Taken from *Reason to Believe: A Response to Common Objections to Christianity* by Robert Charles Sproul Trust. Copyright © 1978 by G/L Publications. Used by permission of Zondervan, Grand Rapids, Mich.

Philosophy — A Professor Reconstructed

Adapted from a chapter by Mary Poplin in *Gladly Learn, Gladly Teach* by John Marson Dunaway. Copyright © 2005, Mercer University Press, Mercer, Ga. Used by permission.

Week 14

Philosophy — The Sleep of Death

Excerpt is from *The Call: Finding and Fulfilling the Central Purpose of Your Life* by Os Guinness. Copyright ©1998, Thomas Nelson Inc., Nashville, Tenn. Used by permission.

Week 15

Philosophy — Blaise Pascal: Genius, Mind, and Heart

Reprinted by permission from *The Call: Finding and Fulfilling the Central Purpose of Your Life* by Os Guinness. Copyright ©1998. Thomas Nelson Inc., Nashville, Tenn.

Literature — T. S. Eliot and Julian of Norwich

Excerpt from "Little Gidding," in *Four Quartets* by T. S. Eliot. Copyright © 1942 by T. S. Eliot and renewed 1970 by Esme Valerie Eliot. Reprinted by permission of Harcourt, Inc., Orlando, Fla.

Arts — Real Art: The Hope Beyond Ground Zero

From "The Hope Beyond Ground Zero" by Charles Colson, *BreakPoint*, February 21, 2007. Reprinted with permission of Prison Fellowship, *www.breakpoint.org*.

Contemporary Culture — The Future and the Wonder of Being

Reprinted by permission from *The Wonder of Being* by Charles Malik. Copyright © 1974. Thomas Nelson Inc., Nashville, Tenn. A portion of *Wonder of Being* appeared in *Finding God at Harvard*, Kelly Monroe, editor. Copyright © 1996, Zondervan, Grand Rapids, Mich.

A Sense of Wonder

1. Charles Malik, *The Wonder of Being* (Waco, Tex.: Word, 1974).

About the Contributors

1. Thomas Dubay, *The Evidential Power of Beauty: Science and Theology Meet* (Ft. Collins, Colo.: Ignatius, 1999).

Week 1

1. Portions of this text adapted from *The Bible and Its Influence* by Cullen Schippe and Chuck Stetson. Copyright © 2006, all rights reserved, The Bible Literacy Project, Front Royal, Va. The adaptations and their use are with permission of the publisher.

2. Madeleine L'Engle, in a talk at a Veritas forum, University of California, Santa Barbara, 2001.

3. Andrew Niccol, *The Truman Show*, directed by Peter Weir, starring Jim Carrey (Hollywood: Paramount Pictures, 1998).

4. Frederica Mathewes-Green, in a conversation with Lael Arrington in 2004.

5. Lael Arrington, *Godsight: Renewing the Eyes of Our Hearts* (Wheaton, Ill.: Crossway, 2005).

6. John Eldredge, *The Sacred Romance: Drawing Closer to the Heart of God* (Nashville: Nelson, 1997).

Week 2

1. Portions adapted from *The Bible and Its Influence* by Cullen Schippe and Chuck Stetson (Front Royal, Va.: Bible Literacy Project, 2006).

2. "Woodstock," words and music by Joni Mitchell (New York: Siquomb, 1969); http://udel.edu/~dsilver/phil367/WOODSTOCK.htm.

3. James Taylor, "New Hymn," *Live* CD, Disc One (New York: Columbia Records, 1993).

4. Pablo Picasso, in a 1950s radio interview with Libro Nero, and later in *National Review*, November 19, 1990. From ORIGIN 12, January 1964, Cid Corman, editor (Kyoto, Japan).

5. Neal Gabler, *Life: The Movie: How Entertainment Conquered Reality* (New York: Vintage, 2000).

6. Daniel Boorstin, cited by Gabler in *Life: The Movie*.

7. Richard Stoley, cited by Gabler in *Life: The Movie*.

Week 3

1. Portions adapted from *The Bible and Its Influence* by Cullen Schippe and Chuck Stetson (Front Royal, Va.: Bible Literacy Project, 2006).

2. Beth Moore, Daniel study, *lifeway.com*; *www.lifeway.com/lwc/files/lwcF_plp_Daniel_Sample_Week1_Day1_pdf.pdf*.

3. C. S. Lewis, *The Last Battle* (New York: HarperCollins, 1984).

4. Bruce Edwards, *Further Up and Further In: Understanding C. S. Lewis's the Lion, the Witch, and the Wardrobe* (Nashville: Broadman, 2005).

5. C. S. Lewis, October 18, 1931, in *The Collected Letters of C. S. Lewis: Family Letters 1905 – 1931*, edited by Walter Hooper (San Francisco: HarperSanFrancisco, 2004).

6. C. S. Lewis, *Mere Christianity* (New York: HarperCollins, 1952).

Week 4

1. Hugh Ross, *www.reasons.org/resources/fff/2000issue03/index.shtml#big_bang_the_bible_taught_it_first*.

2. Dallas Willard, "My Assumptions about the Bible," *The Divine Conspiracy* (San Francisco: HarperSanFrancisco, 1998).

3. Available from Project Gutenberg, *www.gutenberg.org*.

4. Christopher Marlowe, *The Tragical History of Doctor Faustus* (c. 1604 or c. 1616).

5. G. K. Chesterton, *Orthodoxy* (1908).

6. David Aikman, *Jesus in Beijing*, 2nd rev. ed. (Thousand Oaks, Calif.: Monarch, 2006).

Week 5

1. Carl Sagan, *Pale Blue Dot: A Vision of the Human Future in Space* (New York: Random House, 1994).

2. Mark Galli and Ted Olsen, *131 Christians Everyone Should Know* (Nashville: Broadman, 2000), 107 – 8.

3. Ibid.

4. Ibid.

5. Henri J. M. Nouwen, *Return of the Prodigal Son* (New York: Doubleday, 1992).

6. Ibid.

Week 6

1. Francis Schaeffer, *How Should We Then Live? The Rise and Decline of Western Thought and Culture* (Wheaton, Ill.: Crossway, 1976).

2. Cullen Murphy, *Are We Rome? The Fall of an Empire and the Fate of America* (New York: Houghton Mifflin, 2007).

3. Fred Adams and Greg Laughlin, *The Five Ages of the Universe: Inside the Physics of Eternity* (New York: Free Press, 1999).

4. Os Guinness, *The Call: Finding and Fulfilling the Central Purpose of Your Life* (Nashville: Nelson, 1998).

Week 7

1. C. S. Lewis, cited by Nancy Pearcey in *Total Truth*, from *Surprised by Joy: The Shape of My Early Life* by C. S. Lewis (New York: Harcourt Brace, 1955).

2. Portions adapted from *The Bible and Its Influence* by Cullen Schippe and Chuck Stetson (Front Royal, Va.: Bible Literacy Project, 2006).

Week 8

1. Gerard Manley Hopkins, "Terrible Sonnet," *The Norton Anthology of English Literature*, gen. ed. M. H. Abrams, vol. 2, 3rd ed. (New York: Norton, 1974).

2. Ibid.

3. Ibid.

4. Patrick Kavanaugh, *Spiritual Lives of the Great Composers* (Grand Rapids, Mich.: Zondervan, 1996).

5. Patrick Kavanaugh, EMI Christian Music Group, *Spiritual Lives of the Great Composers* (Grand Rapids, Mich.: Zondervan, 1996).

6. Francis Schaeffer, *How Should We Then Live?* (Wheaton, Ill.: Crossway, 1976).

7. Patrick Kavanaugh, *Spiritual Lives of the Great Composers* (Grand Rapids, Mich: Zondervan, 1996), citing Karl Geiringer, *Johann Sebastian Bach: Culmination of an Era* (New York: Oxford University Press, 1966).

Week 9

1. John Winthrop, sermon "A Modell of Christian Charity" (1630).

2. Perry Miller, *Errand into the Wilderness* (Cambridge, Mass.: Harvard, 1956).

3. R. Kent Hughes and Bryan Chapell, *1 and 2 Timothy and Titus: To Guard the Deposit* (Wheaton, Ill.: Crossway, 2000).

4. Jonathan Edwards, *The Religious Affections: The Works of Jonathan Edwards*, edited by John E. Smith (New Haven, Conn.: Yale University Press, 1959).

5. Robert Wright, *Three Scientists and Their Gods: Looking for Meaning in an Age of Information* (New York: HarperCollins, 1989).

6. William Blake, "Auguries of Innocence," *www.artofEurope.com*.

7. Marvin Olasky, *World* magazine (July 14, 2007).

8. Ibid.

9. Archibald MacLeish, in papers of Archibald MacLeish, Intelligence Report 35, 1942.

10. Norman Rockwell, *Norman Rockwell: My Adventures as an Illustrator* (New York: Harry N. Abrams, 1988).

11. *Smithsonian* (May 2007), 73.

12. Ibid.

13. Larry Harvey, "Burning Man, what is it?" *www.Pspyk.com*.

14. "Bonfire of the Techies," *Time*, August 25, 1997.

15. Larry Harvey, from a lecture, "La Vie Boheme — A History of Burning Man," at Walker Art Center, Minneapolis, Minn., February 24, 2000; *www.burningman.com/whatisburning man/lectures/lavie.html*.

16. Ibid.

Week 10

1. David Brooks, *On Paradise Drive: How We Live Now (And Always Have) in the Future Tense* (New York: Simon & Schuster, 2004).

Week 11

1. Calvin DeWitt, quoted in *Thorns in the Garden Planet: Meditations on the Creator's Care* by Vera C. Shaw (Nashville: Nelson, 1996).

Week 12

1. C. S. Lewis, in "The Weight of Glory," *Theology* (November 1941).

Week 13

1. Benjamin Franklin, *The Autobiography of Benjamin Franklin*, or *Memoirs*, written between 1771 and 1790.

2. James Emery White, *Serious Times: Making Your Life Matter in an Urgent Day* (Downers Grove, Ill.: InterVarsity, 2006).

3. Ibid.

4. Charles Baird, quoted in "How to Surf the Age Wave," *Time*, August 12, 2002.

5. John Eldredge, *Desire: The Journey We Must Take to Find the Life God Offers* (Nashville: Nelson, 2007).

Week 14

1. W. Graham Scroggie, *The Unfolding Drama of Redemption* (Grand Rapids, Mich.: Kregel, 1994).

2. William Damon, *The Path to Purpose* (New York: Free Press, 2008).

Week 15

1. Adapted from the Christian Vision Project and *Christianity Today*, *www.christianity today.com/ct/2008/march/13.36.html* (March 2008).

2. A. J. Jacobs, *The Year of Living Biblically: One Man's Humble Quest to Follow the Bible as Literally as Possible* (New York: Simon and Schuster, 2007).

3. Malcolm Muggeridge, *The End of Christendom* (Grand Rapids, Mich.: Eerdmans, 1980).

4. Dallas Willard, "God and the Problem of Evil," *www.dwillard.org*.

5. Os Guinness, *The Call: Finding and Fulfilling the Central Purpose of Your Life* (Nashville: Nelson, 1998).

6. Ibid.

7. Ibid.

8. T. S. Eliot, "Little Gidding," *Four Quartets* (New York: Harcourt Brace, 1943).

9. Makoto Fujimura, in an essay "The Fallen Towers and the Art of Tea," *www.makoto fujimura.com/essays/post_911_English1.html*.

Share Your Thoughts

With the Author: Your comments will be forwarded to the author when you send them to *zauthor@zondervan.com*.

With Zondervan: Submit your review of this book by writing to *zreview@zondervan.com*.

Free Online Resources at
www.zondervan.com

Zondervan AuthorTracker: Be notified whenever your favorite authors publish new books, go on tour, or post an update about what's happening in their lives at www.zondervan.com/authortracker.

Daily Bible Verses and Devotions: Enrich your life with daily Bible verses or devotions that help you start every morning focused on God. Visit www.zondervan.com/newsletters.

Free Email Publications: Sign up for newsletters on Christian living, academic resources, church ministry, fiction, children's resources, and more. Visit www.zondervan.com/newsletters.

Zondervan Bible Search: Find and compare Bible passages in a variety of translations at www.zondervanbiblesearch.com.

Other Benefits: Register yourself to receive online benefits like coupons and special offers, or to participate in research.

ZONDERVAN®

ZONDERVAN.com/
AUTHORTRACKER
follow your favorite authors